SOUTH FLORIDA AND THE KEYS
TRAVEL·SMART™ TRIP PLANNER

Egret wading near the Keys

SOUTH FLORIDA
AND THE KEYS

TRAVEL✦SMART™ TRIP PLANNER

Marylyn Springer

John Muir Publications
Santa Fe, New Mexico

Acknowledgments
With thanks to all of you who helped piece together this project. Special thanks
to DAS, whose support, devotion, enthusiasm, and humor are my miracle.

John Muir Publications, P.O. Box 613, Santa Fe, New Mexico 87504

Printed in the United States of America.
First edition. First printing October 1997

ISSN 1094-7086
ISBN 1-56261-376-6

Editors: Sarah Baldwin, Nancy Gillan
Graphics Editor: Tom Gaukel
Production: Marie J. T. Vigil, Nikki Rooker
Design: Janine Lehmann, Linda Braum
Typesetting: Melissa Tandysh
Maps Style Development: American Custom Maps—Albuquerque, NM USA
Map Illustration: Kathleen Sparkes, White Hart Design
Printer: Publishers Press
Cover Photo: © Jeff Greenberg/Unicorn Stock
Back Cover Photos: *top*—© Vladpans/Leo de Wys
                    bottom—Florida Keys TDC

Distributed to the book trade by
Publishers Group West
Emeryville, California

HOW TO USE THIS BOOK

The *South Florida and the Keys Travel+Smart Trip Planner* is organized in 13 destination chapters, each covering the best sights and activities, restaurants, and lodging available in that specific destination. Thanks to thorough research and experience, the author is able to bring you only the best options, saving you time and money in your travels. The chapters are presented in logical sequence so you can follow an easy route from one place to the next. If you were to visit each destination in chapter order, you'd enjoy a complete tour of the best of South Florida and the Keys.

Each chapter contains:

- User-friendly maps of the area, showing all recommended sights, restaurants, and accommodations.
- "A Perfect Day" description—how the author would spend her time if she had just one day in that destination.
- Sightseeing highlights, each rated by degree of importance: ★★★ Don't miss; ★★ Try hard to see; ★ See if you have time; and No stars—Worth knowing about.
- Selected restaurant, lodging, and camping recommendations to suit a variety of budgets.
- Helpful hints, fitness and recreation ideas, insights, and random tidbits of information to enhance your trip.

The Importance of Planning. Developing an itinerary is the best way to get the most satisfaction from your travels, and this guidebook makes it easy. First, read through the book and choose the places you'd most like to visit. Then, study the color map on the inside cover flap and the mileage chart (page 12) to determine which you can realistically see in the time you have available and at the travel pace you prefer. Using the Planning Map (pages 10–11), map out your route. Finally, use the lodging recommendations to determine your accommodations.

Some Suggested Itineraries. To get you started, six itineraries of varying lengths and based on specific interests follow. Mix and match according to your interests and time constraints, or follow a given itinerary from start to finish. The possibilities are endless. *Happy travels!*

SUGGESTED ITINERARIES

With the *South Florida and the Keys Travel•Smart Trip Planner*, you can plan a trip of any length—a one-day excursion, a getaway weekend, or a three-week vacation—around any special interest. To get you started, the following pages contain six suggested itineraries geared toward a variety of interests. For more information, refer to the chapters listed—chapter names are bolded and chapter numbers appear inside black bullets. You can follow a suggested itinerary in its entirety, or shorten, lengthen, or combine parts of each, depending on your starting and ending points.

Discuss alternative routes and schedules with your travel companions—it's a great way to have fun, even before you leave home. And remember: don't hesitate to change your itinerary once you're on the road. Careful study and planning ahead will help you make informed decisions as you go, but spontaneity is the extra ingredient that will make your trip memorable.

Pompano Beach

The Best of South Florida Tour

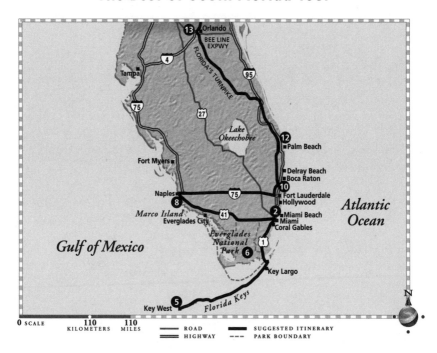

Florida has hundreds of "bests," but here's a list for those who want to see the highlights now—and come back later to see some more!

❷ Miami Beach (Art Deco District, Wolfsonian Foundation)
❺ Key West (Conch Train Tour, Hemingway House, Mel Fisher's Maritime Heritage Museum, Wrecker's Museum)
❻ The Everglades
❽ Naples (Corkscrew Swamp Sanctuary)
❿ Fort Lauderdale and Pompano Beach (Bonnett House, *Jungle Queen*)
⓬ Palm Beach (Henry Morrison Flagler Museum, South Ocean Boulevard)
⓭ Orlando (Cypress Gardens, Sea World of Florida, Universal Studios, Walt Disney World)

Time needed: 2 weeks

Wildlife Lovers Tour

If you *ooh* and *aah* over the world's wild creatures, visit them up close and personal or wild and woolly at the below places.

- ❶ **Miami** (Miami Seaquarium, Gator Park)
- ❸ **Coconut Grove, Coral Gables, and Southern Miami** (Miami MetroZoo, Monkey Jungle, Parrot Jungle and Gardens)
- ❹ **The Keys** (Crane Point, National Key Deer Refuge)
- ❻ **The Everglades** (Anhinga Trail, Eco Pond)
- ❼ **Marco Island and Everglades City** (Parks and preserves)
- ❽ **Naples** (Corkscrew Swamp Sanctuary)
- ❿ **Fort Lauderdale and Pompano Beach** (Kissimmee Billie Swamp Safari, Butterfly World)
- ⓫ **Boca Raton and Delray Beach** (Loxahatchee Wildlife Refuge)
- ⓬ **Palm Beach** (Lion Country Safari)
- ⓭ **Orlando** (Sea World of Florida)

Time needed: 2 weeks

Family Fun Tour

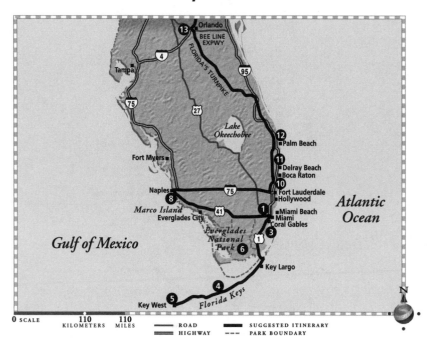

Kids want stuff that bangs and crashes, whirls and whizzes, or is otherwise wild and weird. Here's where to find something to keep everyone happy.

❶ Miami (Museum of Science/Planetarium, airboat tours)
❸ Coconut Grove, Coral Gables, and Southern Miami (Biscayne National Underwater Park, MetroZoo, jungles, Youth Museum)
❹ The Keys (Glassbottom boat, Crane Point, Robbie's Pet Tarpon)
❺ Key West (Conch Tour Train, Ripley's Believe It or Not! Odditorium)
❻ The Everglades (Boat tours, ranger trips, tram tours)
❽ Naples (Teddy Bear Museum of Naples)
❿ Fort Lauderdale and Pompano Beach (Planetarium, swamp safari, Museum of Discovery & Science, Old Dillard Museum)
⓫ Boca Raton and Delray Beach (Museum of Cartoon Art)
⓬ Palm Beach (Lion Country Safari)
⓭ Orlando (Sea World, Universal Studios, Walt Disney World)

Time needed: 2 to 3 weeks

Arts and Architecture Tour

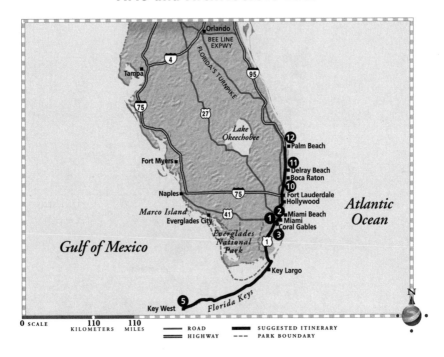

South Florida's architecture runs the gamut from whimsical to grandiose, and its museums feature some of the world's most exciting artwork.

❶ Miami (Vizcaya Museum, Ancient Spanish Monastery of St. Bernard)

❷ Miami Beach (Art Deco District, Wolfsonian Foundation, Bass Museum of Art)

❸ Coconut Grove, Coral Gables, and Southern Miami (Charles Deering Estate, Barnacle State Historic Site, Coral Castle, Merrick House, Lowe Art Museum, Venetian Pool)

❺ Key West (Audubon House, Fort Zachary Taylor, Hemingway House, Heritage House Museum, Key West Lighthouse Museum)

❿ Fort Lauderdale and Pompano Beach (Bonnet House, Museum of Art, Stranahan House)

⓫ Boca Raton and Delray Beach (Museums, Boca Raton Hotel)

⓬ Palm Beach (Museums, South Ocean Boulevard, Breakers Hotel)

Time needed: 1 to 2 weeks

Gardens Tour

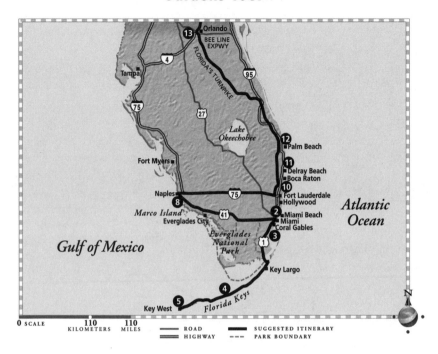

Florida didn't get its floral name for nothing; if you're a flower-lover, you'll delight in the gorgeous gardens throughout the area.

- **②** **Miami Beach** (Ichimura Miami-Japan Garden)
- **③** **Coconut Grove, Coral Gables, and Southern Miami** (Fairchild Tropical Garden, Fruit and Spice Park)
- **④** **The Keys** (Lignumvitae Key State Botanical Gardens)
- **⑤** **Key West** (Nancy Forrester's Secret Garden)
- **⑧** **Naples** (Caribbean Gardens)
- **⑩** **Fort Lauderdale and Pompano** (Flamingo Gardens)
- **⑪** **Boca Raton and Delray Beach** (Japanese Gardens)
- **⑫** **Palm Beach** (Mounts Botanical Garden, Ann Norton Sculpture Gardens)
- **⑬** **Orlando** (Cypress Gardens, Bok Tower Gardens, Leu Gardens, A World of Orchids)

Time needed: 1 to 2 weeks

Romantic Week Tour

Jasmine perfuming the air; full moon gleaming above; candles glittering; waves shushing; palms rustling. Ah, romance. For each destination listed below, I suggest a romantic hotel, restaurant, and nightspot, in that order.

② Miami Beach (Fontainebleau Hilton, The Forge, SoBe/Art Deco District)

③ Coconut Grove, Coral Gables, and Southern Miami (Biltmore Hotel, Norman's, CocoWalk)

⑤ Key West (Marriott's Casa Marina Resort, Louie's Backyard, Sloppy Joe's)

⑩ Fort Lauderdale and Pompano Beach (Hyatt Regency Pier 66, Paesano's, Mai-Kai)

⑪ Boca Raton and Delray Beach (Boca Raton Hotel/The Cloisters, La Vielle Maison, Boston's on the Beach)

⑬ Orlando (Grand Floridian Beach Resort, Maison & Jardin, Church Street Station)

Time needed: 1 week

USING THE PLANNING MAP

A major aspect of itinerary planning is determining your mode of transportation and the route you will follow as you travel from destination to destination. The Planning Map on the following pages will allow you to do just that.

First, read through the destination chapters carefully and note the sights that intrigue you. Then, photocopy the Planning Map so you can try out several different routes that will take you to these destinations. (The mileage chart that follows will help you to calculate your travel distances.) Decide where you will be starting your tour of South Florida. Will you fly into Miami or Orlando, or will you start from somewhere in between? Will you be driving from place to place or flying into major transportation hubs and renting a car for day trips? The answers to these questions will form the basis for your travel route design.

Once you have a firm idea of where your travels will take you, copy your route onto the additional Planning Map in the Appendix. You won't have to worry about where your map is, and the information you need on each destination will always be close at hand.

West Palm Beach skyline

Planning Map: South Florida and the Key

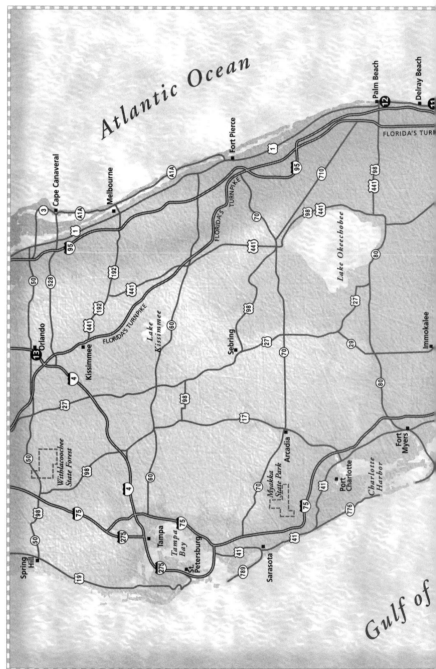

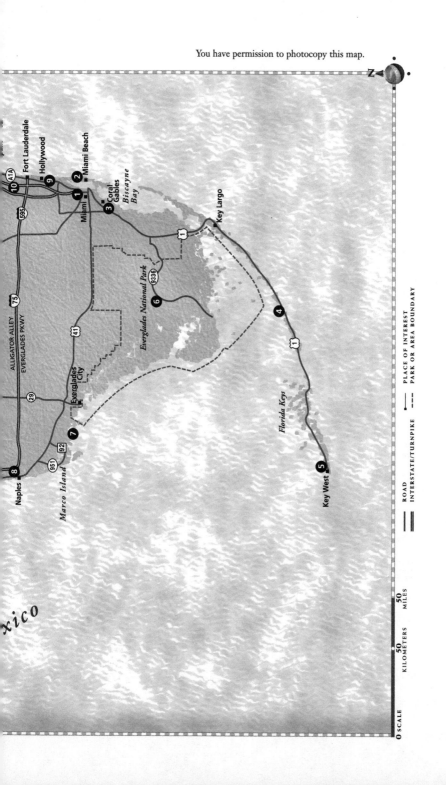

SOUTH FLORIDA AND THE KEYS MILEAGE CHART

	Orlando	Naples	Miami Beach	Miami	Marathon	Key West	Ft. Lauderdale	Everglades Pk.	Coral Gables	Boca Raton
Coral Gables										44
Everglades Pk.									22	62
Ft. Lauderdale								50	27	17
Key West							177	127	149	193
Marathon						49	131	81	105	149
Miami					109	155	22	28	6	39
Miami Beach				8	117	163	23	35	13	40
Naples			114	107	190	236	105	109	108	121
Orlando		187	229	228	227	371	209	243	232	86
Palm Beach	166	147	65	64	175	219	43	92	69	26

WHY VISIT SOUTH FLORIDA?

Why, indeed! Sun, sand, sea, and temperatures so unfailingly warm that *cold* is a four-letter word here—that's why, of course. But South Florida offers more than warmth. Here, in the land that tourism built, you will meet the last word in resortomania and the first word in wilderness, a place of exotic diversity where everything is different, unexpected: Strange blossoms lure living creatures into their lovely, lethal blooms; weird reptiles slither through dank swamps; and birds come in the wildly improbable colors of the sunset, their spectacular plumage matched by golden hibiscus, flaming poinciana trees, and scarlet bougainvillea. Come here chilled from the winter freeze, and you'll be bewitched by an exotic tropical world and seas warm as bathwater. Come in the summer when tropical breezes blow, and you'll revel in cool pools and toasty sands.

Florida is and always has been a place of big dreams, starting with the dreams of those who came here with everything they had and bet it all on this sandy soil. Among those are railroad entrepreneur Henry Flagler; Julia Tuttle, whose foresight and determination created Miami; empire-builder Barron Collier, who created Naples; society architect Addison Mizner, who built most of Palm Beach; avocado farmer John Collins, who dumped his guacamole and sold the land that would become Miami Beach to automobile investor Carl Fisher, who could afford what seemed a very big gamble; Coral Gables' founder George Merrick and Fort Lauderdale's Frank Stranahan; Japanese pineapple planters and Seminoles; Cubans and Miccosukees; a Mouse and many alligators. The list of those who made things happen here goes on and on.

As one who has had sand in her shoes for many a year, I am pleased to introduce you to my chosen place in the world—from the palm-shaded sands of Miami to the pine forests and theme-park nirvana of Orlando, from chic Naples to casual Fort Lauderdale, kooky Key West to posh Palm Beach, wild Lake Okeechobee to even wilder Everglades City and the Ten Thousand Islands, South Florida's varied seductions are hard to resist. Don't try.

HISTORY

It is, of course, those incredibly balmy temperatures that shaped South Florida. Under the sand that squeaks beneath your toes is land half a billion years old, land once underwater and still only a few feet above sea level. Rushing through the limestone base beneath your feet is a huge river of water that is vital to the millions who live here now. Nibbling at your toes is a sea warmed by the Gulf Stream to temperatures so toasty they have created a tourism industry unsurpassed anywhere in the world.

It all started here 6,000 years ago, with the Calusa tribe, who lived along the state's west coast and whose warriors were reputed to be 7 feet tall; and the Tequesta tribe, who ruled at the southern tip of the region. Skeletal remains indicate both tribes survived by hunting and fishing for food—huge clam-shell mounds can still be seen on Marco Island and in the Naples–Fort Myers region. By 1765 both tribes were extinct, killed by disease, war, or the Spanish arrivals.

Enter the Spanish explorers, notably Juan Ponce de León, whose ship anchored off the sands of St. Augustine on Easter Sunday, *Pascua de Florida*, in 1513. Ponce de León set out in search of a fabled fountain of youth, but neither he nor the other Spaniards who visited the region had much luck in Florida—he died from an arrow wound before he could find the elusive fountain. He was followed by Pedro Menéndez de Áviles in 1545, who started the colony's first settlement in St.Augustine.

Meanwhile, the Spanish and the English were feuding. In 1588, when Sir Francis Drake beat the sails off the Spanish Armada, Britain gained sovereignty over the high seas. Later it also acquired Florida in a swap with Spain, which got Cuba. Always a contrary lot, those few settlers living in Florida during the Revolutionary War sided with the British. When Britain lost, the Brits took one look at swampy, mosquito-infested Florida—and what it would cost to keep it—and tossed most of it back to Spain in exchange for the Bahamas, to which many of Florida's Tory sympathizers judiciously fled.

When Thomas Jefferson became president of the United States, he took a look at Florida and decided it really ought to be part of the rest of the country. So he sent General Andrew Jackson down to harass the Spanish. Spain finally tired of the colony, which was expensive and difficult to maintain and, in 1821, agreed to sell it to the United States for $5 million. The United States never actually paid Spain that $5 million—in a style typical of the canny "Cracker" inhabitants of this state, Floridians claimed it all as payment for damages incurred during the Spanish occupation!

By this time, Florida was a land of big plantations that needed growing space. General Jackson tried to get it by ousting the Seminoles, the Native Americans who had settled in the state in the

1700s after breaking from their Creek tribe in the Georgia/Carolinas area. The Seminoles, whose name in Spanish was *Cimarrones*—or wild ones, runaways—fought back with intensity. In 1823 hostilities ended temporarily when the tribe agreed to live on a reservation stretching from Ocala to Lake Okeechobee, but peace did not last; in 1835 the fighting began again when the government decided the best place for the Seminoles was another reservation—in Oklahoma! Fierce and fervent tribal chief Osceola responded to that idea by tossing his long knife into the center of the proposed treaty papers.

For seven years blood ran over the land. Guns roared, plantations burned, and settlers lost their lives in massacres at Colee Hammock in Fort Lauderdale, on Key Biscayne in Miami, and at many other battle sites. When the smoke cleared, the 1,500 Seminoles who had held out for so long against 9,000 soldiers lost, but only by a trick: Osceola was captured, dishonorably, under a flag of truce. Seminole resistance died when their leader perished in a South Carolina prison. Those few hundred who were not shipped off to Oklahoma hid in the impenetrable Everglades, where their descendants still live today. Today the state of the tribe remains technically at war with the United States.

In 1850 the state of Florida consisted of just 60,000 people, scattered about in small settlements, traveling by water and rough roads. During the Civil War, a few battles took place in the north end of the state and a few fortifications went up in Key West, but South Florida played little part in that national nightmare. However, what many feared would happen to plantations without slave labor did happen: during Reconstruction, Florida went broke. But recovery came in the form of Henry Flagler, a millionaire who'd made his fortune helping John D. Rockefeller get Standard Oil off the ground.

Flagler used his money to make more money with railroads that brought wealthy winter travelers south to Florida's sunshine. He spent tens of millions of dollars extending the railroad to Miami and crowned his efforts with the "Railroad That Went to Sea," linking Key West to the rest of Florida. Soon the boom was on, as land developers stampeded into the state to find the pot of gold at the end of a sandy rainbow. South Florida's millionaire-making boom peaked in 1925—and began to crash in 1926, when a vicious hurricane struck South Florida, followed by another storm in 1928 and an equally vicious stock market crash in 1929.

Still standing, however, are a bevy of glamorous hotels from the period—Palm Beach's Breakers, Boca Raton's Cloisters, Coral Gables Biltmore Hotel, and Key West's Casa Marina. In those Roaring

Twenties and Thirties, the sleek and soaring lines of the art deco movement debuted on Miami Beach, creating what is now the world's largest cluster of art deco architecture. As the years passed, some of those hotels and all of the art deco structures moldered, but in the prosperous 1950s and '60s, Florida boomed again. Old hotels were restored and hundreds of new ones were built, turning South Florida into the world's most famous resort.

By the 1970s the state was agog with yet another kind of speculation: where would Walt Disney build the second of its famous theme parks? Orlando was the final answer, an answer that was to change the face of South Florida forever. With the construction of Walt Disney World on thousands of acres of cow pasture on the outskirts of Orlando, the region boomed and is booming still, as that park and others like it expand and multiply. Now a sprawling city that covers the entire center of the state, Orlando is the nation's number-one tourist destination and, indeed, the most popular resort area in the world.

What Orlando lacks, however, is beaches. South Florida is pleased to provide those in abundance. Wherever you travel in the megalopolis that is South Florida, you will never be far from a strip of silica lapped by warm waters, the lure and allure of the southernmost sun capital in the United States—literally and figuratively, the nation's last resort.

CULTURES

South Florida's Tequesta and Calusa tribes were the first to settle into the sunshine, which they had all to themselves for many years. But little by little change came, as Spanish, English, French, and Seminole settlers moved into the north end of the state, which stretched all the way to Louisiana in those days. However, South Florida's swamps, heat, and sandy land remained unappealing to most newcomers—in the 1860 census the population of Miami was just 60! But in the 1920s boom, the population of Miami quadrupled in four years, and it hasn't stopped growing since.

The people of South Florida are as spicy as some of its food, with a long tradition of multicultural influences. By the end of the Civil War, Miami was rife with freed and escaped slaves, army deserters from both sides, Spaniards and Cubans, and others simply seeking to make a new life on land that sold for $1.25 an acre. Bahamians sailed in to work and set up in Coconut Grove—what is now the oldest black community in the region. After the railroad came to Miami in 1897, Southerners moved to the area, and many residents with long lineages still call the city "My-am-ah." During the depression many Jewish entrepreneurs settled in and built small hotels and apartments, many of which form the nucleus of the Art Deco District in Miami Beach. Miami's first mayor was an Irish Catholic, its merchants were Jewish, and John Collins, who created an avocado grove where Collins Avenue now runs, was a Quaker.

Key West became a haven for cigar makers who sailed in from Cuba and stayed for many years before a fire forced them to resettle in Tampa, where those Hav-A-Tampa cigars were born. Fidel Castro's rise to power in Cuba in 1959 led more than half a million Cubans to seek exile in the region, most of them assuming they'd return to Cuba in just a year or two. That was nearly 40 years ago, and Cuban language and traditions are now a vital part of the culture of South Florida. Their enormous influence helped lure many other Central and South American natives, who have been joined by Vietnamese, Thai, Indian, Pakistani, and Chinese immigrants, making South Florida an epicenter of the New World.

THE ARTS

South Floridians have long endured the sneers of those who have called it a cultural wasteland, and they aren't standing for it anymore. Top Broadway shows play throughout the region, and celebrity-watching is an Olympic sport in the trendy SoBe (South Beach) area of Miami Beach. Fort Lauderdale, Palm Beach, Miami, and Naples all have sparkling performing arts centers that lure the most famous names in dance, theater, and music. All four of those cities have ballet and opera companies; Miami City Ballet leads the pack with its ambitious new creations led by artistic director and star Edward Villella.

Hundreds of art galleries can be found throughout the region, and some of the world's great artwork resides in Palm Beach, Fort Lauderdale, and Miami art museums. In February and March, Fort Lauderdale, Coconut Grove, and Winter Park each sponsors a two-day juried art show that draws the nation's top artists and crafts workers.

Festivals celebrate the diversity of the region—more than a million people samba and merengue at the annual Calle Ocho Festival in March. Miami celebrates New Year's Eve with a pre–football game

Orange Bowl Parade, televised nationally. Fort Lauderdale's December Winterfest Boat Parade lights up the night with a celebrity grand marshal atop a massive, decorated yacht, trailed by a hundred or so similarly bejeweled sailing craft.

In Palm Beach the annual spring Sunfest draws throngs of music lovers to a lively jazz festival, and throughout South Florida the region's agricultural roots are saluted in spring county fairs. In May Fort Lauderdale's Shell Air and Sea Show lures a million spectators to a two-day look at fancy flying. Both Miami and Fort Lauderdale have annual film festivals. Seminole Indians get in on the action with patchwork quilting and beading on display at several festivals near Naples, in Hollywood, and at the Brighton Reservation at Lake Okeechobee.

CUISINE

Take lobsters from the Caribbean, *arroz con pollo* and *ropa vieja* (shredded beef stew), jerk pork and cracked conch. Team them up with mangoes and Key limes, sugar cane and citrus, star-shaped carambola and little round sea grapes. Toss with *pad Thai*, dim sum, *capellini*, gyros, *feijoada* (Brazilian black bean stew), tacos, and salsa. Stir with some of the greatest chefs in the nation seeking fame and sunshine in South Florida. Add a few multicultural culinary innovations, and you've got "New World" cuisine, an unusual dining experience that's as diverse as the mix of nationalities that create it.

Thanks to all the nationalities that have merged here, Floridians have acquired a taste for crusty Cuban bread and steaming, thick, black *café Cubano* in thimble-size cups; conch (pronounced "konk") chowder made from conch—that creature that lives inside the pink shells you "listen" to—and hot-hot-hot conch salad marinated in lime juice; tomatoes grown on many acres south of Miami; paella, a rice-and-seafood dish from Spain; *picadillo*, a mix of ground meat, olives, and raisins in a spicy Cuban sauce; Creole gumbo and jambalaya; and pecans, kumquats, mangos, papayas, peppers, and eggplants, all grown around Lake Okeechobee. In South Florida you can nibble a Jamaican meat patty, savor Mexican mole (MOE-lay), try Thai. You can dine in Chinese, Vietnamese, Korean, Brazilian, Indian, Argentinean, Colombian, Venezuelan, and Creole restaurants, among many others.

Talented chefs who have settled here from all over the nation and the world combine the region's many native products into award-winning dishes that have made South Florida one of the nation's culinary capitals. Huge cattle ranches cover much of the state, with Kissimmee and Orlando the center of a beef production area that stretches south to Lake Okeechobee. Florida has more than 21,000 cattle ranches and has more cows than any other state east of the Mississippi. The sea provides more than a billion pounds of good eating, including the oxymoronic jumbo shrimp, succulent lobster, grouper, dolphin (no, not the Flipper kind), kingfish, bay and sea scallops, pompano, swordfish, tuna, red and yellow snapper, mackerel, sea bass, and many others. Topping all of them are stone crab claws, a delicacy harvested only from October to May and only in Naples. The claws are a renewable resource: fisherman capture the crabs, break off one large claw then throw them back into the sea, where they regenerate the missing one.

Where there's food, there's drink. Florida's climate invites a sip of something tall and cool—daiquiris, made popular by Cuban immigrants, margaritas from Mexico, rum punch from the Caribbean. Florida citrus has even been turned into wine, and microbreweries are springing up everywhere, with three in tiny Key West alone, at last count. And, lest we forget the most important drink of all, there's lots of orange juice.

FLORA AND FAUNA

South Florida's symbol is the ubiquitous palm tree, but there is life beyond palms, although some of it is very strange indeed. Strangler figs twine themselves around other trees, eventually cutting off light and nutrients, killing the trees to make way for new life on the forest floor. Gumbo-limbo trees sport bright red bark that has earned them the "tourist tree" moniker for their sunburned look—stick a twig from one of these trees into the ground, and you'll have a new one in weeks. And no matter how you plant a traveler palm, it will twist around to point north, creating a jungle compass and providing, in its trunk, a quart of water for wilderness travelers. Sabal palms, the state tree, often end up in salads as—you guessed it—hearts of palm.

Unusual tree stories go on and on, crowned by the stately royal palm, oak, and mahogany, and bottoming out with the skunk tree that exudes the odor its name suggests. Where the land is high, pine trees prevail; pine forests are common around Orlando and Kissimmee. In Miami's lowlands, red mangroves spread their roots right into the salt water to create a home for microorganisms and begin a complex food chain that supports fish, birds, and ultimately, humans. Black mangroves are just as weird: they send up fields of cigar-like shoots that absorb air and nutrients.

Flowers bloom in amazing profusion, from multicolored hibiscus that grow big as platters to red ixora hedges and rainbow-hued bougainvillea that are a brown-thumber's dream: they thrive on little water and no fertilizer. Queen of the floral world is the orchid, which grows wild here and is easily cultivated in South Florida's subtropical atmosphere.

Along the shores of Orlando's scores of lakes dwell a wide variety of waterbirds, many of them visible at wildlife preserves and theme parks. Farther south in the Everglades and throughout the rest of South Florida, more than 500 species of birds twitter and chirp. Add to those the dozens of species that migrate here each winter, and you have a bird-watcher's paradise.

Leggy cattle egrets can be spotted even on city streets. Snowy egrets fluff out their plumes in a showy courtship display that nearly wiped the birds out when hunters bagged them for ladies' hat feathers. Roseate spoonbills sport platypus-like bills and rosy bodies that resemble South Florida's icon, the flamingo. Other birds you're likely to spot here include black anhingas, hawks, turkey vultures, ospreys, a rare cuckoo found only here, barred owls, herons, woodstorks, cormorants, caracaras, hawks, rare snail kites, white ibis, blue herons, pelicans, gulls, bald eagles, and more.

In the waters are more unusual creatures. Strangest of them all is the no-longer-endangered alligator, which can be found in nearly every body of water in the region and can easily be seen throughout the Everglades. Lake Okeechobee is one of the nation's best bass-fishing lakes, but you can also snag speckled perch, crappie, shellcracker, slabsided bluegill, bream, and freshwater catfish there. In the sea is an enormous variety of creatures ranging from the fearsome shark to playful dolphins and trophy-winning marlin, tarpon, and sailfish. Once a year lobster fans can go in search of their prey, and any time of year anglers can go after snapper, sea bass, sea trout, grouper, dolphin, snook, and the elusive bonefish. Shrimp boats sail from docks in Key West and Miami.

Land-based creatures include tiny Key deer (no bigger than collies), bobcats, river otters, raccoons, muskrats, opossums, marsh rabbits, and even, occasionally, a bear. Reptiles include many varieties of lizards and snakes, with at least three poisonous varieties to avoid—water moccasins, rattlesnakes, and orange-and-black-banded coral snakes.

Endangered species can still be seen here, but no one knows how long they'll last. American crocodiles, found only in the Everglades, have diminished to just a few hundred. Only about 1,200 fat, gentle Florida manatees remain, and sloe-eyed Florida panthers number just 30. Yellow-and-brown swallowtail butterflies and four species of sea turtle are endangered, as is the apple snail that is the only food of the at-risk snail kite.

LAY OF THE LAND

Just think flat, flat, and flatter. You won't find any mountains in South Florida, and after awhile you'll be thrilled at the sight of a high bridge. That said, however, flatlands have a personality all of their own, as you will see. Hammocks, which are jungled rises in the sawgrass prairies that spread across the region, shelter veritable animal villages. Mangrove swamps are home to thousands of birds and animals. Seas are filled with colorful creatures, and the beaches are decorated with shells and sandpipers.

Florida's land is highest on its north end and from there slopes slowly southward into the Atlantic and the Gulf of Mexico. Rolling hills around Orlando flatten out into sawgrass prairies from Lake Okeechobee south. From there the land is so flat that the Everglades' invisible river water "flows" at a record speed of one-quarter mile every 24 hours!

The sea glitters everywhere you look, breaking the flat monotony with its sparkling clarity. The water is at its most beautiful in the Keys, where it is clear and warm as liquid sunlight. But it's also gorgeous in Biscayne Bay, where diamond-tipped waves lap onto tiny island beaches, and you can take in the gleaming panorama as you soar across causeways. In Fort Lauderdale the sea soothes and satisfies, rolling along beside you as you drive.

OUTDOOR ACTIVITIES

Smiled upon by nature, which permits 365 days of outdoor activity, South Florida knows how to play. Every water sport you can dream up is old news here—surfboarding, Jet Skiing, parachute parasailing, windsurfing, water biking, rubber rafting, body surfing, snorkeling, scuba diving—you name it, it's here. Canoeing and kayaking are available in dozens of parks as well as throughout the Keys, with a 99-mile trail through the Everglades and many shorter hops in rivers and lakes. Power-boating is a mania in even the smallest towns along the coast lines, and you will rarely see the sea without also seeing sails. Marinas are huge and packed on both coastlines.

Two strange contraptions offer unusual aquatic transportation: fat-tired swamp buggies, which sit high up on massive tires and can slog through the swamp without stalling, and airboats powered by jet engines that allow the flat-bottomed craft to skim across the shallow marsh waters. More conventional charter boats and drift-fishing craft take you out into the briny in search of a big one, while bass-fishing guides will help you hook a whopper in Lake Okeechobee or in one of Orlando's many lakes.

But South Florida offers outdoor enthusiasts more than water. Nature trails take you through the area's abundant wildlife, and bicycle trails can be found in every city and park. Horseback riding, shooting, hunting, dirt-bike riding, and archery round out the many options available. Lacking only mountain climbing and river rafting, South Florida even has ice skating, rock climbing, ski practice, and ice hockey.

Duffers will find hundreds of golf courses, including some of the best-known competition courses in the world. Thousands of tennis courts await lobbers whose star icons play here in winter. Thousands, perhaps millions, of swimming pools await swimmers, who also have, of course, hundreds of miles of ocean in which to splash. Spectator sports include National League football, baseball, hockey, and basketball teams. You can bet on thoroughbreds, harness horses, greyhounds, and a Spanish Basque country ball game called jai alai.

Finally, thanks to an impressively efficient network of expressways and to vast, unpopulated distances, driving also qualifies as a South Florida sport. Finding a rental convertible in peak winter season may require supernatural assistance.

PRACTICAL TIPS

HOW MUCH WILL IT COST?

Thanks to the state's popularity, which has spawned competition in everything, what you spend depends on when you come here and how high a roller you are. I've tried to pass on some big-splurge suggestions and some low-key, low-cost spots so you can pick according to your own budget and taste among the wide range of offerings. However, there are some South Florida experiences that are simply worth it, no matter what they cost.

To keep expenses down, plan your trip for the off-season, when prices are lowest throughout the region. Throughout this book, I've quoted peak-season rates to give you an idea of the most your trip would cost. High season throughout the region stretches from about mid-December to late April or, more succinctly, from Christmas to Easter. After that prices plummet. Hotel rates drop as much as 50 percent or more in most parts of South Florida, although the popularity of the Keys and Orlando keeps prices up in many hotels in those regions, even in summer. (Orlando is an exception to nearly every rule, with many motels in Kissimmee, the bedroom to Walt Disney World, offering rates of $25 or $30 even in peak season, and a host of fast-food spots competing for your dollar.)

You can also save money by seeking out small motels—Fort Lauderdale has a particularly active small-hotels community, with its own brochure and marketing efforts, called Superior Small Hotels. Small hoteliers also are often willing to bargain down their rates for long stays. Heat, insects, and increasing urbanity have made camping a less appealing option here than in some other parts of the country. Primitive camping is possible but difficult.

Expect to pay $70 to $125 for budget accommodations in winter and about half that in summer. If you're camping, budget $25 to $35 a night per person in the high season. Add $25 to $50 or more a day per person for meals, depending on what kind of dining your moods and budget dictate. Also add $10 to $20 per person for each attraction you plan to visit—considerably more for Orlando theme parks—and figure in some cash for souvenirs and gifts. If you have time to plan ahead, call the regions you intend to visit (see contact names and numbers under Resources, at the end of this chapter)—many offer books full of discount coupons that can save you a bundle.

WHEN TO GO

M ost people are drawn to South Florida in winter, when the rest of the world is frozen. However, for my money spring is the most beautiful time of year here; with the bulk of tourists gone, restaurants and accommodations tend to be more accessible and less expensive, and yet the weather is still cool and dry. October and November are good months to visit for similar reasons. If you plan a late spring trip, be forewarned: frequent short but torrential rains during late spring and summer make for lots of mud; if you're visiting Lake Okeechobee or other remote areas, come prepared.

During the summer beachfront locations are blessed with breezes, and everything, absolutely everything, everywhere is air-conditioned. Mosquitoes with voracious appetites are at their most avaricious in the Everglades and other areas with heavy undergrowth but are not usually much of a problem in cities, where spraying programs control the critters. In general, the festivals, cultural events, and recreational activities that fill the winter months occur less frequently in the heat of summer. Orlando, which is far inland, can be hot and muggy in the summer, while in winter it is often colder than coastal cities.

CLIMATE

S outh Florida is dry from November to May, wet thereafter. It even rains differently in Florida, rarely producing long gloomy days of dreary gray. Instead, rain arrives with ear-splitting thunderclaps and scudding black clouds crackling with lightning that flashes and flickers before torrents pour from the sky. Then, suddenly, it's all over, with nothing left but white wispy clouds racing across the sky and leftover drops arcing into a showy rainbow. An hour of sunshine dries it all to a memory.

From June to November, South Floridians keep a close watch on the weather, ever fearful of the hurricanes that periodically wreak havoc here. Although only a few have done serious damage, those few have been memorable, indeed. Hurricanes are frightening, but they are never a surprise, thanks to a hardworking weather service that tracks every big wind. When a storm is brewing, South Floridians know about it many days in advance, and they know how to prepare. As a visitor you will know in plenty of time to leave the area if a big wind is on the way. Even if you stay, however, you are likely to weather the storm safely, thanks to a network of shelters and strict building codes designed to keep structures safe in a storm. Although the official hurricane season lasts all summer, storms occur most often between August and November.

Temperatures in winter are in the 60 to 80°F range, rarely dropping below 50°F; in summer they rise to 80 to 90°F, rarely higher. However, humidity is high in the summer, often 80 to 90 percent, so the heat is muggier than in winter.

No matter how cloudy you think it is, that Florida sun is powerful enough to melt macadam, so use your head for more than a sunglasses rack—skin that has not seen sunshine for months is no match for the relentless rays. Bring sun hats, sunglasses, and sunscreen, and take extra precautions with babies. Don't try to get a tan in one day, and do stay out of the noonday sun. If you don't take my advice, take my medicine: aloe, a gelatin-like plant, soothes the burn and is available in burn preparations as well as in many Florida gardens and grocery stores.

SOUTH FLORIDA AND THE KEYS

Average daily temperatures in degrees Fahrenheit, plus monthly precipitation in inches.

	Miami	Key West	Naples	Palm Beach	Orlando
Jan.	67	69	64	64	59
	3.1	4.2	4.4	3.9	1.5
Mar.	74	74	71	72	68
	4.6	1.9	.75	2.4	2.1
May	82	84	80	81	80
	2.9	.66	4.0	.83	4.2
July	86	85	82	83	82
	6.4	2.9	NR	6.9	5.1
Sept.	84	84	83	82	82
	10.4	4.4	10.9	7.5	3.6
Nov.	74	75	72	71	66
	2.5	00	.59	1.5	1.7

TRANSPORTATION

If you're flying here, you have your pick of at least five airports—Miami International and Orlando International, the state's busiest airports, followed by Fort Lauderdale/Hollywood International, Palm Beach International, and the smallest, Southwest Florida International Airport, in Fort Myers. All welcome a variety of domestic and international flights, and Miami is now a hub for most South American and many European airlines. A few regularly scheduled carriers also fly into Naples Municipal Airport.

Car rental agencies are locked in fierce competition in Florida, which provides you with some of the least expensive rental rates in the nation. Alamo, Value, and Dollar are the low-price leaders, with weekly rates under $100 for subcompact cars, including unlimited mileage. Recreational vehicles can also be rented but are considerably more expensive, as are convertibles, the car of choice for many in this sunny clime.

Roads throughout the region are excellent. Florida's Sunshine State Parkway (more commonly called the Florida Turnpike) cuts through the center of the state past Orlando and heads east to run parallel to the coastline. I-95 runs from Miami north along the east coast. Alligator Alley (SR 84) joins I-75 to go west from Fort Lauderdale to Naples and north to Tampa. Tamiami Trail (U.S. 41) connects Miami to Naples. I-4 joins Daytona to Tampa through Orlando. One road only, U.S. 1, goes past the entrance to the Everglades and on through the Florida Keys to Key West.

Connecting those major throughways are many smaller highways and roads. Unfortunately, traffic is part of the package, but if you avoid peak traffic hours in urban areas—7 to 9 a.m. and 4 to 6 p.m.—you'll rarely get steamed. Some rules of the road: Seat belts are mandatory in Florida; right turns on red lights are permitted; interstate speed limit is now 70 miles per hour outside urban areas, 55 to 60 elsewhere.

Amtrak trains connect South Florida along the coastline and travel to Orlando and Tampa. An Amtrak Auto-Train carries you and your car between Sanford, Florida (just north of Orlando), and Lorton, Virginia (not far from Washington, D.C.), in an overnight trip. Tri-Rail commuter trains connect West Palm Beach to Miami, where MetroMover and MetroRail circle the inner city and unite it with the suburbs. Greyhound buses serve large and small cities in South Florida.

CAMPING, LODGING, AND DINING

South Florida has plenty of campgrounds, particularly around Orlando, where family budgets are blessed with plenty of inexpensive options, and in the Naples/Marco/Everglades areas, where many retirees visit and live. Rates vary rather widely according to park facilities, which often are as elaborate as resorts. You'll pay $25 to $40 in winter for an RV site with water, sewer, and electrical hookups, less in other seasons; if you're visiting in winter, reserve a space well in advance.

The large, historic hotels and chic, contemporary ones are more expensive, of course, than their smaller, less glamorous counterparts; however, the larger hotels often offer deep discounts and toss in complimentary breakfasts or theme park discounts in nonpeak months. Big-splurge hotels require a substantial outlay of cash in winter, but they'll make you feel like royalty.

Smaller hotels and inns have lower overheads and are often willing to bargain for your business, especially if you're staying a week or more. Large hotels, with higher overheads and employees tuned to the bottom line, don't wheel and deal, although it's always wise to ask for special rates and vacation packages. These days, almost everyone belongs to some organization—AAA, AARP, gasoline clubs, airline clubs, even your large-company employer—so ask, then ask again. You may be amazed at the response.

Many motels are also available, some of them furnished with antiques and lots of chintz and lace. Bed-and-breakfast establishments are becoming more common in Florida, but it's a slow process. Orlando now has a few, and Key West, with its abundant Victorian architecture, has many. Bed and breakfasts in Florida, however, tend to be as expensive as many hotels.

Dining options vary widely in price as well as in cuisine. This book gives you a sampling of all the options. Fast-food chains aren't included—we all know what those are, and they're everywhere in Florida, although an interesting, little-known chain, Steak 'n' Shake, in the Orlando area, does fast food right. As is true anywhere, the best way to keep down meal costs is to rein in your consumption of alcoholic beverages and such extras as appetizers, desserts, specialty coffees, and side orders. Because many of Florida's trendiest and most lauded restaurants become history in a matter of months, I've generally suggested dining spots that have been in business for years, in the hope that they'll still be there when you get here. If you want the hottest spot on the block, ask around and check local newspaper and magazine restaurant reviews.

RECOMMENDED READING

Florida and South Florida have always been popular literary subjects—with research done in February, of course—and hundreds of books have been written about the state. Here are a few of my favorites, books that will help you see beneath the surface and into the heart of this lovely land.

Start with Ernest Hemingway, whose novel *To Have and Have Not* is based in Key West. Then pick up Marjorie Stoneman Douglas' *The Everglades: River of Grass*, which was the catalyst for restoration and preservation of the state's most famous wilderness area. Marjorie Kinnan Rawlings put Florida on many a map decades ago when her novel *The Yearling* won a Pulitzer Prize, and a later novel, *Cross Creek*, detailed her experiences in the countryside not far from Orlando.

For historical perspective, have a look at Robert Wilder's novels. Wilder left an advertising career to write about Florida and the Bahamas, to which the state has long been closely tied. *Wind from the Carolinas* describes the early Tory immigration to the Bahamas, much of it from Florida. Another Wilder novel, *Bright Feather*, details Seminole chief Osceola's vain struggle against the destruction of the Seminole tribes. Way back in 1791, William Bartram, son of a botanist, wrote about his Florida travels in a book called *Travels Through North and South Carolina, Georgia and East and West Florida* (my, how we've changed). Patrick Smith's *A Land Remembered* is a prize-winning novel that covers a century of developments in the state through the eyes of a pioneer family. *The True Sea*, by F. W. Belland, is one of several books to tackle the tale of Henry Morrison Flagler and his railroad empire.

Gloria Jahoda's *The Other Florida* provides a charming look at the region and the state (it's out of print, but check used bookstores). Anne Morrow Lindbergh, wife of the famous aviator, spent many vacations in the Naples area; here she wrote *Gift from the Sea*, which offers some haunting observations on the ties that bind us to the sea and to each other.

For a frivolous look at some of the shenanigans that take place here, there are few better storytellers than the late mystery writer John D. MacDonald, who lived on Florida's west coast for many years. His detective Travis McGee lived on a yacht in Fort Lauderdale's Bahia Mar yacht basin and was visited by lots of dames with problems. Following in MacDonald's footsteps (but in his own style) is *Miami Herald* columnist Carl Hiaasen, who has written several novels focusing on the steamy—and seamy—side of South Florida.

Contemporary nonfiction books that will help you enjoy Florida and its diversions include *A Field Guide to Southeastern and Caribbean Seashore* by Eugene Kaplan; *Florida Wildlife Viewing Guide* by Susan Cerulean and Ann Morrow; *A Birder's Guide to Florida* by James Lane; *Adventure Guide to the Everglades & Florida Keys* by Joyce and Jon Huber; *Adventuring Along the Gulf of Mexico* by Donald Schueler; *Florida Parks* by Gerald Grow; *The Hiker's Guide to Florida* by Timothy O'Keefe; and *Diver's Guide to Florida and the Florida Keys* by Jim Stachowicz.

Filmmakers love Florida, which rivals California as the top filmmaking state in the nation. Hundreds of films have been made here, the most famous of which is *Key Largo*, starring Humphrey Bogart and Lauren Bacall. *Where the Boys Are*, a 1960s film based on Fort Lauderdale's one-time popularity as a spring-break haven for college students, put Fort Lauderdale on a map it didn't want to be on—those days of suds and sun are history now. *Tony Rome*, with Frank Sinatra and Raquel Welch, was filmed here, as were Robert De Niro's *Cape Fear*; the James Bond *Goldfinger* thriller; *Cross Creek*, about Rawlings' life; *Creature from the Black Lagoon*, a sci-fi classic; and two of Burt Reynolds' *Smokey and the Bandit* films. Television series focusing on south Florida were topped by *The Golden Girls* and the famous—or infamous—*Miami Vice*.

RESOURCES

Every village, town, and city in Florida—far more than can be listed here—has a Chamber of Commerce that specializes in statistics. Here's a look at the region's other major information sources.

Central Florida Convention and Visitors Bureau: 600 North Broadway, Suite 300, Bartow, FL 33830; (941) 534-4375 or (800) 828-7655. For Lake Wales, Haines City, Winter Haven, Polk City, Lakeland information.
Department of Agriculture and Consumer Services, Division of Forestry: 3125 Conner Boulevard, Tallahassee, FL 32399; (904) 488-6611. For state forest information.
Department of Business and Professional Regulations, Division of Parimutuel

Wagering: 8405 NW 53rd Street, Suite C250, Miami, FL 33166; (305) 470-5675. For information on horse and greyhound racing and jai alai dates.

Department of Environmental Protection, Office of Fisheries Management and Assistance: Mail Station 250, 3900 Commonwealth Boulevard, Tallahassee, FL 32399; (904) 488-7326. For saltwater fishing information.

Destination Florida: The first Website devoted to Florida, run by the *Miami Herald.* You can reach it at www.goflorida.com.

Florida Association of Canoe Liveries and Outfitters: P.O. Box 1764, Arcadia, FL 33821; (941) 494-1215.

Florida Association of Dive Operators: Tallahassee, FL 32303; (904) 386-5245.

Florida Attractions Association: P.O. Box 10295, Tallahassee, FL 32302; (904) 222-2885.

Florida Campground Association: 1340 Dickers Drive, Tallahassee, FL 32303; (904) 562-7151.

Florida Department of Agriculture and Consumer Services: Room 416, Mayo Building, Tallahassee, FL 32399; (904) 488-9682. For information on equestrian trails.

Florida Department of Environmental Protection, Office of Recreation and Parks: Mail Station 535, 3900 Commonwealth Boulevard, Tallahassee, FL 32399; (904) 488-9872. For state park information.

Florida Department of State, Bureau of Historic Preservation: R. A. Gray Building, 500 South Bronough Street, Tallahassee, FL 32399; (904) 487-2333.

Florida Department of Transportation: 605 South Suwanee Street, Tallahassee, FL 32399; (904) 487-1200. For bicycling information.

Florida Game and Fresh Water Fish Commission: 620 South Meridian Street, Farris Bryant Building, Tallahassee, FL 32399; (904) 488-1960 or (904) 488-2975. For hunting and fishing licenses.

Florida Hotel/Motel Association: 200 West College Avenue, Tallahassee, FL 32301; (904) 224-2888.

Florida Keys and Key West: P.O. Box 866, Key West, FL 33041; (305) 296-1552 or (800) FLA-KEYS.

Florida Sports Foundation: 107 West Gaines Street, Suite 466, Tallahassee, FL 32399; (904) 488-8347. Includes golf, baseball spring training, and fishing information.

Florida Tourism Marketing Corp.: This is the state's visitor information center—ask for the *Florida Vacation Guide.* 661 East Jefferson or

107 West Gaines Street, Tallahassee, FL 32301; (904) 488-5607 or (904) 487-1462.

Florida Trail Association: P. O. Box 13708, Gainesville, FL 32604; (904) 378-8823.

Fort Lauderdale/Hollywood International Airport: off U.S. 1 south of SR 84, 1400 Lee Wagener Boulevard, Fort Lauderdale; (954) 359-6100.

Greater Fort Lauderdale Convention and Visitors Bureau: 1850 Eller Drive, Suite 303, Fort Lauderdale, FL 33316; (954) 765-4466 or (800) 22-SUNNY.

Greater Miami and The Beaches Hotel Association: 407 Lincoln Road, Suite 10G, Miami Beach, FL 33139; (305) 531-3553 or (800) SEE-MIAMI.

Greater Miami Convention and Visitors Bureau: 701 Brickell Avenue, Suite 2700, Miami, FL 33131; (305) 539-3000 or (800) 283-2707.

Key West International Airport: 3491 South Roosevelt Boulevard, Key West, FL 33040; (305) 296-7223.

Kissimmee–St. Cloud Convention and Visitors Bureau: P.O. Box 422007, Kissimmee, FL 34742; (407) 847-5000 or (800) 327-9159.

Lake County Convention and Visitors Bureau: 20763 U.S. Highway 27, Groveland, FL 34736; (352) 429-3673 or (800) 798-1071. For Leesberg, Tavares, Clermont, Howey in the Hills, and Mount Dora information.

Marathon Airport: MM52, Marathon; (305) 743-2155.

Marco Island and The Everglades Convention and Visitors Bureau: 1102 North Collier Boulevard, Marco Island, FL 33937; (941) 394-7549 or (800) 788-MARCO.

Miami International Airport: I-95 at NW 36th Street/Le Jeune Road, Miami; (305) 876-7077.

Naples Area Tourism Bureau: P.O. Box 10129, Naples, FL 33941; (941) 262-2712 or (800) 605-7878.

Naples Municipal Airport: Airport-Pulling Road, Naples; (941) 643-0733.

Office of Greenways and Trails: 325 John Knox Road, Building 500, Tallahassee, FL 32303; (904) 487-4784.

Orlando/Orange County Convention and Visitors Bureau/Visitors Center: 8723 International Drive, Orlando, FL 32819; (407) 363-5871 or (800) 643-9492.

Palm Beach County Convention and Visitors Bureau: 1555 Palm Beach Lakes Boulevard, Suite 204, West Palm Beach, FL 33401; (561) 471-3995 or (800) 544-7256.

Palm Beach International Airport: I-95 at (headed south) Exit 51, Belvedere Road, or (headed north) Exit 50, Southern Boulevard, West Palm Beach; (561) 471-7400.

Seminole County Convention and Visitors Bureau: 105 International Parkway, Heathrow, FL 32746; (407) 328-5770 or (800) 800-7832. For Altamonte Springs, Sanford, and Casselberry information.

Southwest Florida International Airport: 16000 Chamberlin Parkway, Suite 8671, Fort Myers; (941) 768-1000 (automated service) or (941) 768-4700.

Sunny Isles Beach Resort Association: 17100 Collins Avenue, Suite 208, Sunny Isles Beach, FL 33160; (305) 947-5826.

U.S. Forest Service: 227 North Bronough Street, Suite 4061, Tallahassee, FL 32301; (904) 681-7265.

U.S. Tennis Association, Florida Section: 1280 SW 36th Avenue, Suite 305, Pompano Beach, FL 33069; (954) 652-2866.

1
MIAMI

A t the turn of the century, the very same things that bring millions of travelers to South Florida each year brought a man and a woman who were to change the history of this region. That woman was feisty pioneer Julia Tuttle, who realized that South Florida would prosper if the railroad, which then stopped in Jacksonville, were extended to Miami. So when a freeze killed citrus groves as far south as West Palm Beach, including the oranges for railroad magnate Henry Flagler's morning juice, Julia sent him a note—and oranges from Miami. That did it. Flagler extended the railroad to South Florida's sunshine. And the boom was on.

So quickly did pieces of these beaches sell that "binder boys" peddled deeds on street corners, shoving bucks and binders into shoeboxes. One booming winter day, so many trains full of sun-seeking tourists arrived that there was no place for the trains to turn around to get back out again!

Miami's skyline has changed radically since those early days, but its brash and bullish outlook hasn't altered much. Verve, élan, and a determined *joie de vivre* have made Miami the undisputed economic center of Florida and the Caribbean, home to the world's largest cruise port, center of the state's aviation industry, and certainly the most sophisticated city in Florida. Just as Flagler once did, the hopeful continue to arrive here in search of two weeks of sunshine or a lifetime of leisure. Miami has capitalized on this diversity to create a chic, cosmopolitan urbanity that is, indeed, a New World. ◼

MIAMI

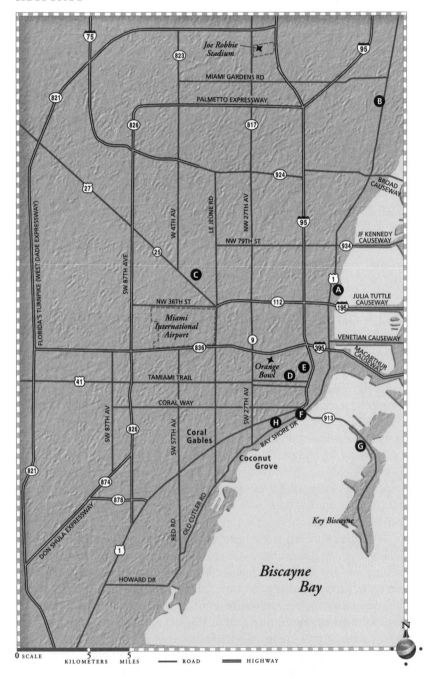

Sights

- Ⓐ American Police Hall of Fame and Museum
- Ⓑ Ancient Spanish Monastery of St. Bernard
- Ⓒ Hialeah Park
- Ⓓ Historical Museum of Southern Florida
- Ⓔ Miami Art Museum
- Ⓕ Miami Museum of Science and Space Transit Planetarium
- Ⓖ Miami Seaquarium
- Ⓗ Vizcaya Museum and Gardens

A PERFECT DAY IN MIAMI

Pack up some bagels and o.j., find a shady spot along Key Biscayne's Rickenbacker Causeway, and breakfast beside the sea. Then drop into the city's past in the massive magnificence of Villa Vizcaya, Miami's first mansion. Add a contemplative element to your exploration of the past at the elegant Spanish Monastery. For a change of pace, visit Lolita the killer whale at the Miami Seaquarium. On the way back, shop for handmade cigars, a colorful *piñata*, sinful pastries, and Cuban coffee along Calle Ocho, Little Havana's main street. Then head to Bayside Marketplace for tapas and plan a late dinner and dancing at one of the area's into-the-wee-hours clubs.

SIGHTSEEING HIGHLIGHTS

★★★ **Miami Seaquarium**—A killer whale that plants a wet smooch on her trainer's cheek and pirouettes with all the grace of a skilled, if rather hefty, ballerina is the star here. Large as she looms in the star category, Lolita the killer whale gets plenty of competition from television superstar Flipper, a talented dolphin who squeaks and squeals to his fans. One of the state's oldest attractions, the Seaquarium also introduces you to a flock of toothy sharks, thousands of rainbow-hued tropical fish, and some chubby manatees. Details: 4400 Rickenbacker Causeway; (305) 361-5705; open daily 9:30 a.m. to 6 p.m. Admission $19.95 adults, $14.95 children ages 3 to 9. (4 hours)

★★★ **Vizcaya Museum and Gardens**—Miami's most beautiful house, this enchanting private villa built in 1916 by James Deering (the Chicago International Harvester millionaire) cost $15 million way back then. All that money created a 70-room Renaissance palace that took over five years and more than 1,000 craftspeople to complete. Set in the middle of a tropical jungle and adorned with formal gardens, Vizcaya overlooks the sea and is dotted with fountains, statuary, reflecting pools, and a magnificent "moored" stone barge that doubles as a breakwater. Inside you can visit 34 rooms with frescoed ceilings, tapestries, priceless paintings, and a huge indoor swimming pool. Details: 3251 South Miami Avenue; (305) 250-9133; open daily (except Christmas) 9:30 a.m. to 5 p.m.; ticket booth closes at 4:30 p.m. Admission $10 adults, $5 children ages 6 to 12. (3 hours)

★★ **Ancient Spanish Monastery of St. Bernard**—In today's world tranquility is rare, but you will find it here in this ancient monastery believed to be the oldest building in the Western Hemisphere. Publisher William Randolph Hearst, famous for his San Simeon mansion in California, dismantled this monastery built in 1141 in Segovia, Spain, and shipped it to California. Before it got there, however, it met up with Miami customs officers, who, fearing hoof-and-mouth bacteria in the wooden crates, ordered them burned, leaving a huge jumble of masonry. It took five years to solve the resultant jigsaw puzzle and reconstruct the building, now home to a priceless medieval art collection. Details: 16711 West Dixie Highway, North Miami Beach; (305) 945-1462; open Monday through Saturday 10 a.m. to 4 p.m., Sunday noon to 4 p.m. Admission $4 adults, $1 children under age 12. (1 hour)

★★ **Hialeah Park**—Often dubbed the world's most beautiful racetrack, this handsome thoroughbred track is now a National Historic Place. Acres and acres of floral gardens, tropical jungles, and royal palms surround striking, tile-roofed, Mediterranean architecture with ivy-covered walls and sweeping stone staircases. In the center of it all lives a colony of flamingos that circle the course after the seventh race in a spectacular display of black-tipped pink plumage. Details: East 4th Avenue between 21st and 32nd Streets, Hialeah; (305) 885-8000; open daily except the two weeks prior to the racing season, 9 a.m. to 5 p.m. Admission to the grounds free; $1 to the grandstand, $2 to the clubhouse during racing season. (1–2 hours)

★★ **Historical Museum of Southern Florida**—Board an antique trolley car that once clanged its way around Miami and get a close look at a Seminole chickee hut, an old-time sailing ship, and a Spanish fort. A hands-on spot, the museum features changing exhibits that have focused on such eclectic items as cigar-label art, a slave ship, and objects from Miami's 1996 100th birthday celebration. Details: 101 West Flagler Street; (305) 375-1492 or 375-1621; open Monday through Saturday 10 a.m. to 5 p.m., Thursday to 9 p.m., Sunday noon to 5 p.m. Admission $4 adults, $2 children ages 6 to 12. (2 hours)

★★ **Miami Art Museum**—Miami is proud of its Metro Dade Cultural Center, a tripartite facility that includes this museum, the Historical Museum of Southern Florida, and the city's library. Designed by famed architect Philip Johnson, this soaring museum showcases post–World War II Americas art. Details: 101 West Flagler Street, parking at 50 NW 2nd Avenue; (305) 375-1700; open Tuesday through Friday 10 a.m. to 5 p.m., Thursday to 9 p.m., Saturday and Sunday noon to 5 p.m. Admission $5 adults, $2.50 students, children under age 12 free; free to all Tuesday and Thursday 5 p.m. to 9 p.m. (2 hours)

★★ **Miami Museum of Science and Space Transit Planetarium**— Things crackle, zap, thunder, and thwack in this hands-on science museum, where you learn why the world does what it does by getting right in there and trying out the more than 140 exhibits. Shipwrecks, sunken treasure, birds of prey, and reptiles are all part of the fun. In the Planetarium you get a closer look at the moon over Miami, and quite a lot of the stars as well, on a 65-foot dome with multimedia star shows. You can walk on a rock from Mars, and weekends feature laser shows to the music of the Beatles and Led Zeppelin. Details: 3280 South Miami Avenue; (305) 854-4247, museum; 854-2222, cosmic hotline; open daily 10 a.m. to 5 p.m. Admission $6 adults, $4 children ages 3 to 12; planetarium admission: $6 adults, $3 children for laser shows; $5 adults, $2.50 children for planetarium shows. (3 hours)

American Police Hall of Fame and Museum—Handcuffs, badges, nightsticks, and an electric chair? If you've ever wanted to see *those* things, this is certainly the least stressful way to do it. All the accouterments of law life are on display at this unusual museum, which salutes the world's fallen police officers and displays more than 10,000 cop-shop items, from uniforms to photos to firearms. Details: 3801 Biscayne Boulevard; (305) 573-0070; open daily (except Christmas) 10 a.m. to 5:30 p.m. Admission $6 adults, $3 children ages 6 to 12, free to police officers. (2 hours)

GREAT BEACHES

Crandon Park Beach, 4000 North Crandon Park Boulevard, in Key Biscayne, has 4 miles of alluring sand shaded by palms and sea grapes as well as waterspots, restaurants, and shops. At the tip of Key Biscayne is the tranquil **Bill Baggs Cape Florida State Recreation Area**, 1200 South Crandon Park Boulevard, with plenty of shallow water and shady seclusion, a picnic area, a fast-food kiosk, and an historic lighthouse. Park entry is $2.50 for the driver, $1.50 for each passenger. **Virginia Key Beach**, Rickenbacker Causeway, in Key Biscayne, has an area that's widely known as a clothing-optional beach, but you didn't hear it here.

SHOPPING

Bayside Marketplace, 401 Biscayne Boulevard, (305) 577-3344, occupies a dramatic waterside setting within sight of massive cruise ships, yachts, and sailboats. There's always something popping here at this roofed, open-air, bilevel shopping center that sports 150 shops, lounges, a food court, and restaurants. It's particularly easy to find at night—a huge neon guitar looms over the Hard Rock Café. Street performers warble and juggle to provide free entertainment, and national chains team with tiny kiosks brimming with unusual products from around the world. It's open Monday through Thursday 10 a.m. to 10 p.m., closes at 11 p.m. weekends, and is open Sunday 11 a.m. to 8 p.m.

   Downtown Miami's shopping district stretches from Biscayne Boulevard to NE 3rd Avenue between SE 1st Street and NE 3rd Street, (305) 379-7070, encompassing more than 300 stores. A highlight is the **Miami Jewelry District**, anchored by the dozens of glittering showcases that fill ten floors of the Seybold Building at 37 East Flagler Street. Downtown you'll also find many electronic shops as well as department stores, including Burdines and Marshall's. Many small cafés have walk-up windows where you can order a Miami favorite: tiny cups of thick, industrial-strength *café Cubano* sweetened with plenty of sugar. For a lower-level caffeine jolt, order a *café Americano*.

   Miami International Arts & Design District, which stretches from NE 36th to 41st Streets between NE 2nd Avenue and North Miami Avenue, offers a potpourri of restaurants and shops focusing on furniture, antiques, and artwork. It's open Monday through Friday 10 a.m. to 5 p.m.

An old-fashioned carousel is the focal point of **Omni International Mall**, 1601 Biscayne Boulevard, (305) 374-6664, with 75 stores, including a cluster of upscale designer boutiques, a ten-screen theater, and many restaurants. Hours are Monday through Saturday 10 a.m. to 9 p.m., Sunday noon to 5:30 p.m. At the northern end of the city, **Aventura Mall**, 9501 Biscayne Boulevard, (305) 935-1110, has more than 200 shops, anchored by Macy's, Lord & Taylor, and Sears. It's open Monday through Saturday 10 a.m. to 9:30 p.m., Sunday 11 a.m. to 6 p.m.

Sample the flavor of the Caribbean at **Caribbean Marketplace**, 5925 NE 2nd Avenue, (305) 751-2251, where a wildly colorful shuttle called a "tap-tap" scoots around, evoking the Haitian spirit that infuses this part of town. Caribbean arts, crafts, and food, a flea market operating Friday through Sunday 10 a.m. to 7 p.m., and the Marketplace (open daily 10 a.m. to 9 p.m., closing at 7 p.m. Sunday), are all part of the fun. Bargain hunters spend weekends at the **Opa-Locka/Hialeah Flea Market**, 12705 NW 42nd Avenue, (305) 688-8080, where 1,200 vendors can be found wheeling and dealing Thursday through Sunday 5 a.m. to 7 p.m.

FITNESS AND RECREATION

With round-the-year warmth and round-the-town water, Miami has been a favorite place to play for more than a century. More than 40 golf courses and hundreds of tennis courts exist within a 35-mile radius. Professional golfers tee off—and get teed off—in the Doral-Ryder Open, which offers a $1.5-million prize, while tennis fans battle for tickets to see their favorite tennis stars at the Lipton Championships on Key Biscayne. Tops among the many golf courses in Miami are the five at **Doral Golf Resort & Spa**, 4400 NW 87th Avenue, (305) 592-2000, which include the legendary 7,000-yard **Blue Monster**, and the course at Turnberry Isle, 19999 West Country Club Drive, (305) 932-6200, where the 18th hole is on an island!

Key Biscayne offers both sheltered and open waters, so it's one of the best spots in Miami for water play. Rent a Jet Ski at **Tony's Jet Ski Rentals**, 3501 Rickenbacker Causeway, Key Biscayne, (305) 361-8280, or **Fun Watersports**, Miami Airport Hilton Marina, 5101 Blue Lagoon Drive, (305) 261-7687, for $50 to $60 an hour. Or go sailing with **Key Biscayne Boat Rentals**, 3301 Rickenbacker Causeway, (305) 361-7368.

To see the seas that surround Miami, head for Bayside Marketplace, where many tour and party boats are moored. Walk around the marina and read the brochures until you find a boat that's doing what you want to do. Excursions range from tours of Biscayne Bay mansions to party evenings with dancing at sea. There's even a gondola, complete with a singing gondolier, that offers romantic little sojourns around the quieter inlets.

If you'd like to go deep-sea fishing, seek a charter boat at the **Bayside Marketplace Marina**, 401 Biscayne Boulevard, (305) 579-6955. Expect to pay about $400 for a half-day to $700 for a full day of fishing for up to six people—and don't be afraid to bargain. More boats are at **Pelican Harbor Marina**, 1275 NE 79th Street Causeway, North Bay Village, (305) 754-9330. For more information on fishing and boating, see the Miami Beach chapter in this book.

Miami is proud to have top teams in all the spectator sports. **Miami Heat**, the city's National Basketball Association team, plays at the **Miami Arena**, 701 Arena Boulevard, (305) 577-HEAT, from April to October. Miami has hosted the Super Bowl several times, and the city's National Football League team, the **Miami Dolphins**, has played in it five times. You can see the Dolphins at play from August through December at **Pro Player Stadium**, 2269 NW 199th Street, (954) 452-7000. Tickets are $20 to $40. Or take in a **University of Miami Hurricanes** (305-284-2655) football game there from September through November or the January Orange Bowl clash between two of the nation's top collegiate football teams. Miami's **Florida Marlins** baseball team (305-626-7400) plays there, too, from April through October.

South Florida's hockey team, the **Florida Panthers** (305-530-4444) play 41 games a year against National Hockey League opponents and can be seen at Miami Arena until 1998, when they move to a new Fort Lauderdale arena.

Greyhounds, thoroughbreds, and jai alai players provide both wagering and watching opportunities. Greyhounds race at **Flagler Dog Track**, 401 NW 38th Court, (305) 649-3000, with purses up to $125,000, a clubhouse dining room, and racing at 7:30 p.m. nightly with a 12:30 p.m. matinee on Tuesday, Thursday, Saturday, and holidays. Admission is $1, clubhouse seating $3. Racing dates change each year in an exchange with the Hollywood Dog Track.

Thoroughbreds run at **Calder Race Course**, 21001 NW 27th Avenue, (305) 625-1311, where post time is 1 p.m. Thursday through Sunday and admission is $2 to $4, with the racing season here usually May to November. **Hialeah Park** (see Sightseeing Highlights, above), a beautiful racetrack with classic architecture, usually has races from mid-March to June, exchanging dates with Gulfstream Park. Post time is 1 p.m., and admission is $1 to $4.

Jai alai fans can see this exciting game at **Miami Jai Alai**, 3500 NW 37th Avenue, (305) 633-6400, open year-round with matinees at noon and night games at 7 p.m., daily except Tuesday and Sunday. Admission is $1 to $5.

FOOD

Miami's diverse population means a wide range of culinary options and has even led to the region's own signature culinary style, called New World cuisine. At **Le Pavillion** in the Hotel Inter-Continental, 100 Chopin Drive, (305) 577-1000, you dine in elegant settings on such unusual treats as gold and black fettucini with Florida lobster and curried lamb. Chef Allen Susser has won many an award for the New World cuisine he serves at **Chef Allen's**, 19088 NE 29th Avenue, North Miami Beach, (305) 935-2900, where the setting is as simple as the food is complex and the prices high. **Il Tulipano**, 11052 Biscayne Boulevard, (305) 893-4811, considered by some the best Italian restaurant in Miami, serves innovative Italian flavors in a cozy, country-chic atmosphere—the *agnolotti* is to die for.

Hundreds of Cuban restaurants offer both elegant and simple dining. Mirrors reflect Cuban *media noche* (grilled ham and cheese "midnight" sandwiches), and the creamy *batidas* (milkshakes) star at **Versailles**, 3555 SW 8th Street, (305) 444-0240, an inexpensive café that's a political gathering spot often visited by U.S. presidential candidates. **La Carreta** has five restaurants in the region, including one on Little Havana's Calle Ocho at 3632 SW 8th Street, (305) 444-7501, serving moderately priced Cuban specialties. **Casa Juancho**, 2436 SW 8th Street, (305) 642-2452, claims the nation's rarest collection of Spanish wines, served with oak-grilled meats and strolling musicians. All are open until midnight or later.

Stone crabs are a South Florida favorite, grown right here on the southwest coast near Naples. For $35 you can eat as many as you can cram in at **Mike Gordon's**, 1201 NE 79th Street, (305) 751-

4429, but you can buy fewer for less at this waterside spot that's been in business for more than 50 years. For bargain-priced seafood, dress down and head on over to **East Coast Fisheries**, 350 West Flagler Street, (305) 372-1300, where you can choose from a huge, moderately priced menu of seafood straight from the fishing boats docked there. At **The Fish Peddler**, 8699 Biscayne Boulevard, (305) 757-0648, where the crowds are huge and chic, the decor rustic, and the price right, you can dine on such treats as black grouper, pan-fried yellowtail, shrimp steamed in beer, Maryland oysters, and fried clams.

Three kinds of Asian cuisine team up at **Two Dragons**, in the Sonesta Beach Hotel, 6450 Ocean Drive, Key Biscayne, (305) 361-2020, where you select from Japanese tempura or sushi, Thai treats, and Chinese delicacies in exotic pagoda surroundings. Two other Key Biscayne restaurants, **Sundays on the Bay**, 5420 Crandon Boulevard, (305) 361-6777, and **Rusty Pelican**, 3201 Rickenbacker Causeway, (305) 361-3818, are popular spots, particularly for Sunday brunch. Both have great sea views and moderate prices.

For steak and seafood in an unusual setting near the airport, try **94th Aero Squadron**, 1395 NW 57th Avenue, (305) 261-4220, where World War I flying machines and their pilots are the center of attention. You can watch planes land and hear their radio communications on a headset as you dine.

LODGING

Downtown Miami, which includes the area around the airport and Key Biscayne, is a resort and business-traveler destination, so many area accommodations are both elaborate and expensive. **Hyatt Regency Miami**, 400 SW 2nd Street, (305) 358-1234 or (800) 233-1234, occupies enviable acreage along the Miami River a block from Biscayne Bay, with an acclaimed restaurant, fitness center, and pool in a 615-room hotel that charges $160 to $175 in peak season. A cluster of historic buildings were joined to create the 40-room **Miami River Inn**, 118 South River Drive, (305) 325-0045 or (800) HOTEL-89, nestled alongside the Miami River and charging a reasonable $89 to $129 in peak season.

A triumvirate of hotels, close together and near the Bay, the MetroMover monorail, and the port, make a convenient place to settle in downtown Miami. **Doubletree Grand Biscayne Bay**, 1717 North Bayshore Drive, (305) 372-0313 or (800) 872-7749; **Biscayne Bay**

Marriott Hotel and Marina, 1633 North Bayshore Drive, (305) 374-3900 or (800) 228-9290; and **Crowne Plaza Miami** (formerly the Omni), 1601 Biscayne Boulevard, (305) 374-0000 or (800) 2-CROWNE, are all just steps away from Omni Mall. Each sports handsome furnishings and great views of glittering city lights or gleaming Biscayne Bay. Rates fall in the $150 to $210 range in peak season.

In the airport area **Crown Sterling Suites**, 3974 NW South River Drive, (305) 871-6000 or (800) 772-3787, is a pleasant spot just a few minutes' drive from the terminal. All rooms have a living room and basic kitchen facilities for winter rates of $155 to $165. Nearby, **Hotel Sofitel**, 5800 Blue Lagoon Drive, (305) 264-4888 or (800) 258-4888, salutes its French connections in 281 attractive rooms, an acclaimed French restaurant, tennis courts, fitness facilities, and winter rates in the $195 to $205 range. **Sheraton River House**, 3900 NW 21st Street, (305) 871-3800 or (800) 933-1100, near the airport, has two lively lounges, a pool, restaurant, tennis courts, and fitness center for $155 to $175 in peak season. Not far away, **Doral Resort & Spa**, 4400 NW 87th Avenue, (305) 592-2000 or (800) 71-DORAL, is a huge resort with 694 fine rooms, five championship golf courses, 15 tennis courts, four swimming pools, and a showy spa. Rates in peak season are $245 to $390.

North of town, **Turnberry Isle Resort & Club**, 19999 West Country Club Road, (305) 936-2929 or (800) 223-1588, sprawls over many acres with six restaurants, five lounges, four swimming pools, two golf courses, a fitness center, and 24 tennis courts; winter rates are in the $295 to $405 bracket.

On Key Biscayne, **Sonesta Beach Resort Key Biscayne**, 250 Ocean Drive, Key Biscayne, (305) 361-2021 or (800) SONESTA, spreads across the sands with 300 rooms, four restaurants, a swimming pool, tennis courts, and lounge at winter rates of $285 to $350. A smaller property on the island, **Silver Sands**, 301 Ocean Drive, Key Biscayne, (305) 361-5441, has long been beloved by locals for its oceanside location and $149 to $300 room and cottage rates.

NIGHTLIFE

Performing Arts

Miami is a cosmopolitan city with a cultural mix that allows you to roam the musical and theatrical globe without ever leaving town.

MIAMI

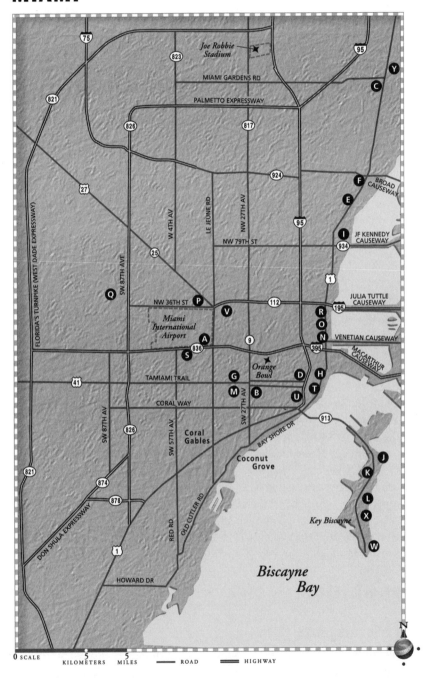

Joe Robbie Stadium

MIAMI GARDENS RD

PALMETTO EXPRESSWAY

BROAD CAUSEWAY

JF KENNEDY CAUSEWAY

NW 79TH ST

JULIA TUTTLE CAUSEWAY

NW 36TH ST

Miami International Airport

VENETIAN CAUSEWAY

MACARTHUR CAUSEWAY

Orange Bowl

TAMIAMI TRAIL

CORAL WAY

Coral Gables

BAY SHORE DR

Coconut Grove

Key Biscayne

FLORIDA'S TURNPIKE (WEST DADE EXPRESSWAY)

SW 87TH AVE

SW 87TH AVE

SW 57TH AVE

SW 27TH AVE

RED RD

OLD CUTLER RD

DON SHULA EXPRESSWAY

HOWARD DR

W 4TH AV

LE JEUNE RD

NW 27TH AV

Biscayne Bay

N

0 SCALE
KILOMETERS   MILES   ROAD   HIGHWAY

Food

Ⓐ 94th Aero Squadron

Ⓑ Casa Juancho

Ⓒ Chef Allen's

Ⓓ East Coast Fisheries

Ⓔ The Fish Peddler

Ⓕ Il Tulipano

Ⓖ La Carreta

Ⓗ Le Pavillion

Ⓘ Mike Gordon's

Ⓙ Rusty Pelican

Ⓚ Sundays on the Bay

Ⓛ Two Dragons

Ⓜ Versailles

Lodging

Ⓝ Biscayne Bay Marriott Hotel and Marina

Ⓞ Crowne Plaza Miami

Ⓟ Crown Sterling Suites

Ⓠ Doral Resort & Spa

Ⓡ Doubletree Grand Biscayne Bay

Ⓢ Hotel Sofitel

Ⓣ Hyatt Regency Miami

Ⓤ Miami River Inn

Ⓥ Sheraton River House

Ⓦ Silver Sands

Ⓧ Sonesta Beach Resort Key Biscayne

Ⓨ Turnberry Isle Resort & Club

Flamenco from Spain, storytellers and reggae singers from Jamaica, the Vienna Boys Choir, Thai and African dancers, South American singers—the list goes on, as many nationalities add to the cultural mélange. Find out what's happening in the *Miami Herald*'s "Showtime," published every Friday, and in local magazines usually available free in hotel rooms or lobbies.

Productions take place in a variety of venues, ranging from the city's ornate and nicely restored **Gusman Center for the Performing Arts**, 174 East Flagler Street, (305) 372-0925, to the floating **Key Biscayne Marine Stadium**, 3601 Rickenbacker Causeway, Key Biscayne, (305) 361-6732, a stars-under-the-stars stage. Other centers include **Dade County Auditorium**, 2901 West Flagler Street, (305) 545-3395; **James L. Knight Center**, 400 SE 2nd Avenue, (305) 372-0277; and **Miami Arena**, 721 NW 1st Avenue, (305) 530-4400.

Ballet Flamenco La Rosa, 1031 NE 72nd Street, (305) 747-8475, salutes the music and dance of Spain; and **Black Door Dance Ensemble**, (305) 385-8960, specializes in jazz, gospel, and African-Caribbean dance.

Florida Grand Opera, (305) 854-1645 or (800) 741-1010, now one of the ten largest opera companies in the nation, performs five operas November through May at Dade County Auditorium, 2901 West Flagler Street. The **Philharmonic Orchestra of Florida** (see Chapter 10) performs at Gusman Center and Jackie Gleason Theater.

Clubs and Bars

To see heel-clacking, castanets-clicking flamenco, stop in at **Malaga**, 740 SW 8th Street, (305) 858-4224, where there's a two-drink minimum but no cover charge for the lively show. **Tobacco Road**, 626 South Miami Avenue, (305) 374-1196, holds the first liquor license ever granted in Miami—75 years ago—and was a Prohibition speakeasy, gangster den, gambling parlor, and jazz club, with a secret staircase. It's still rocking every night into the wee hours for a $6 cover charge.

A favorite among sports bars is **Don Shula's All-Star Café**, in Don Shula's Hotel & Golf Club, Main Street, Miami Lakes, (305) 362-7487, where you can sometimes spot the famed Dolphins coach. Find more of the same at **Shuckers Bar & Grill**, 1819 NE 79th Street Causeway, North Bay Village, (305) 866-1570.

You can call a **blues hotline** at (305) 666-6656 for information on upcoming jazz and blues events. Miami also has an **Activity Line**, (305) 557-5600, with recorded messages on dining and entertainment options. (See Miami Beach, Chapter 2, for more nightlife options.)

2
MIAMI BEACH

For many years, the dozens of 1920s buildings on Miami's South Beach deteriorated, growing steadily shabbier. As building after building faced the wrecker's ball, a few determined preservationists, led by the late Barbara Capitman, fought off highrise-minded developers with all the ferocity of starving tigers.

Finally the tide turned, and the wonderland that is now the largest collection of art deco buildings in the world became a National Historic Preservation District. Little by little, preservation and restoration money poured in; today the area from 40th Street to the southern tip of the island is a whimsical wonderland of color and furbelowed architecture. By day, pastel hues climb the sides of buildings, color on color. By night, wildly colorful neon in pink and purple, emerald and ochre, twists and soars over doors, windows, and walls.

A dream come true for some and a dream world for everyone, this immense collection of art deco architecture is now trendy South Beach—call it "SoBe"—a hugely popular playground for photographers and models from around the world, for Rollerbladers and bikinis, bohemians and billionaires. By night, celebrity sighting is practically guaranteed: Madonna, Gloria Estefan, Sly Stallone, and dozens of others play here. North of the district, the island and its sands run on for miles, lined with hotels and restaurants now basking in the glamour spawned by a collection of aging architecture once considered worthless. ◼

MIAMI BEACH

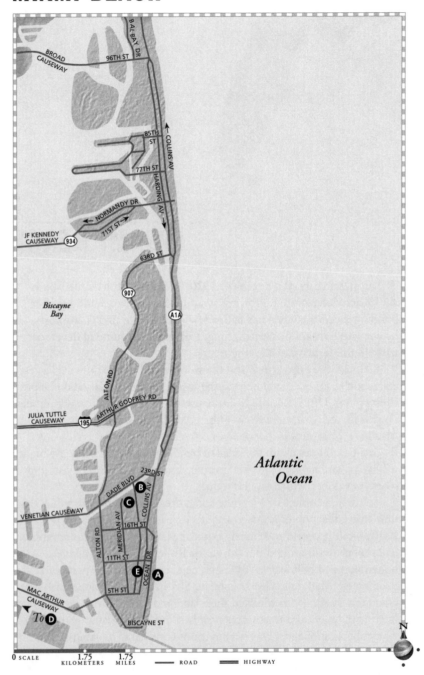

Sights

Ⓐ Art Deco District Welcome Center
Ⓑ Bass Museum of Art
Ⓒ Holocaust Memorial
Ⓓ Ichimura Miami-Japan Garden
Ⓔ Wolfsonian Foundation

A PERFECT DAY IN MIAMI BEACH

Breakfast at the News Café to discover which of the hot clubs are hottest that night, then stop by the Art Deco District's Welcome Center to join a walking tour or begin your own self-guided tour among the teensy boutiques along Española Way and through the city's antique post office. At lunchtime drive up the beach for a look at the kitschy plaster signs—a giant maiden with flowing hair, a stagecoach, and plaster horses—that once were popular attention-getters. Lunch beside the historic Fontainebleau Hotel's glamorous pool, then stop for a contemplative moment at tranquil Japanese Garden on Watson Island. To see some of the priceless memorabilia of the art deco era, stop in at the Wolfsonian Foundation, one of the finest period collections in the world. Wander the shops and cafés along Lincoln Road to find a spot for dinner, then spend the evening in the weird and wild clubs of SoBe, where anything goes and usually does.

SIGHTSEEING HIGHLIGHTS

★★★ **Art Deco District Welcome Center**—This is the center of the Art Deco District and a great spot to find real art deco pieces and good-looking posters and reproductions. Walking tours depart from here Saturday at 10:30 a.m. and Thursday at 6:30 p.m.; bicycle tours leave Sunday at 10:30 a.m. from Miami Beach Bike Center, 601 5th Street, Miami Beach. Occasionally the Miami Design Preservation League, the driving force behind preservation here, sponsors bus or boat tours of homes. Details: 1001 Ocean Drive; (305) 531-3484 or 672-2014; open daily 11 a.m. to 11 p.m. Admission free for the Welcome Center, $10 adults, $5 children ages 8 to 12 for tours, $5 for a cassette self-guided tour. (2 hours)

✮✮✮ **Wolfsonian Foundation**—One of Miami's newest museums, this amazing collection of contemporary design pieces was compiled by entrepreneur Mitchell Wolfson, who has a similar museum in Genoa. Dramatic displays of more than 70,000 objets d'art and rare books complement the wonderland of art deco design outside the ornate doors of this museum. Details: 1001 Washington Avenue; (305) 531-1001; open Tuesday, Thursday, and Saturday 10 a.m. to 6 p.m., Friday to 9 p.m., Sunday noon to 5 p.m. Admission $7 adults, $5 children ages 6 to 12. (3 hours)

✮✮ **Bass Museum of Art**—An eclectic collection of Old Masters' paintings, textiles, period furniture, sculpture, and ecclesiastical artifacts, this museum has changing exhibitions of contemporary and historic art. Details: 2121 Park Avenue; (305) 673-7530; open Tuesday through Saturday 10 a.m. to 5 p.m., Sunday 1 to 5 p.m., second and fourth Wednesday 1 to 9 p.m. Admission $5 adults, $3 students and children ages 6 to 12. (1 hour)

✮ **Holocaust Memorial**—Devoted to the memory of the 6 million Jews killed by the Nazi movement, this somber memorial chronicles the death camps in a tunnel-like passage and features a photographic mural and Memorial Wall with victims' names. Details: 1933–1945 Meridian Avenue; (305) 538-1663; open daily 9 a.m. to 9 p.m. Admission free. (1 hour)

✮ **Ichimura Miami-Japan Garden**—Japanese serenity reigns in this quiet spot tucked away on Watson Island. An octagonal pavilion is the centerpiece of the garden, which also includes a granite Hotei—the Japanese god of prosperity—a rock garden, a pond, and a 300-year-old stone pagoda. Details: north side of Watson Island off MacArthur Causeway; (305) 575-5240; open Monday through Friday 8 a.m. to 3 p.m., Saturday 10 a.m. to 4 p.m., Sunday noon to 4 p.m. Admission free. (1 hour)

GREAT BEACHES

Great beaches stretch from the tip of South Beach to Haulover Park Beach at the north end of the county. For a look at some of the most glamorous bodies in Miami, head for Miami Beach's **SoBe** (South Beach), which stretches from the southern tip of the island to about 27th Street. Photographers from around the world come here for winter photo shoots, and models can usually be found posturing on the sands. One designated area of **Haulover Park Beach**, at 10800 Collins Avenue, is an unofficial bare-it beach.

SHOPPING

Lincoln Road Mall, 924 Lincoln Road, (305) 532-3442, is 10 blocks of pedestrian shopping area that has undergone an amazing renaissance to become the trendiest sector of SoBe. On this wide pedestrian mall, you'll find more than 160 boutiques, 40 restaurants, 30 art galleries, and an avant-garde movie house. There's street music and street art, and you can watch the dancers of the Miami City Ballet at practice. At posh **Bal Harbour Shops**, 9700 Collins Avenue, Bal Harbour, (305) 866-0311, you're greeted by a parking attendant togged out in a plumed helmet and snappy red and white uniform. That sets the stage for the elegant boutiques and restaurants nestled among waterfalls, pools, and towering palms. Tiffany & Co., Louis Vuitton, Gucci, Cartier, Hermès, Fendi, and Bottega Veneta are all here, with Neiman Marcus and Saks Fifth Avenue staring each other down at either end of this attractive open-air center. The **Mall at 163rd Street**, 1421 NE 163rd Street, North Miami Beach, (305) 947-9845, has 120 specialty shops anchored by Burdine's, Mervyn's, and Marshall's.

FITNESS AND RECREATION

Golf courses abound, including two public courses: **Bayshore Golf Course**, 2301 Alton Road, (305) 532-3350, and **Normandy Golf Course**, 2401 Biarritz Drive, (305) 865-6381. Greens fees, including cart, are $20 to $45.

Fishing fans can drop a hook over the sides of bridges at **MacArthur Causeway** or piers in **Haulover Park**, 10800 Collins Avenue, Miami, (305) 947-3525; **South Point Park**, 1 Washington Avenue, (305) 673-7224; and **Sunny Isles Pier**, 170th Street and Collins Avenue. For drift-fishing, try the **Kelley Fishing Fleet**, 10800 Collins Avenue in Haulover Marina, Sunny Isles, (305) 945-3801, which charges $26 for four-hour trips that depart at 9 a.m., 1:45 p.m., and 8 p.m. daily.

At **Miami Beach Marina**, 300 Alton Road, (305) 673-6000, you can rent a power boat from **Club Nautico of Miami Beach**, (305) 673-2502, or go deep-sea fishing with **Kozy Charters**, (305) 674-8607. Sailboats and other water-sports equipment can be rented at the **Fontainebleau Hilton Hotel**, 4441 Collins Avenue, (305) 538-2000.

You can rent a Jet Ski for $80 an hour or go on a five-hour Jet Ski tour for $150 with **D & D Water Sports**, Pan American Hotel, 17875 Collins Avenue, Miami Beach, (305) 932-8445 or (800) 805-8445.

Try kayaking in the Oleta River with a rental kayak from **Urban Trails Kayak**, Haulover Park, 10800 Collins Avenue, North Miami Beach, (305) 947-1302. Rates are $8 an hour, $20 for four hours. If surf's up, the top surfing spots are **Haulover Park**, 10800 Collins Avenue, Miami, (305) 947-3525, and **South Beach**, where areas are set aside for surfers. **Miami Beach Recreation, Culture and Parks Department**, 1700 Convention Center Drive, (305) 673-7730, can help you find tennis and other sports facilities.

FOOD

Dozens of cafés have sprouted along the oceanfront on Ocean Drive and on Washington Avenue, a block away. So close together are the sidewalk cafés and veranda bistros that it's difficult to tell where one ends and the next begins. The top spot is the 24-hour **News Café**, 800 Ocean Drive, (305) 538-6397, where much of the Beach gossip—and there is much—is exchanged. Start there and just wander, reading the menus as you go until you find your favorite in cost and cuisine.

Baroque and opulent with stained glass, Viennese crystal chandeliers, Art Nouveau touches, and antiques from every era, **The Forge**, 432 Arthur Godfrey Road, (305) 538-8533, is lavishly elegant, with an enormous wine cellar, adjoining lounge, and award-winning nouvelle cuisine. Among the poshest restaurants in Miami Beach is the **Dining Galleries**, in the Fontainebleau Hilton Hotel, 4441 Collins Avenue, (305) 538-2000, where you dine in one of four gilded, mirrored restaurants filled with flowers and glowing with soft lighting. Perfect service and fine food for lofty prices. Both restaurants open for dinner and Sunday brunch.

Yuca, 501 Lincoln Road, (305) 532-9822, is a tribute to a starchy tuber beloved by Cubans and doubles as an acronym for Young Cuban Americans. Cuisine here is called Nuevo Latino, marrying Cuban flavors with contemporary zing; moderately priced and open for lunch and dinner daily.

Joe's Stone Crabs, 227 Biscayne Street (*not* Boulevard), (305) 673-0365, is a Miami Beach institution and the city's most visited restaurant. For 70 years this jam-packed spot at the southern tip of the island has been playing to crowds that get no respect—and no breaks—

from the harried maitre d'. What they do get is fat stone crab claws and other seafood as well, crispy hash-brown potatoes, unusual coleslaw, and creamy Key lime pie.

China Grill, 404 Washington Avenue, (305) 534-2211, a branch of the New York operation of the same name, plays to huge crowds, and word has it that you need dinner reservations weeks, if not months, in advance. Big, brash, and good, the Grill (despite its name) serves international cuisine with an Asian flair.

Strand, 671 Washington Avenue, (305) 532-2340, grabbed a major spot in the sun here from the day it opened and continues to be a place to see and be seen. Awash in black-and-white checks and deco design, the Strand serves grilled seafood, steaks, and the like until the wee hours of the morning.

Massive cruise ships sail by so close you can almost touch them at **South Point Seafood**, 1 Washington Avenue, (305) 673-1708, where you can dine inside or out on lots of fresh seafood or beef, washed down with the restaurant's own beer.

For more than 50 years, **Curry's**, 7433 Collins Avenue, (305) 866-1571, has been a mainstay of Beach budget dining. Chopped liver and clam chowder, baked ham and broiled pork chops, spareribs and steak, joltingly brusque service and no atmosphere, but who cares when you're paying just $8 to $12 for dinner?

Shells, 1813 NE 163rd Street, North Miami Beach, (305) 274-5552, is another cheap shot on the Beach with good seafood. There's a line early every night at **Wolfie Cohen's Rascal House**, 17190 Collins Avenue, Sunny Isles, (305) 947-4581. Copious quantities of everything make this a mecca for gourmands who dine on potato pancakes and sour cream, matzoh ball soup, mile-high sandwiches, big dinner platters, and free pickles, served 24 hours a day.

LODGING

Miami Beach hotels are so many and so varied that people often drive down the beach just to look at them all. In North Miami Beach and Sunny Isles, many small family-style motels/hotels line the beachfront, offering basic accommodations and comparatively inexpensive rates.

Farther south, plush Bal Harbour has two very attractive oceanfront resort hotels with all the amenities. The premier hotel is **Sheraton Bal Harbour Beach Resort**, 9701 Collins Avenue, Miami, (305) 865-7511 or (800) 998-9898, a 668-room hotel with a two-story

MIAMI BEACH

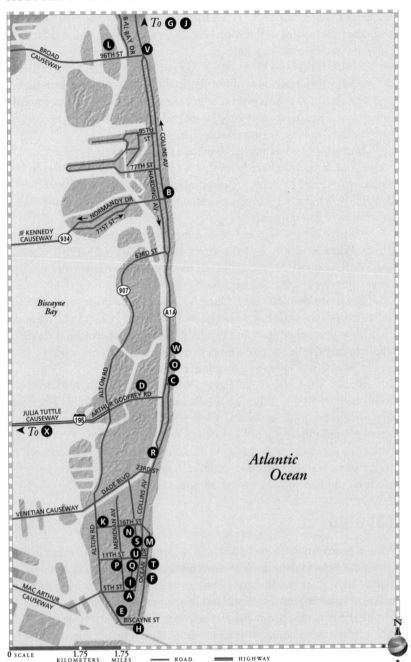

Food

(A) China Grill
(B) Curry's
(C) Dining Galleries
(D) The Forge
(E) Joe's Stone Crabs
(F) News Café
(G) Shells
(H) South Point Seafood
(I) Strand
(J) Wolfie Cohen's
    Rascal House
(K) Yuca

Lodging

(L) Bay Harbor Inn
(M) The Cardozo

Lodging (Continued)

(N) The Delano
(O) Eden Roc Resort & Spa
(C) Fontainebleau Hilton
    Resort and Spa
(P) Hotel Astor
(Q) Hotel Impala
(R) Indian Creek Hotel
(S) The Kent
(T) The Leslie
(U) Marlin
(V) Sheraton Bal Harbour
    Beach Resort
(W) Westin Resort Miami Beach

Camping

(X) KOBE Trailer Park

Note: Items with the same letter are located in the same place.

atrium, fountain cascading down the center, jade marble floors and large rooms, some with balconies overlooking the sea. Four restaurants, three pools, tennis courts, and a fitness facility round out the entertainment. Rates in peak season are $289 to $389.

Bay Harbor Inn, 9660 East Bay Harbor Drive, Bay Harbor Island, (305) 868-4141, is a jewel. Nestled along one of the region's Venice-like waterways, it has two-room suites furnished with four-poster beds, antiques, and Victorian couches in rooms that aren't on the water for $112 in peak season, chic contemporary decor in rooms along the water for $126. Rates include breakfast, a newspaper, and parking. Neighboring Surfside is home to a number of smaller, family-run properties charging moderate rates.

On the north end of Collins Avenue, from about 40th to 70th Streets, are many large, elegant, and expensive hotels, capped by the grande dame of beachfront hotels, the classic **Fontainebleau Hilton Resort & Spa**, 4441 Collins Avenue, (305) 538-2000 or (800) 548-8886. A massive and historic resort whose 1,206 rooms wrap around nearly half a mile of oceanfront, the "Font" has hosted such celebrities as Joan Crawford, Frank Sinatra, Gary Cooper, Joe DiMaggio, and Lana Turner. In recent years a multimillion-dollar renovation transformed the swimming pool into a huge rock grotto that surrounds a five-story, half-acre artificial mountain with the Lagoon Saloon swim-up bar. A calypso band plays outside an open-air café that is one of seven restaurants. Winter rates are $275 to $325.

Westin Resort Miami Beach, 4833 Collins Avenue, (305) 532-3600 or (800) 228-3000, formerly the Doral Beach Hotel, is another beautifully restored property, where big closets retain built-in dressers and shoe racks once demanded by well-heeled guests who stayed all winter. Chic and elegant, the hotel is topped by a glassed-in restaurant with beautiful sea views. Rates are $225 for city views, $325 for oceanfront rooms in peak season. **Eden Roc Resort & Spa**, 4525 Collins Avenue, (305) 531-0000 or (800) 327-8337, one of the oldest hotels on the Beach, has been renovated from sea to summit. It now sports beautiful decor and a great spa complete with the only rock-climbing wall in South Florida and a sports bar named for current Dolphins football coach Jimmy Johnson. Rates in peak season are $195 to $325.

The award-winning **Indian Creek Hotel**, 2727 Indian Creek Drive, (305) 531-2727 or (800) 491-2772, was built in the flapper era and restored, with antiques as lovely as its location near Indian Creek and an oceanfront boardwalk. Rates in peak season at this three-story beauty are $120 for rooms and $200 for suites; its Pancoast Restaurant is renowned for intimate dining and buffet breakfasts.

In the Art Deco District are dozens of small hotels offering a variety of prices. **The Cardozo**, 1300 Ocean Drive, (305) 535-6500 or (800) 782-6500, is the flagship of the art deco restoration effort. Here you'll find original terrazzo floors, deco furnishings, an etched-glass elevator door, and a bar returned to the spot it occupied when the hotel was built in the '30s. Rates are $120 to $145. Other top deco hotels include the **Hotel Astor**, 956 Washington Avenue, (305) 531-6146 or (800) 270-4981, with the acclaimed Astor Place Restaurant, a great location right in the middle of lively Washington Avenue, and plenty of soundproofing when you want to get away from it all; the all-suites **Marlin**, 1200 Collins Avenue, (305) 673-8770 or (800) OUTPOST, a stylish yet funky spot that charges $250 to $400; **The Leslie**, 1244 Ocean Drive, (305) 534-2135 or (800) 338-9076, one of the first deco hotels to be restored, charging $145; and **The Kent**, 1131 Collins Avenue, (305) 531-6771 or (800) OUTPOST, a 53-room hotel in the heart of the Deco District, charging $120. **Hotel Impala**, 1228 Collins Avenue, (305) 673-2021 or (800) 646-7252, was restored by some of the same folks who turned an old apartment building into the magnificent Ocean Drive home of designer Gianni Versace; winter rates are $189.

A new avant-garde hotel is really an old hotel gone contemporary; dubbed **The Delano**, 1685 Collins Avenue, (305) 538-7881 or (800) 555-5001, and reconstructed by New York hotel developer Ian Schrager, the hotel is frequented by celebrities who love its Dali-esque touches: a chair in the pool, mirrors leaning on palm trees, and the Blue Door Restaurant (frequented by singing star Madonna). Peak rates are $295 to $395.

CAMPING

Kobe Trailer Park, 11900 NE 16th Avenue, Miami, (305) 893-5121, is 2 miles from Miami Beach, across the causeway in Miami, and has shaded sites plus tennis and shopping nearby.

NIGHTLIFE

Performing Arts

New World Symphony, 541 Lincoln Road, (305) 673-3331, under the direction of Michael Tilson Thomas, has earned accolades in a very short time. It performs from October through May. Various shows take place at **Miami Beach Convention Center**, 1700 Washington Avenue, (305) 539-3000.

Big, blockbuster Broadway touring companies take to the boards at **Jackie Gleason Theater of the Performing Arts** (TOPA), 1700 Washington Avenue, (305) 673-8300, which has hosted *Les Misèrables, Annie, Cats*, and *Miss Saigon*, among many others. Miami has three ballet companies. The best known is the **Miami City Ballet**, 905 Lincoln Road, (305) 532-4880, which recently celebrated its tenth anniversary with worldwide acclaim for its innovative productions. Under the artistic direction of star Edward Villella, the company performs at Miami Beach's TOPA from September through March.

Clubs and Bars

Nightlife changes nightly in SoBe, where the club of the moment is just that. To find out what's hot, check the *Miami Herald*'s Friday "Showtime" listings or ask around at cafés and shops. SoBe clubs are beloved by the region's gay population, but people of all persuasions go to them. Long on the "hot" list are these: **Warsaw**, 1450 Collins Avenue, (305) 531-4555; **Amnesia**, 136 Collins Avenue, (305) 531-5535; **Bash**, a celeb hangout at 655 Washington Avenue, (305) 538-2274; **Liquid**, 1435 Washington Avenue, (305) 532-9154; **Oceanside Promenade**, 1052 Ocean Drive, (305) 538-9029; **Rezurrection Hall** at Club Nu, 245 22nd Street, (305) 532-4340; **Salvation**, 1775 West Avenue, (305) 673-6508; and **Penrod's**, 1 Ocean Drive, (305) 538-1111. For a spangled, high-steppin', high-energy, Las Vegas–style revue, head for **Club Tropigala**, in the Fontainebleau Hilton Resort & Spa, 4441 Collins Avenue, (305) 538-2000.

3
COCONUT GROVE, CORAL GABLES, AND SOUTHERN MIAMI

Coconut Grove is to Miami what Greenwich Village is to New York.
Bohemians, Bahamians, and billionaires mix easily here, all of them
dedicated to retaining the jungled magnificence of this antique enclave
first settled in the 1860s. They've succeeded. Huge old oak trees canopy
the oldest streets in the county. Tiny cottages and impressive mansions
are tucked into a wilderness of greenery. Now part of Miami, the Grove
retains its identity with determined vigor, and it continues to attract
artists, writers, wealthy escapists, and chic boutiques.

Neighboring Coral Gables developed in quite another direction.
Here massive coral-rock entranceways trim shady streets, and stately
Mediterranean architecture nestles along waterways and manicured golf
courses. In 1921 developer George Merrick, a man of great vision and
great fortune, decided to turn his inherited citrus groves into a glamorous
city. By 1925 Coral Gables was a city, but 1926's hurricane and the
resulting financial crash doomed Merrick's dream. His vision remains,
however, in the towering City Hall, the lovely Venetian Pool, the
Douglas Road Entrance, and the huge Biltmore Hotel.

As you wade farther south, urban sights give way to pasture and
farmland. Here at the south end of Dade County grow many of the
fruits and vegetables that end up on your winter table. Homestead,
long a horse, cattle, and rodeo town, now also hosts the rip-roaring
annual Miami Grand Prix. Which brings us back to diversity... ◼

COCONUT GROVE, CORAL GABLES, AND SOUTHERN MIAMI

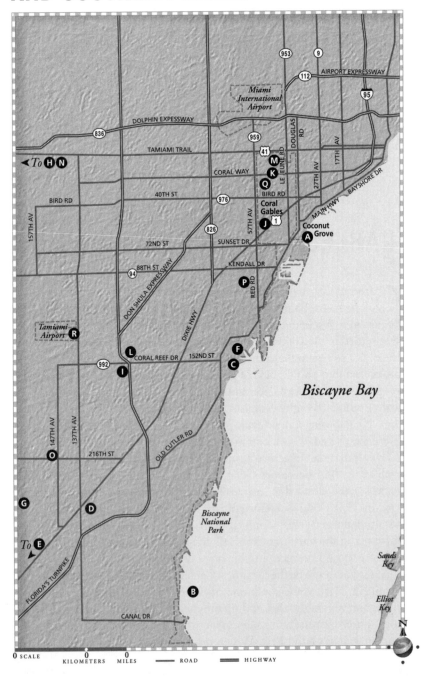

Sights

Ⓐ Barnacle State Historic Site

Ⓑ Biscayne National Underwater Park

Ⓒ Charles Deering Estate

Ⓓ Coral Castle

Ⓔ Everglades Alligator Farm

Ⓕ Fairchild Tropical Garden

Ⓖ Fruit and Spice Park

Ⓗ Gator Park

Ⓘ Gold Coast Railroad Museum

Ⓙ Lowe Art Museum

Ⓚ Merrick House

Ⓛ Miami MetroZoo

Ⓜ Miami Youth Museum

Ⓝ Miccosukee Indian Gaming

Ⓝ Miccosukee Indian Village and Airboat Tours

Ⓞ Monkey Jungle

Ⓟ Parrot Jungle and Gardens

Ⓠ Venetian Pool

Ⓡ Weeks Air Museum

Note: Items with the same letter are located in the same place.

A PERFECT DAY IN COCONUT GROVE, CORAL GABLES, AND SOUTHERN MIAMI

After breakfast in a Coconut Grove sidewalk café, stroll Peacock Park for a look at sailboats bobbing in the bay. Take a drive down scenic Main Highway and into Coral Gables past the huge City Hall and its coral entry pillars. Splash among the waterfalls at Venetian Pool, then lunch amid the columned magnificence of the Biltmore Hotel. Walk and talk with the animals at cageless MetroZoo or at the amusing Parrot or Monkey Jungles. A don't-miss for garden enthusiasts: the exotic tropical greenery at Fairchild Tropical Gardens or Fruit and Spice Park. Later, dine with one of Coral Gables' award-winning chefs and party late into the night at Coconut Grove clubs.

SIGHTSEEING HIGHLIGHTS

★★★ **Biscayne National Underwater Park**—Forests of coral 20 feet high shelter a colorful array of sea creatures that you watch through the glass bottom of the park's tour boat. If you want to be among them, cheerful park rangers will take you on scuba or snorkeling expeditions aboard a speedy catamaran that also sails on island tours. Or you can rent a canoe and paddle around on your own in this 180,000-acre park that is one of the largest underwater parks in the world. Details: U.S. 1 at SW 328th (Canal) Street, Homestead; (305) 230-1100; open daily 9 a.m. to 5:30 p.m. Admission to the park requires "just a smile," rangers say; glass-bottom boat tours at 10 a.m. daily are $19.95 adults, $9.95 children under age 12; scheduled snorkeling, scuba, and island tours require reservations and are $21 to $34.50; canoe rentals are $7 an hour. (4 hours)

★★★ **Charles Deering Estate**—When James Deering settled into his massive Vizcaya homestead up the road, his brother Charles decided Miami's sun and sea looked pretty good to him too. So, in 1914, he built his own mansion on a beautiful limestone bluff surrounded by 100 acres of mangroves, pineland, and a towering stand of royal palms that show you what a natural wonder this part of the state once was—and here still is. Currently under restoration, the handsome home with 10-inch-thick walls is scheduled to reopen in 1998. Details: 16701 SW 72nd Avenue, Miami; (305) 235-1668; hours and admission to be announced. (2 hours)

★★★ **Fairchild Tropical Garden**—One of the most renowned gardens in Florida, this massive collection of tropical plants sprawls over 83 acres complete with rain forest, sunken garden, hibiscus garden, vine pergola, and a conservatory filled with rare blooms. You can scoot around on a tram to see it all, then go back and wander in scenic silence. Details: 10901 Old Cutler Road, Miami; (305) 667-1651; open daily 9:30 a.m. to 4:30 p.m. Admission $8 adults, free for children under age 13. (2 hours)

★★★ **Miami MetroZoo**—Mom gorillas cuddle their babies and tigers whap each other across the nose in this huge, artfully designed, cageless zoo, where you're separated from the animals by moats, not bars. See white tigers, warthogs, and rhinos, two of only four fearsome Komodo dragons in the United States, cute koalas, and bouncy kangaroos—900 animals in all, representing 240 species. In the Children's Fun Center, the youngsters can ride an elephant, pet a baby deer, and see ecology and wildlife shows. Details: 12400 SW 152nd Street, Miami; (305) 251-0400; open daily 9:30 a.m. to 5:30 p.m., ticket booth closes at 4 p.m. Admission $8 adults, $4 children ages 3 to 12. (3 hours)

★★★ **Miccosukee Indian Village and Airboat Tours**—When the Seminoles broke from the Creek tribes in Georgia and set off on their own, the Miccosukee branch of the tribe settled in the Everglades and never left. They are there still, offering visitors a look at their culture and way of life at this attraction deep in the swamp. Here artisans demonstrate the art of patchwork quilting and dollmaking, wood-carving, beadwork, and the inevitable alligator wrestling. The highlight of a visit is an airboat ride into the swamp. Details: U.S. 41, 27 miles west of the Florida Turnpike, Miami; (305) 223-8380; open daily 9 a.m. to 5 p.m. Admission $5 adults, $3.50 children ages 5 to 12. Airboat rides are $7, children under age 6 free. (2 hours)

★★★ **Monkey Jungle**—Look over there, swinging from that tree! Isn't that your ex-boss? Darwin's theories come to life here at this attraction in which people roam through caged walkways while dozens of swinging monkeys hang out in a made-for-monkeys environment. Shows include a monkey swimming-pool party, Hangin' With Orangs, and a lowland gorilla King of Our Jungle show. Details: 14805 SW 216th Street, Miami; (305) 235-1611; open daily 9:30 a.m. to 5 p.m. Admission $11.50 adults, $6 children ages 4 to 12. (3 hours)

★★★ **Parrot Jungle and Gardens**—Squawking and wisecracking since 1936, these parrots flit around in feathery splendor, turning this attraction's magnificent jungle greenery into a rainbow-hued wonder-land. Some of the 1,200 rare and exotic birds who live here entertain visitors with displays of their special talents. You can breakfast in the midst of a winged wonderland at the Parrot Café and talk back to the birds in a petting room. Details: 11000 SW 57th Avenue, Miami (the attraction is slated to move to Watson Island near downtown Miami in 1998); (305) 666-7834; open daily 9:30 a.m. to 6 p.m. Admission $12.95 adults, $8.95 children ages 3 to 10. (3 hours)

★★ **Barnacle State Historic Site**—Commodore Ralph Munroe sailed in here and was so captivated by the sun and sand that he never sailed out again. A yacht builder, he constructed this octagonal house himself in 1891 from timber salvaged from sunken ships. When the family outgrew the house, he just lifted it up and built a new first floor of concrete block, wrapping it with an inviting porch cooled by sea breezes. Details: 3485 Main Highway, Coconut Grove; (305) 448-9445; open Friday through Sunday 9 a.m. to 4 p.m., with tours at 10 a.m., 11:30 a.m., 1 p.m., and 2:30 p.m. Admission $1 adults, children under age 6 free. (2 hours)

✯✯ **Coral Castle**—Built by a lovelorn Latvian named Edward
Leedskalnin, who spent 30 years hoisting huge hunks of coral rock into
this "castle" in hopes of winning the heart of his lady love, Coral Castle
was mysteriously constructed in the 1920s without the use of any modern
lifting equipment. Sad to say, this rock-solid valentine didn't work. How
could she resist a solid rock rocking chair? Details: 28655 South Dixie
Highway (U.S. 1), Homestead; (305) 248-6344; open daily 9 a.m. to 6
p.m. Admission $7.75 adults, $5 children ages 7 to 12. (1 hour)

✯✯ **Everglades Alligator Farm**—Those toothy critters that seem to be
synonymous with Florida are the stars of this attraction, offering you a
look into the life and loves of Florida's most fearsome creatures. Here an
intrepid crew caters to the whims of more than 3,000 'gators, a bevy of
snakes, and a cluster of Everglades animals. You can whiz around the
attraction's acreage on an airboat ride or take a self-guided walking tour
of the farm, complete with alligator and snake shows. Details: 40351 SW
192nd Avenue, Homestead; (305) 247-2628; open daily 9 a.m. to 6 p.m.
Admission for airboat tours $12.50 adults, $6 children ages 4 to 12; for
the self-guided tour $7 adults, $3 children. (2 hours)

✯✯ **Fruit and Spice Park**—There's always something to taste here in
this 50-year-old park, where more than 200 species and 500 varieties of
fruits, nuts, and spices grow on 20 acres of shady grounds. Discover
how one tree creates nutmeg, allspice, and mace all at one time at this
unusual botanical garden that shows you what your spice-jar powders
look like before they're pulverized. Details: 24801 SW 187th Avenue,
Homestead; (305) 247-5727; open daily 10 a.m. to 5 p.m. Admission $2
adults, 50 cents children under age 12. (2 hours)

✯✯ **Gold Coast Railroad Museum**—Train buffs will adore this
museum's showy collection of antique railroad cars, including its star, the
snappy Ferdinand Magellan presidential railroad car. Details: 12450 SW
152nd Street, Miami, next door to MetroZoo; (305) 253-0063; open
Monday through Friday 11 a.m. to 3 p.m., Saturday and Sunday to 4
p.m. Admission $5 adults, $2 children. Railroad buffs also periodically
sponsor a "Mystery on the Sunshine Express," traveling between Miami
and Palm Beach and Fort Lauderdale. (2 hours)

✯✯ **Merrick House**—George E. Merrick was an artist, a visionary,
and a canny developer who knew a good thing when he saw it. A

builder on the grand scale, in 1898 Merrick used natural coral rock to build huge pillared city entranceways and, in the 1920s, his own two-story house. You can see his honeymoon cottage—he married Elizabeth Peacock, whose family owned Coconut Grove's Peacock Inn, now a park—nearby at Granada Boulevard and Coral Way. Details: 907 Coral Way, Coral Gables; (305) 460-5361; house open Wednesday and Saturday 1 to 5 p.m., grounds open sunrise to sunset. Admission $2 adults, 50 cents children ages 6 to 12. (1 hour)

★ **Gator Park**—An airboat tour of this 'gator-infested park gives you a close look at those fearsome creatures that are so much a part of South Florida. At a wildlife show, you can also meet a Florida panther, now an endangered species—only a few wild panthers remain in the Everglades—plus snakes, lemurs, and more. Details: 24050 SW 8th Street; (305) 559-2255; open daily 9 a.m. to 6 p.m. Admission $12 adults, $6.50 children. (2 hours)

★ **Lowe Art Museum**—A lauded collection of Renaissance and Baroque art is the centerpiece of this museum, which also houses Spanish masterpieces, nineteenth- and twentieth-century American art, and galleries devoted to pre-Columbian, Asian, Native American, African and East Indian artwork. Details: University of Miami, 1201 Stanford Drive, Coral Gable; (305) 237-3603; open Tuesday through Saturday 10 a.m. to 5 p.m., Sunday noon to 5 p.m. Admission $4 adults, $2 students, free to children under age 6. (2 hours)

★ **Miami Youth Museum**—Kids can dress up in a suit of armor, weave baskets, crawl into a caveman's cave, roll through a kid-sized grocery story, visit a tiny police and fire station, see themselves on television, become editor in a pint-sized newsroom, and more. Details: Miracle Center, 3301 Coral Way, Level U, Miami; (305) 446-4386; open Monday through Thursday 10 a.m. to 5 p.m., Friday to 9 p.m., Saturday and Sunday 11 a.m. to 6 p.m. Admission $4. (2 hours)

★ **Venetian Pool**—Carved from coral rock, this historic spring-fed landmark is South Florida's most beautiful pool. Designed in the city's early days, the pool is as close as you can come to a Venetian lagoon (outside of Venice of course), with caves, stone bridges, and waterfalls; there's also a café. Details: 2701 DeSoto Boulevard, Coral Gables; (305) 460-5356; open Tuesday though Sunday 10 a.m. to 4:30 p.m. Admission

$5 adults, $4 for swimmers ages 13 to 17, and $2 for children ages 3 to 12; children under 3 not permitted in the pool. (2 hours)

Miccosukee Indian Gaming—Miccosukees were among the first tribes in the nation to create tribal revenue with high-stakes bingo. They've since added poker, table games, and video gambling. Details: 500 SW 177th Avenue; (305) 222-4600; open daily 24 hours. Free admission. (2–4 hours)

Weeks Air Museum—Aircraft buffs will love this display of restored World War I and II planes, including the last WWII Grumman Duck seaplane left in the world and a B-29 Super Fortress, the plane that ended the war with Japan. Youngsters—or not-so-youngsters—can play pilot in a real jet airliner cockpit. Details: Kendall-Tamiami Airport, 14710 SW 128th Street, Miami; (305) 233-5197; open daily 10 a.m. to 5 p.m. Admission $6.95 adults, $4.95 children under age 13. (1 hour)

GREAT BEACHES

Matheson Hammock Park, 9610 Old Cutler Road, in Miami near Coconut Grove, is one of Miami's best-kept secrets, wrapped around a scenic lagoon with barbecue grills, picnic shelters, a refreshment stand, a walking trail, a bike path, and fishing. Admission is $3.50 a car; open daily sunrise to sunset. Quite a few miles south but worth the ride is **Biscayne National Underwater Park**, near Everglades National Park at U.S.1 and SW 328th (Canal) Street in Homestead—a gorgeous spot for sun, sand, sea, and solitude.

SHOPPING

Coral Gables' downtown shopping center was dubbed **Miracle Mile** many years ago and so it remains, lined by a bevy of boutiques and cafés. In the middle is **Miracle Center**, 3301 Coral Way, (305) 444-8890, a cluster of shops including Gap, Victoria's Secret, and other national chain stores, plus a Play City for kids and a ten-screen theater. **Dadeland Mall**, 7535 North Kendall Drive, Miami, (305) 665-6226 or (800) 665-6226, is anchored by Burdines, Saks Fifth Avenue, and Lord & Taylor, with more than 175 specialty stores and a food court. It would be difficult to find a shopping center more tropical than **The**

Falls, U.S. 1 at SW 136th Street, Miami, (305) 255-4570, with water-falls cascading into pools, glittering lakes, and lush landscaping. Indoor and outdoor restaurants and more than 60 shops are anchored by Bloomingdale's. **Mayfair Shops in the Grove**, 2911 Grand Avenue, Coconut Grove, (305) 448-1700, is a study in Spanish tile and feathery greenery surrounding chic, upscale boutiques and restaurants.

FITNESS AND RECREATION

Golf courses and tennis courts abound, topped by the **Biltmore Golf Course**, 1210 Anastasia Avenue, Coral Gables, (305) 460-5366, which surrounds one of the oldest hotels in South Florida. **Metro-Dade Parks and Recreation Department**, 50 SW 32nd Road, Coconut Grove, (305) 533-2000, can guide you to various sports facilities.

Water-sports activities center on Coconut Grove, where you can rent a sailboat at **Castle Harbor Sailboats**, Dinner Key Marina, 3400 Pan American Drive, (305) 858-3212, or a power boat at **Club Nautico**, Monty's Marina, 2560 South Bayshore Drive, Coconut Grove, (305) 858-6258. Fishing boats can also be found at Dinner Key Marina in Coconut Grove. Expect to pay $400 (half-day) to $700 (full day) for fishing, but you can often bargain lower rates or pay just a few dollars to fish off the **Dinner Key Pier** in Coconut Grove.

On the first weekend in March, stars of the race-car circuit turn up in Miami to roar around the **Homestead Motorsports Complex**, 1 Speedway Boulevard, Homestead, (305) 230-5200 at the annual **Miami Grand Prix**. You'll find the racetrack east of U.S. 1 at Palm Drive, off the Florida Turnpike at Exit 6. Tickets are $40 to $100.

For the daring: instructors at **Sky-Dive Miami**, 28700 SW 217th Avenue, Homestead, (800) 759-3483 or (800) 275-9348, will fall out of the sky with you on Saturday and Sunday from 7 a.m. to dark and on weekdays by appointment.

FOOD

Coconut Grove and Coral Gables are Miami's culinary capitals—prices are on the high side, but the food's worth it. To see what New World cuisine is all about, head straight for **Norman's**, 21 Almeria Avenue, (305) 446-6767, where Chef Norman Van Aken has won international accolades for his innovative cuisine. Learn about New Miami Cuban cuisine at **Victor's Café**, 2340 SW 32nd Avenue, Coral

COCONUT GROVE, CORAL GABLES, AND SOUTHERN MIAMI

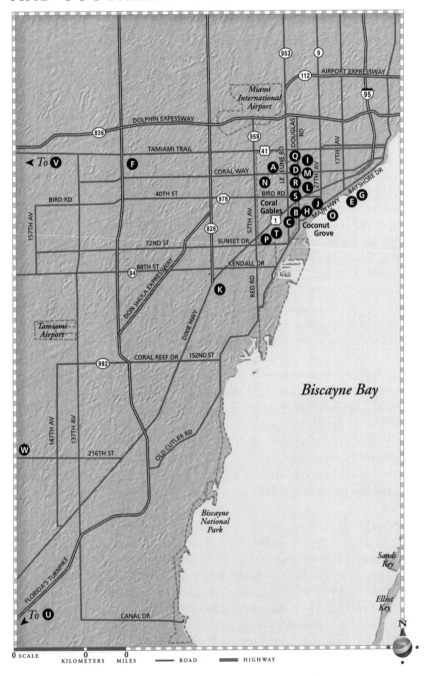

Food

- **A** Caffe Abbracci
- **B** Café Sci Sci
- **C** Café Tu Tu Tango
- **D** Christy's
- **E** Grand Café
- **F** Lila's
- **G** Monty's Seafood House
- **H** Murphy's Law Irish Pub & Restaurant
- **I** Norman's
- **J** Señor Frog
- **K** Shorty's Bar–B–Q
- **L** Tony Roma's – A Place for Ribs
- **M** Victor's Café

Lodging

- **N** Biltmore Hotel
- **E** Grand Bay Hotel
- **O** Grove Isle Club & Resort
- **P** Holiday Inn–University of Miami
- **Q** Hotel Place St. Michel
- **R** Hyatt Regency Coral Gables
- **S** Omni Colonnade Hotel
- **T** Riviera Court Motel

Camping

- **U** City of Florida City Camp Site & RV Park
- **V** Gator Park
- **W** Miami/Homestead KOA

Note: Items with the same letter are located in the same place.

Gables, (305) 445-1313, a café born in New York and transferred here, where it's been captivating local audiences with flavorful combinations of regional Cuban dishes and Caribbean touches.

Caffe Abbracci, 318 Aragon Avenue, Coral Gables, (305) 441-0700, combines Italian flavors with award-winning contemporary styles in an intimate room trimmed with two-tone wood, dark green marble, and mirrors. Think black fettucini *alla* vodka, *scampi grattinati*, lobster *fra Diavolo*, and *agnolotti Verdi* in salsa *tartufata*, then run, don't walk to **Café Sci Sci**, 3043 Grand Avenue, Coconut Grove, (305) 446-5104, where the indoor-outdoor dining's as attractive as the moderately priced food. **Grand Café** at Grand Bay Hotel, 2669 South Bayshore Drive, Coconut Grove, (305) 858-9600, is one of the most elegant restaurants in the region, with a gourmet menu to match.

Meat-and-potatoes folks will love **Christy's**, 3101 Ponce de Leon Boulevard, Coral Gables, (305) 446-1400, and its award-winning thick, juicy steaks and seafood fare. **Monty's Seafood House**, 2550 South Bayshore Drive, Coconut Grove, (305) 858-1431, started out as a gas station and became this restaurant that mesmerizes crowds with huge platters of stone crabs and other seafood served waterside.

For budget-priced dining, try shepherd's pie at **Murphy's Law Irish Pub & Restaurant**, 2977 McFarlane Road, Coconut Grove, (305) 446-9956; slabs of barbecued ribs at **Tony Roma's—A Place for Ribs**, 2665 SW 37th Avenue, Coral Gables, (305) 443-6626; great open-pit barbecue and the world's best coleslaw at **Shorty's Bar-B-Q**, 9200 South Dixie Highway, South Miami, (305) 670-7732; ethnic specialties at **Café Tu Tu Tango**, 301 South Grand Avenue, Coconut Grove, (305) 529-2222; or moo or peep flutes—that's beef or chicken *flautas*—and chicken in a *mole verde* sauce at **Señor Frog**, 3008 Grand Avenue, Coconut Grove, (305) 448-0999; **Lila's**, 8518 SW 24th Street, Miami, (305) 553-6061, is a favorite spot for steaks that lop over the plate and are buried under a mountain of French fries.

LODGING

Large, luxury resorts, a jewel of a small hotel, and moderately priced properties mean a wide range of choices for visitors to the area.

Coconut Grove has two standout hotels. An intimate hostelry with just 50 rooms, **Grove Isle Club & Resort**, 4 Grove Isle Drive, (305) 858-8300 or (800) 88-GROVE, on a small island just off South Bayshore Drive, is one of the region's most elegant and exclusive hotels. Posh and popular with celebrities, Grove Isle has luxurious quarters, tennis courts, a fitness room, formal sculpture gardens, and two restaurants. Winter rates are $295 to $420.

A bright red Alexander Calder sculpture looms over the entrance to the **Grand Bay Hotel**, 2669 South Bayshore Drive, (305) 858-9600 or (800) 327-2788, where an elaborate afternoon tea in the elegantly appointed lobby is a high spot of the day. The best of everything includes a showy site overlooking Dinner Key and an acclaimed restaurant. Rates are $295 to $350 in peak season.

Coral Gable's grande dame is the stately **Biltmore Hotel**, 1200 Anastasia Avenue, (305) 445-1926 or (800) 727-1926. For many years, this massive hotel was a veterans' hospital, but today its magnificent domed, frescoed ceilings have been restored to their original 1926 splendor. In its glory days Ginger Rogers, Rudy Vallee, and Bing Crosby walked its elegant hallways, and Johnny "Tarzan" Weissmuller taught swimming in a pool so huge that it was used for water-ski shows. A luxury property from its massive, sunset-peach Mediterranean architecture to its fine restaurants and lounges, hand-carved headboards, antique armoires, and iron chandeliers, the Biltmore charges $259 to $279 in peak season. The hotel has its own golf course, tennis courts, and fitness center.

Tucked away in the middle of downtown Coral Gables, **Hotel Place St. Michel**, 162 Alcazar Avenue, (305) 444-1666 or (800) 848-HOTEL, is a lovely spot with just 27 rooms, each elegantly resurrected from a 1950s overlay of shoddy "improvements" that covered elaborately stuccoed walls, pretty terrazzo floors, vaulted arches, and high ceilings. There's an outstanding restaurant here, too, also called St. Michel. Peak rates are $165 and $200.

Attendants garbed in Italian Renaissance costumes signal what is to come at **Hyatt Regency Coral Gables**, 50 Alhambra Plaza, (305) 441-1234 or (800) 233-1234. Occupying a flashy location right in the downtown business area, the hotel has 242 well-appointed rooms and an array of showy suites. Rates in peak season are $280 to $295 including a continental breakfast. Still another showplace in Coral Gables is **Omni Colonnade Hotel**, 180 Aragon Avenue, (305) 441-2600 or (800) THE-OMNI, part of a fascinating reconstruction of a 1926 building built by George Merrick. Crowned by a massive, 75-foot-high marble rotunda, the hotel has appealing rooms with mahogany furniture and armoires, brass lamps, and black marble sinks and bars. More marble in the lobby plays backdrop to Oriental rugs and crystal chandeliers. There's an impressive colonnaded pool, whirlpool, two chic restaurants, and a rooftop health club. Rates in peak season are $145 to $225.

Holiday Inn–University of Miami, 1350 South Dixie Highway, (305) 667-5611 or (800) HOLIDAY, is convenient to the university and has a pool, restaurant, and lounge. It charges $119 for a double in winter months. Not far away is the budget **Riviera Court Motel**, 5100 Riviera Drive, (305) 665-3528 or (800) 368-8602, a simple, family-run spot with a pool and basic amenities. Rates are $68 or $78 for efficiencies with cooking facilities.

CAMPING

If you'd like to experience what little wilderness is left around Miami, try **Gator Park**, 24050 SW 8th Street, Miami, (305) 559-2255 or

(800) 559-2205, which is way out on Tamiami Trail (the other name for SW 8th Street), 12 miles west of the Florida Turnpike and deep in the heart of the Everglades. Full hookups on a private lake with a restaurant are $25. You'll also find camping facilities at **City of Florida City Camp Site & RV Park**, 601 NW 3rd Avenue, Florida City, (305) 248-7889, about 25 miles south of Coral Gables, for $16.31 a day. **Miami/ Homestead KOA**, 20675 SW 162nd Avenue, Homestead, (305) 233-5300 or (800) 562-7732, offers sites amid avocado and mango groves but close to local attractions. Rates are $36.95 for full hookups.

NIGHTLIFE

Performing Arts

Both avant-garde and traditional theater productions, often with major stars, take the stage at the **Coconut Grove Playhouse**, 3500 Main Highway, (305) 442-2662, now more than 40 years old and one of the largest regional theaters in Florida. Performances are Tuesday through Sunday from November through April. **Ring Theater**, 1380 Miller Drive, Entrance #6, Coral Gables, (305) 284-3355, is part of the University of Miami's Department of Theater Arts, which has spawned many a nationally known star. Students and guest actors take to the boards from September to May.

Clubs and Bars

Plunked down in the heart of chic Coconut Grove, lively **CocoWalk**, 3015 Grand Avenue, (305) 444-0777, has indoor and outdoor cafés that are busy every night and jammed on weekends. It's open daily 11 a.m. to 10 p.m., 'til 3 a.m. on weekends. Among the diversions at CocoWalk are **Baja Beach Club**, where the bartenders are as much fun as the patrons; **Howl at the Moon Saloon**, which pretty much gives you the idea of what goes on there; and **Dan Marino's American Sports Bar & Grill**, where the famed Dolphins' quarterback is occasionally in attendance. Just down the road: **Planet Hollywood**, 3390 Mary Street, (305) 445-7277, where wild decor and Hollywood-star memorabilia lures a lively crowd of celebs and wanna-bes. In Coral Gables, **Explosion Latina** at **Victor's Café**, 2340 SW 32nd Avenue, (305) 445-1313, is just what the name suggests, an eruption of Latin song and dance—volatile stuff indeed—ranging from hypnotic Afro-Cuban drums to sultry rumba sounds.

4

THE KEYS

C ascading off the end of Florida like a ribbon on a gift package, these islets in the stream are the steam-heat of cold winter dreams, the deserted isles of Robinson Crusoe yearnings. Here, mañana seems altogether too much pressure, and "ASAP" conveys no sense of urgency. Magic takes over the minute you streak across the merged waters of the Atlantic and the Gulf of Mexico. In a flash of aquamarine sea and golden sand, you're transported from a rush-and-ready world to the lazy life that has long drawn pirates and poets to these shores.

As you roll down 113 miles of the Highway That Goes to Sea, leapfrogging over 42 bridges, you're following a route spanned by another dreamer: railroader Henry Flagler, who pushed his "Flagler's Folly" tracks to the nation's tip, only to see a vicious hurricane turn his seaborne steam engines into a mass of twisted metal, his dreams to dust. But that railroad proved more foresight than folly—it paved the way for this highway, today traversed by millions.

From its beginning at Key Largo, the legendary isle of the steamy Bogart-Bacall film of the same name, the highway rolls on to Islamorada, water-sports capital of the Keys. In between is Marathon, named by Flagler's 3,000 workers, who claimed getting the railroad here was a marathon endurance test. It has always been thus on these islands, where geography and meteorology demanded daring and determination, candor and canny vision that sees much and overlooks plenty—quite a good definition, in fact, of the determinedly independent "Conch" families who have called these islands home for generations. ◼

THE KEYS

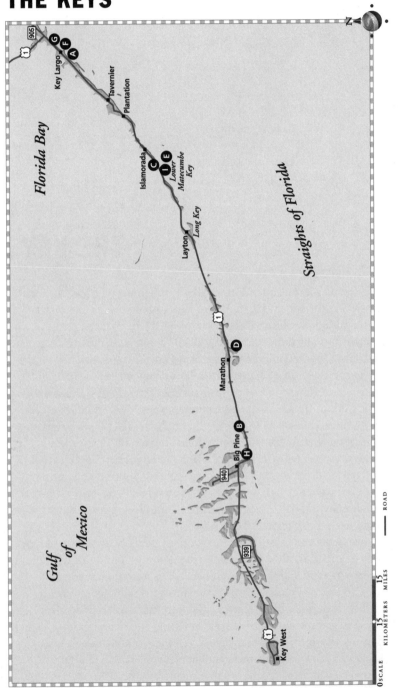

Gulf of Mexico

Florida Bay

Straights of Florida

Key Largo

Tavernier

Plantation

Islamorada

Lower Matecumbe Key

Long Key

Layton

Marathon

Big Pine

Key West

905

1

1

940

939

1

G F A

C I E

D

B H

N

0 SCALE
15 KILOMETERS
15 MILES

——— ROAD

Sights

Ⓐ *African Queen*

Ⓑ Bahia Honda State Park

Ⓒ Coral Sea Glassbottom Boat

Ⓓ Crane Point Hammock/Museum of
National History of the Florida Keys

Ⓔ Indian Key State Historic Site/Lignumvitae
Key State Botanical Gardens

Ⓕ John Pennekamp Coral Reef State Park

Ⓖ Key Largo Undersea Park

Ⓗ National Key Deer Refuge

Ⓘ Robbie's Pet Tarpon

A PERFECT DAY IN THE KEYS

What you do with your day depends on where you're staying along the
113-mile length of the Keys. Here are a variety of options to help you
decide what to do if you just have one day to spend in the Keys: After
breakfast, head for John Pennekamp Coral Reef State Park to spend
the morning in a watery wilderness of multihued coral and impossibly
colored fish. Or sink into the history of the Keys, and their exotic flora
and fauna at Indian or Lignumvitae Keys. Later, schedule a fishing trip
into the crystalline waters of the Atlantic, where prize-winning catches
await. Or try a kayaking tour of the Keys' backcountry, where little has
changed in centuries. If you're not too far away, end the day at
National Key Deer Refuge to watch deer no bigger than collies
scamper to watering holes. After dinner, find your own watering hole
and enjoy a barefoot evening with cool sips and hot sounds.

SIGHTSEEING HIGHLIGHTS

Little green signs called Mile Markers—indicated in addresses by
MM—mark addresses in the Keys, making it easy to find your way to
the hundreds of businesses here. Numbers begin with 1 in Key West
and rise to 113 in Key Largo. Sometimes islanders add an O to
indicate oceanside, B to indicate bayside.

★★★ **Bahia Honda State Park**—Here in the shadow of Flagler's railroad trestles is the most scenic swimming spot in the Keys, where you can paddle from the warm waters of the Gulf of Mexico to the crystalline glitter of the Atlantic. Fat tarpon and sassy game fish cruise about beneath the bridge, and three popular campgrounds are packed year-round. Details: MM37, Big Pine Key; (305) 872-2353; open daily 8 a.m. to sunset. Admission $4 per car plus 50 cents each occupant. (4 hours)

★★★ **Crane Point Hammock/Museum of National History of the Florida Keys**—A living record of Keys' history, Crane Point Hammock's 63 acres are home to endangered ibises and rare tree snails living among hundreds of native and exotic plants. Inhabited for centuries, this site has yielded a wealth of prehistoric Indian artifacts and historic structures including an "Indian- and hurricane-proof" home. Museum displays range from shipwreck gold to ancient pottery and a dugout canoe. Details: MM50, Marathon; (305) 743-9100; open Monday through Saturday 9 a.m. to 5 p.m., Sunday noon to 5 p.m. Admission $5 adults, $2 students, children under age 12 free. (3 hours)

★★★ **Indian Key State Historic Site/Lignumvitae Key State Botanical Gardens**—A microcosm of Keys life, these two small islands are fascinating spots to learn about the fiercely independent Conchs and their island world. On **Indian Key**, you'll hear how pioneer Jacob Housman stole his father's boat and headed south to make his fortune, only to make contact with a reef. Wreckers saved his life then stole his cargo. Housman was a quick study: he became a wrecker, too. When he noticed that many ships went aground in Key Largo, he bought Indian Key so he'd be, well, close to the office. Next, he created a county—so he wouldn't have to turn over half his wrecker-booty to Key West. He then built a hotel for Cuba-bound travelers, but his empire collapsed after Indians attacked and burned his small settlement. **Lignumvitae Key**, a 280-acre island just a mile away, still has a stand of the rare "tree of life" that once proliferated here before development. Virtually untouched in centuries, the key hosts an amazing variety of rare tropical plants and trees. You can reach either key by boat. Details: Robbie's Marina, MM77.5, Islamorada; (305) 664-9814; sailing at 8:30 a.m. and 12:30 p.m. for Indian Cay, at 9:30 a.m. and 1:30 p.m. for Lignumvitae. Fare $15 adults for one island, $25 for both, $10 for children; park rangers charge $1 for an island tour. (4 hours)

★★★ **John Pennekamp Coral Reef State Park**—One of the most famous parks in the nation, this underwater garden 25 miles long and 3 miles wide is a fairyland of 55 feathery corals and 600 species of rainbow-colored fish. In the middle of it all is a towering underwater Christ of the Deep statue that's a popular site for underwater weddings. In the park are a 30,000-gallon aquarium and two nature trails. On scuba trips you can visit caves, rays, moray eels, and shipwrecks. Details: MM102.5, Key Largo; (305) 451-1202; open daily 8 a.m. to sunset. Admission $4 per car, 50 cents each occupant. Glass-bottom boat and snorkeling trips depart at 9 a.m., noon, and 3 p.m., sailing/snorkeling catamaran trips at 9 a.m. and 1:30 p.m. Admission $13 adults, $8.50 children for glass-bottom boat trips; $23.95 adults, $18.95 children under age 18 for snorkeling trips; $28.95 adults, $23.95 children under 18 for snorkeling/sailing trips. (2–3 hours)

★★★ **National Key Deer Refuge**—Tiny, sloe-eyed Key deer are protected here at this refuge, where they can be seen in the morning and at sunset, when they come out to graze on the 2,300 acres—but please don't feed them. A deep hole dug by Flagler's crews is today the Blue Hole, inhabited by alligators, birds, and turtles. Watson's Hammock, a nature preserve, and the Great White Heron Refuge also are part of the park. Details: MM30.5, Big Pine Key; (305) 872-2239; open daily sunrise to sunset. Admission free. (1 hour)

★★ *African Queen*—In addition to *Key Largo*, Humphrey Bogart starred in another famous movie filmed in the area, with Katharine Hepburn and that ragamuffin boat, the *African Queen*, still sailing here. Details: Holiday Inn Key Largo Marina, MM100, (305) 451-2121; by appointment between 11 a.m. and 3 p.m. Admission $15 adults, $7.50 children under age 12. (1 hour)

★★ **Coral Sea Glassbottom Boat**—See what's going on in the busy reef, just offshore through a glass floor. Details: Bud 'n' Mary's Dive Center, MM79, Islamorada; (305) 554-2211 or (800) 344-7352; sails daily at 1:30 p.m. Admission $15 adults, $7.50 children under age 7. (1 hour)

Florida Keys TDC

Snorkeling near Marathon

✭✭ **Key Largo Undersea Park**—If you're a little timid about getting too deep into the wild blue ocean, start with a snorkeling or scuba trip in this sheltered lagoon. Professional instructors accompany you into the water to see a shipwreck, explore an underwater research laboratory, watch marine archaeologists, and observe two most unusual sights—an underwater art studio and an underwater hotel (see Lodging). Details: MM103.2; (305) 451-2353; open daily 9 a.m. to 3 p.m. Admission free, self-guided snorkeling tours $10; scuba diving $20 to $30 for a one-tank dive. (2–4 hours)

✭ **Robbie's Pet Tarpon**—Get a close look at a huge tarpon that weighs in at 200 pounds and hang around the docks waiting for a handout. Details: Robbie's Marina, MM77.5, Islamorada; (305) 664-9814; open daily 8 a.m. to 5 p.m. Admission $1. (1 hour)

GREAT BEACHES

Coral reefs keep the sand from washing up on the shoreline in the Upper Keys, so you won't find any natural beaches there; however, there are many manmade beaches at **John Pennekamp Coral Reef State Park** and at **Harry Harris County Park** in Tavernier. In the Lower Keys **Bahia Honda State Park** has 2½ miles of natural sand.

SHOPPING

Treasure Village, MM86.2, Islamorada, (305) 852-0511, has stained glass, pottery, and leathercraft artists' demonstrations in shops open daily 9 a.m. to 7 p.m., as does the **Rain Barrel**, MM86, Islamorada, (305) 852-3084.

FITNESS AND RECREATION

Acclaimed as one of the top sportfishing grounds in the world, the waters of the Keys are filled with sailfish, tarpon, kingfish, cobia, amberjack, tuna, dolphin, wahoo, bonefish, snook, snapper, grouper, yellowtail, and sharks. Hundreds of charter and rental boats chase them. Find a local captain/guide at **Holiday Isle Marina**, MM84, Islamorada, (305) 664-2321 or (800) 327-7070; **Whale Harbor Marina**, MM84, (305) 664-4959; and **Bud 'n' Mary's Fishing Marina**, MM79.8, Islamorada, (305) 664-2461 or (800) 742-7945, which also arranges dive trips. Extensive water-sports facilities are available at **Cheeca Lodge**, MM82, (305) 664-2777 or (800) 934-8377.

One of the more unusual ways to explore the Keys is by kayak, paddling in the Gulf of Mexico backcountry area, where shallow water shelters fragile mangrove islands, and rocky flats are home to sponges, soft corals, lobsters, turtles, stingrays, and even the occasional shark, barracuda, and tarpon. Kayaks are stable enough even for children to handle, and both guided tours and rental boats are available at **Florida Bay Outfitters**, MM104, Key Largo, (305) 451-3018, which has trips to Everglades National Park, Lignumvitae, and Indian Keys.

Papa Joe's Marina, MM79.7, Islamorada, (305) 644-8065, has single and double kayaks for rent, as does **Ocean Paddlers Nature Tours**, MM48.5, Marathon, (305) 743 0131 or (305) 743-6139, which has additional locations on Islamorada, Summerland, and Big Pine Keys. **Reflections Kayak Nature Tours**, MM28.5, Little Torch Key, (305) 872-2896, offers trips into the Great White Heron National Wildlife Refuge and Everglades National Park for $25 to $80.

Lost World Adventures, Jig's Bait and Tackle, MM30.5, Big Pine Key, (305) 872-1040, has guided tours into the Great White Heron Refuge, the Key Deer Refuge, and the Coupon Bight Aquatic Preserve for $45 per person.

SWIM WITH A DOLPHIN

If you've always dreamed of a date with Flipper, there's no better place to chase your dream than here in the Keys, where three facilities offer dolphin swim programs. Walk and talk—and swim—with the animals at **Dolphin Research Center**, MM59, Grassy Key, Marathon Shores, (305) 289-1121, known for its expertise in caring for wounded or sick dolphins. Dolphin Research lavishes love on its charges, and they return the favor by hauling visitors around the swimming pool. You can meet one of these bottle-nosed guys fin-to-fin for a $90 contribution; or, for $75, researchers will take you on a DolphinSight Program for an in-depth look at these gentle creatures. Walking tours are Wednesday through Saturday, $9.50 for adults and $6 children 4 to 12.

Dolphins Plus, MM99.5, Key Largo, (305) 451-1993, has dolphin interaction programs with both untrained and trained dolphins and charges $30 to $135 for a swimming and instructional session. At **Theater of the Sea**, MM84.5, Islamorada, (305) 664-2431, you can jump right in and swim with Flipper—but if that seems chummier than you want to get with a sea creature, just pat one on the nose or go cuddle up to a sea lion. Special programs teach you the care, feeding, and training of dolphins, and those with nerves of steel can touch a shark . . . carefully. Curtain's up here daily 9:30 a.m. to 4 p.m., but dolphin swims are by reservation. Admission is $14.75 adults, $8.25 children 3 to 12. Dolphin swim programs are $75 to $80, and a four-hour dolphin snorkeling adventure exploring the flora and fauna is $50 adults, $30 children 6 to 12.

FOOD

All of the following restaurants are moderately priced, casual spots full of character and, occasionally, characters. A bilevel bistro with beautiful views, **Marker 88**, MM88, Islamorada, (305) 852-9315, whips up such award-winning treats as baby snapper with mangoes, papayas, bananas, and pineapples in a lemon-parsley sauce and shrimp curry with mango chutney. **Whale Harbor Inn**, MM83.5, Whale Harbor Docks, Islamorada, (305) 664-4959, is easy to find—just look for the lighthouse. Owners here waited out a hurricane up top, while the chairs floated around downstairs. Fresh seafood and a view of boats bobbing in the marina makes for delightful, moderately priced dining. **Ziggie's Conch Restaurant**, MM83.5, Islamorada, (305) 664-3391, is a cozy, casual spot that serves pasta with unusual sauces, fluffy conch fritters, lobster de jonghe, and lots more. **Sid & Roxie's Green Turtle Inn**, MM81.5, Islamorada, (305) 664-9031, is a must-stop on a Keys trip. Pin your business card on the wall— everybody does—then dine on good seafood and steaks, famed turtle soup and conch chowder canned here. Bouillabaisse and banana bread are two of the specialties at **Squid Row Restaurant**, MM80.9, Islamorada, (305) 664-9865, which has local seafood and hand-cut steaks.

LODGING

What other place in the world is so tied to water that you can even *sleep* in it? At **Jules Undersea Lodge**, MM103.2, Key Largo, (305) 451-2353, you can nod off underwater in a two-room suite from which you can watch the action outside your window while dining on lobster or filet prepared by a diver-butler who brings you dinner. Tell that at your next party! If you're not a certified diver, you can take a three hour course ($75 for one, $50 each for other participants) to get you

THE KEYS

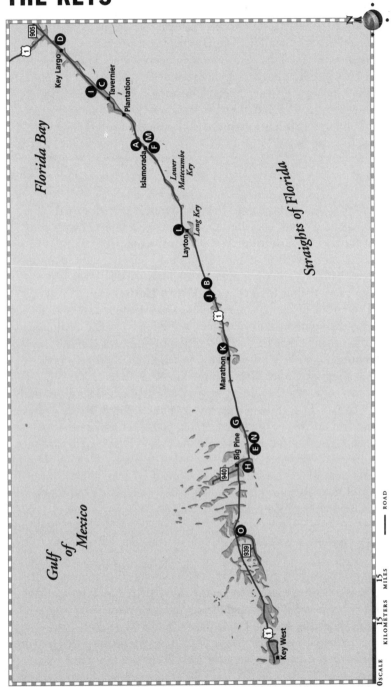

Gulf of Mexico

Florida Bay

Straights of Florida

Key Largo
Tavernier
Plantation
Islamorada
Lower Matecumbe Key
Long Key
Layton
Marathon
Big Pine
Key West

905
1
1
940
939
1

SCALE

0   15
KILOMETERS   MILES
15

ROAD

A B C D E F G H I J K L M N O

Food

- (A) Marker 88
- (A) Sid & Roxie's
  Green Turtle Inn
- (A) Squid Row Restaurant
- (A) Whale Harbor Inn
- (A) Ziggie's Conch Restaurant

Lodging

- (A) Harbor Lights Resort
- (B) Hawk's Cay Resort
  and Marina
- (C) Historic Tavernier Hotel
- (D) Jules Undersea Lodge
- (A) Key Lantern Motel
- (E) Little Palm Island
- (E) Parmer's Place
- (D) Sheraton Key Largo
- (F) Sugarloaf Lodge

Camping

- (D) America Outdoors
- (G) Bahia Honda State Park
- (H) Big Pine Key Fishing Lodge
- (I) Calusa Camping Resort
- (D) Florida Keys RV Resort
- (D) John Pennekamp Coral Reef
  State Park
- (J) Jolly Roger Travel Park
- (D) Key Largo Campground
  and Marina
- (K) Knights Key Park
- (L) KOA Fiesta Key
- (M) Lazy Lakes Resorts
- (L) Long Key State
  Recreation Area
- (N) Sunshine Key Camp
- (O) Venture Out

Note: Items with the same letter are located in the same town or area.

down there safely. An underwater adventure includes dinner, breakfast, and an aquanaut certificate for $295 per person.

Sheraton Key Largo, MM97, (305) 852-5553 or (800) 826-1006, sprawls over bayfront acreage with three restaurants, a lounge, two pools, a private beach, water sports, children's center, tennis, a nature trail, marina, and 200 well-appointed rooms. Rates are $219 to $269.

Historic Tavernier Hotel, MM91.8, (305) 852-4131 or (800) 515-4131, was built in 1928 as a movie theater but never showed the first film. Instead it became a hotel and today is a cluster of pretty pink buildings with a hot tub and fitness center clustered around a tropical garden and a restaurant that serves fresh bread and French pastry. Rates are $99 to $129.

Two comparatively inexpensive spots are **Key Lantern Motel**, MM82.1, Islamorada, (305) 664-4572, adjacent to a trailer park and charging $45 to $58 in winter; and **Harbor Lights Resort**, MM84.9, (305) 664-3611 or (800) 327-7070, which has simply decorated rooms (some with screened porches) and shares the Holiday Isle beach for rates of $85 to $145 in peak season.

Hawk's Cay Resort and Marina, MM62, Duck Key, (305) 743-7000 or (800) 432 2242, is a rambling, Caribbean-style resort on its own island with lots of wicker paddle-fan atmosphere in handsome rooms. Fishing, boating, tennis, whirlpools, water sports, lagoon where dolphins swim with you, and a kids' club are all part of the action here. Rates in peak season are $210 to $350.

Dozens of small motels, only one with more than 50 rooms, line the Overseas Highway in the Lower Keys. Head of the class is **Little Palm Island**, MM28.5, Little Torch Key, (305) 872-2524 or (800) 343-8567, a hedonist's paradise whose 30 suites are reachable only by the resort's private launch. Once there, you live in luxuriously appointed, thatch-roofed suites with whirlpool, bar, and walled-in but open-air shower—no phones, no televisions. You dine in elegance, indoors in the candle glow or on the sand in the glow of sunset; swim in a waterfall-fed pool; imbibe at a tiki bar; loll in a sauna. A posh and exclusive resort, Little Palm charges $545 per night.

Sugarloaf Lodge, MM17, (305) 745-3211 or (800) 553-6097, is the largest resort in the Lower Keys, with 55 brightly decorated paneled rooms tucked away in one- and two-story buildings. There's an airstrip, tennis courts, mini-golf, and a glass-walled restaurant overlooking the water where tame dolphins cavort. Rates in peak season are $110 to $120. **Parmer's Place**, MM28.5, Little Torch Key, (305) 872-2157, has casual waterfront cottages with motel rooms and apartments, a heated pool, boat launch ramp, and rates of $70 to $125.

CAMPING

You'll find plenty of camping opportunities in the Keys, beginning with **John Pennekamp Coral Reef State Park**, MM102.5, Key Largo, (305) 664-9814 (see Sightseeing). Rates for full hookups are $23 to $26. **Florida Keys RV Resort** (MM106, Key Largo, 800-252-6090), **Calusa Camping Resort** (MM101.5, Frank's Key, 305-451-0232), **Key Largo Campground and Marina** (MM101.5, Key Largo, 305-451-1431), and **America Outdoors** (MM97.5, Key Largo, 305-852-8054) have land- and water-view sites for $30 to $40.

In the Middle Keys, look for **Long Key State Recreation Area**, MM67.5, Long Key, (305) 664-4815, where you'll find waterside camp-sites, guided nature walks, and lecture programs for $28 to $30. **KOA Fiesta Key**, MM70, Long Key, (305) 664-4922, charges $54 to $68 for one of its 300 oceanside sites with heated pool, hot tubs, café, pub, and marina. **Jolly Roger Travel Park**, MM59, Grassy Key, (305) 289-0404, charges $35 to $45 for hookups, and **Knight's Key Park**, MM47, Mara-thon, (305) 743-4343, has water and electric hookups for $42 to $56.

In the Lower Keys, **Bahia Honda State Park**, MM37, Big Pine Key, (305) 872 2353, is very popular for its beautiful Gulf and Atlantic beaches; it charges $26. **Big Pine Key Fishing Lodge**, MM33, Big Pine Key, (305) 872-2351, has a heated pool, recreation and game room, marina, boat rentals, nature trail, and $26 rates.

Sunshine Key Camp, MM39, Ohio Key, (305) 872-2217, charges $49 for full hookups and use of the camp's pool, tennis courts, and horseshoes. **Venture Out** at Cudjoe Cay, MM23, Summerland Key, (305) 745-1333, charges $38 to $44, and **Lazy Lakes Resorts**, MM19.8, Sugarloaf Key, (305) 745-1079, has 100 campsites for $39 to $42.

A free camping guide to the Lower Keys is available by calling (305) 872-2411 or (800) USA-ESCAPE.

NIGHTLIFE

Caribbean Club, MM103, Key Largo, (305) 451-9970, a local watering hole famed for, among other things, its great views of fiery sunsets, was the locale for a certain famous film starring Humphrey Bogart and Lauren Bacall. **Key Largo Casino Cruises**, Holiday Inn Resort and

Marina, MM100, (305) 451-0000 or (800) THE-KEYS, has added a neat gimmick to the shipboard casino: the ship anchors at sea, while water taxis scoot out to the main ship every 90 minutes so you can arrive and leave whenever you like. Light dining's available on board the ship, which departs at 2 p.m., returning at 3 a.m. Water-taxi trips are at 5, 7, 9, and 11 p.m. Admission is free; water-taxi round-trip is $10.

Partying never stops at **Holiday Isle**, MM84, Islamorada, (305) 664-2321 or (800) 327-7070, and you'll find suds and fun at **Woody's**, MM82, Islamorada, (305) 664-4335; **Señor Frijoles**, MM103.9, Key Largo, (305) 451-1592; Snappers, 139 Seaside Avenue, Key Largo, (305) 852-5956; **Coconuts**, 529 Caribbean Drive, Key Largo, (305) 451-4107; **Breezers** at Marriott Bay Beach, MM103, Key Largo, (305) 453-0000; **Lorelei**, MM82, Islamorada, (305) 664-4656; and my favorite, **No Name Pub**, MM30, No Name Key, turn right at stoplight on Big Pine Key, (305) 872-9115. No Name bills itself, rightfully, as "a nice place . . . if you can find it."

5
KEY WEST

Key West is elegant and antique, contemporary and a little crazy, a world of its own 100 miles—and light years—from Miami. Just 5 miles long and 3 miles wide, it was first spotted by the Spanish, who sailed gold-laden galleons through its treacherous waters. In 1733 a fleet of those galleons had a bad Friday the 13th, foundering in a gale that sent $68 million in gold to the bottom, where it remains the dream of many a modern treasure-hunter.

Purloined gold created quite a snappy lifestyle in Key West, as canny settlers discovered the rewards of shipwreck salvage. To expedite the inevitable, folks here soon found methods of ensuring that there would be shipwrecks. Soon everyone was involved in wrecking, including a minister whose view from the pulpit allowed him to be the first to spot a wreck one Sunday—so he finished his sermon on the way to the door, to ensure he'd be the first to claim wrecking rights!

Conchs, as longtime islanders call themselves, suffer little from slavish adoration of tradition and are quick to adjust to whatever comes their way. Unamazed by the amazing array of lifestyles here, they open their homes and their hearts to a stream of visitors that over the years has included hordes of celebrities, from writer Ernest Hemingway and playwright Tennessee Williams to designer Calvin Klein, actor Dustin Hoffman, and singer Jimmy Buffett. All found just what you will find: a welcome as warm as the temperatures, and days and nights as glittering as the seas around this island in the stream. ◙

KEY WEST

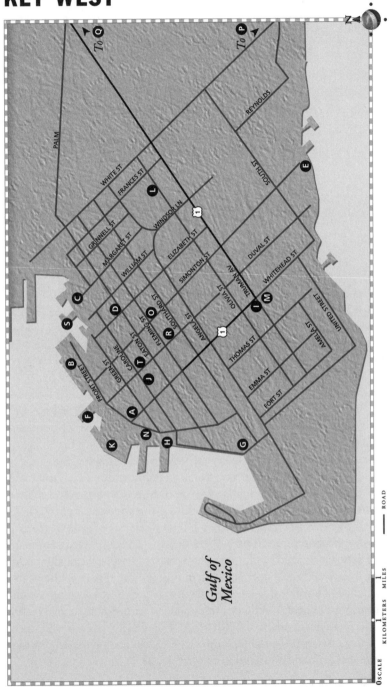

Sights

Ⓐ Audubon House and Gardens

Ⓑ Conch Tour Train

Ⓒ Discovery Undersea Tours

Ⓓ Donkey Milk House

Ⓔ East Martello Tower Museum and Art Gallery

Ⓕ *Fireball* and *Pride of Key West* Glassbottom Boat Rides

Ⓖ Fort Zachary Taylor State Historic Site

Ⓗ Harry S. Truman Little White House Museum

Ⓘ Hemingway House

Ⓙ Heritage House Museum

Ⓚ Key West Aquarium

Ⓛ Key West Cemetery

Ⓜ Key West Lighthouse Museum

Ⓝ Mel Fisher Maritime Heritage Society Museum

Ⓞ Nancy Forrester's Secret Garden

Ⓟ Old Town Trolley Tours

Ⓠ Personalized Tours of Key West

Ⓡ Ripley's Believe It or Not! Odditorium

Ⓢ Turtle Kraals

Ⓣ Wrecker's Museum

A PERFECT DAY IN KEY WEST

Hear the lore and gossip of old Key West aboard a Conch Tour, then fill the morning with cannons and antique bricks in the city's early Fort Zachary Taylor and East Martello Towers. Stop at Key West Lighthouse for a look at the wreckers' favorite reefs, then see the golden treasure that was their dream in shipwreck-finder Mel Fisher's museum. Learn the rules of wrecking at the Wrecker's House, then immerse yourself in the antique architecture and jungle gardens of Key West, with visits to Audubon House, Hemingway House, Heritage House, Donkey Milk House, or—sssssh!—the little-known Nancy Forrester's Secret Garden. Sunset absolutely must find you at Mallory Dock, where even if you don't see the amazing "green flash" that sometimes can be spotted as the sun goes down, you'll certainly see *something* amazing. By night, join the ghosts of Hemingway and many others at Sloppy Joe's Bar.

SIGHTSEEING HIGHLIGHTS

★★★ **Audubon House and Gardens**—You'll see beautiful antique furnishings in one of the island's oldest homes and also the work of famous bird artist John James Audubon, who visited here in 1832. Details: 205 Whitehead Street; (305) 294-2116; open daily 9:30 a.m. to 5 p.m. Admission $7.50 adults, $2 children ages to 6 to 12. (1 hour)

★★★ **Conch Tour Train**—Aboard this narrated tour that toots its way around town in open-sided cars, relating the weird and wonderful history of Key West, you'll learn four ways the first settlers air-conditioned their houses and how they made a living wrecking ships. Details: 501 Front Street; (305) 294-5161; open 9:30 a.m. to 4:30 p.m. Admission $14 adults, $6 children ages 6 to 12. (2 hours)

★★★ **Donkey Milk House**—No, they never milked donkeys here, but they did use them to pull milk wagons and pick up the produce behind this charming house, which has been owned by the Williams family for more than 120 years. Built in 1866, it's decorated in period style and still has its original bathroom plumbing, parlor, and butler's pantry. Details: 613 Eaton Street; (305) 296-1866; open daily 10 a.m. to 5 p.m. Admission $5 adults, children under age 13 free. (1 hour)

★★★ **Fort Zachary Taylor State Historic Site**—How the
southernmost point in the nation became a Union stronghold during
the Civil War is an odd story you'll hear at this small fort, where a
ranger and his son have unearthed the nation's largest buried arsenal of
Civil War cannons. Details: end of Southard Street, Truman Annex;
(305) 292-6713; open 8 a.m. to sunset, with tours at noon and 2 p.m.
Admission $1.50 for walkers or cyclists; in cars, $2.50 for driver, $2.50
second person, 50 cents each additional person. (1 hour)

★★★ **Hemingway House**—Thirty of writer Ernest Hemingway's
most prolific years were spent in this house, where he lived with six-
toed cats whose descendants remain here, enjoying their own fountain
created from an olive jar Hemingway swiped from his bar-owner
buddy, Sloppy Joe. You'll hear those and other stories about the famous
author at this handsome home. A $10 Writers Walk tour, (305) 293-
9291, departs from here Sunday at 10:30 a.m. Details: 907 Whitehead
Street; (305) 294-1575; open daily 9 a.m. to 5 p.m. Admission $6.50
adults, $4 children ages 6 to 12. (1 hour)

★★★ **Key West Cemetery**—This good-humored spot is as amusing
as it is historic. As unusual as the Keys folks who now occupy space
here, the stones bear such inscriptions as "I Told You I Was Sick" and
"At Least I Know Where He's Sleeping Tonight." A memorial honors
the many buried here after the U.S. battleship *Maine* was sunk in
Havana in 1898, touching off the Spanish-American War. One unusual
crypt, not yet occupied by its owner, has already been inscribed with
his 17 nicknames, including "Nuts," and this last request: "Call Me For
Dinner." Details: Angela and Margaret Streets; no phone; open sunrise
to dusk. Admission free. Guided tours for $5 led by the Historic
Florida Keys Preservation Board, Old City Hall, 510 Greene Street,
(305) 292-6829. (1 hour)

★★★ **Mel Fisher Maritime Heritage Society Museum**—For
decades Key West treasure-seeker Mel Fisher dreamed of and hunted
for sunken treasure. Even as bankruptcy loomed, he pored over old
maps. Suddenly, his dream came true: he located the galleon *Nuestra
Señora de Atocha* and retrieved the $400 million in gold, silver, and
emeralds, some of it on display here. Details: 200 Greene Street; (305)
294-2633; open daily 9:30 a.m. to 5 p.m. Admission $6 adults, $2
children ages 6 to 12. (1 hour)

Hemingway House

Florida Keys TDC

★★★ **Wrecker's Museum**—ere, in the oldest home in Key West, once owned by wrecker Capt. Francis Watlinson, you can learn all about the wrecker's game—including the rules. Yes, there were rules! Historic documents, ship models, and paintings detail this unusual occupation. Details: 322 Duval Street; (305) 294-9502; open daily 10 a.m. to 4 p.m. Admission $4 adults, 50 cents children. (1 hour)

★★ **East Martello Tower Museum and Art Gallery**—This Civil War–era fortification today features exhibits of the city's cigar-making and sponging industries and tells the story of the railroad's tumultuous times. Next door, West Martello Tower is home to a lovely tropical garden. Details: 3501 South Roosevelt Boulevard; (305) 296-3913; open 9:30 a.m. to 5 p.m. daily. Admission $5 adults, $1 children ages 6 to 12. (1 hour)

★★ **Harry S. Truman Little White House Museum**—Our bucks-stops-here president brought his bucks here each winter, when he ran the nation from this "Winter White House," now restored and showing a video. Details: 111 Front Street; (305) 294-9911; open 9 a.m. to 5 p.m. Admission $7 adults, $3.50 children under age 12. (1 hour)

★★ **Heritage House Museum**—A shipwreck that came to be known as the "wreck of the German brides" ended with the marriage of one rescued woman to this home's owner. Today you'll see authentic Keys furnishings collected from five generations of the Porter family, who hosted writers John Dos Passos, Thornton Wilder, and Tennessee Williams. Poet Robert Frost was such a frequent visitor that the family named the cottage and gardens after him. A $10 Writers Walk tour, (305) 293-9291, departs from here at 10:30 a.m. Saturday. Details: 410 Caroline Street, Key West; (305) 296-3573; open Monday through Saturday 10 a.m. to 5 p.m.; Sunday noon to 5 p.m. Admission $6 adults, students $3, children under age 12 free. (1 hour)

★★ **Key West Lighthouse Museum**—Get your daily workout here by climbing the 88 steps to the top of the observation tower for a pelican's eye view of the city. One of the three oldest lighthouses in Florida, this brick tower was built in 1847, and its museum details the history of Keys lighthouses. Details: 938 Whitehead Street; (305) 294-0012; open daily (except Christmas) 9:30 a.m. to 5 p.m. Admission $5 adults, $1 children ages 7 to 12. (1 hour)

★★ **Nancy Forrester's Secret Garden**—Key West's homes are secreted behind walls and thick greenery, but here you can peek into the privacy of an old Conch house. So tranquil and dramatically beautiful is this collection of rare palms and beautiful blooms that you'll want to stay forever. Details: 1 Free School Lane; (305) 294-0015; open daily 10 a.m. to 5 p.m. Admission $5 adults, $2 children under age 12. (1 hour)

★★ **Old Town Trolley Tours**—To tour at your own pace, just get on and off these trolleys that traverse an 18-mile course through the city with 12 stops and narration. Details: 1910 North Roosevelt Boulevard; (305) 296-6688; open daily 9 a.m. to 5 p.m. Admission $15 adults, $6 children ages 4 to 12. (1½ hours)

★★ **Ripley's Believe It or Not! Odditorium**—Weird. Weird, weird, weird. Shrunken heads, a collection of 10,000 neckties, a painted torture chamber, a giant shark, a slanted room, a ball that rolls uphill, and 1,500 other exhibits that are . . . weird. Details: 527 Duval Street; (305) 293-9686 or (800) 998-4418; open daily 10 a.m. to 11 p.m. Admission $9.95 adults, $6.95 children ages 4 to 12. (1½ hours)

★ **Discovery Undersea Tours**—See the subsurface action from an underwater viewing room in which you can watch the daily life of a coral reef. Details: Lands End Village & Marina, 251 Margaret Street; (305) 293-0099; trip times vary by season, but offices are open 9:30 a.m. to 5:30 p.m. daily. Admission $18 adults, $12 children ages 6 to 12. (2–3 hours)

★ *Fireball* **and** *Pride of Key West* **Glassbottom Boat Rides**—You can get a close look at the colorful inhabitants of Key West's famous living coral reef aboard these glass-bottomed craft. Details: 2 Duval Street; (305) 296-6293; trips daily at noon, 2, and 4:30 p.m. Admission $20 adults for day cruises, $25 for the champagne sunset trip, $10 and $12.50 for children ages 5 to 12. (2 hours)

Key West Aquarium—Sea turtles, colorful tropical fish, and game fish live in this aquarium, where you can watch a shark feeding frenzy and even pet one of the feeders in a "touch tank." Details: 1 Whitehead Street; (305) 296-2051; open daily 9 a.m. to 6 p.m. Admission $6.50 adults, $3.50 children ages 8 to 15. (1 hour)

Personalized Tours of Key West—Bill and Anita Schwessinger run a variety of auto and walking tours of Key West, showing you the many sides of this fascinating city and even taking you right into their friends' backyards for a look at tropical life and lifestyles. Details: 81 Bay Drive; (305) 292-TOUR; by arrangement. Charges are $60 to $70 by car; $15 per person by foot. (2 hours)

Turtle Kraals—A holding pen is home to a collection of turtles, sharks, rays, huge crawfish, and tropical fish. Details: 2 Land's End Village at the foot of Margaret Street in the Turtle Kraals Restaurant; (305) 294-2640; open daily 11 a.m. to 10:30 p.m. Admission free. (1 hour)

GREAT BEACHES

Key West has only one beach of note, **Smathers Beach**, on South Roosevelt Boulevard near the airport. Small, but large enough to accommodate island tan fans.

SHOPPING

Hundreds of boutiques and gifts shops are tucked into every alley and inlet. You're on your own—with just these few suggestions. **FastBuck Freddie's**, 500 Duval Street, (305) 294-2007, is worth a stop just to see what they're stocking in this spot that's been here forever. Next door is Jimmy Buffett's store called—what else?—**Margaritaville**, also at 500 Duval Street, (305) 296-3070. Take home a very–Key West souvenir from **Key West Hand Print Fabrics**, 201 Simonton Street, (305) 294-9535, or **Key West Fragrances**, 524 Front Street, (305) 294-5592, which features such scents as frangipani and white ginger. Key West was once the cigar center of Florida, and you can still see the little cylinders being rolled at **Caribbean Cigar Factory**, 112 Fitzpatrick Street, (305) 292-9595. Finally, don't even *try* to take home a yellow-lime delicacy from **Key West Key Lime Pie Company**, 701 Caroline Street (rear), (305) 294-6567 or (800) 872-2714—you'll be lucky to get out the door without finishing it off.

FITNESS AND RECREATION

Sail off aboard the swift **Fury Catamarans**, 201 Front Street, (305) 294-8899 or (800) 201-2369, which fly across the waters for reef

snorkeling trips at 9:30 a.m. and 1 p.m. and sunset trips at 5 p.m.
Admission is $38 adults for snorkeling and $28 for sunset cruises, $19
and $14 for children ages 7 to 13.

Sebago Catamarans, 200 Williams Street, Key West, (305) 294-
5687, sails a 60-footer on $28 snorkeling and $22 champagne sunset
cruises, and offers a snorkeling/kayaking combo that includes lots of
food, drink, and underwater sights for $69.

Skilled divers can dive the ultimate, the *Atocha* site, discovered by
treasure-hunter Mel Fisher. Arrange expeditions at the Mel Fisher
Maritime Heritage Society Museum, 200 Greene Street, (305) 294-2633.

Fishing is fabulous in Key West, where the fighting fish of
choice is the bonefish, an elusive devil that's smarter than most
anglers. If you'd like to try your luck, stop by the **Garrison Bight
Marina**, on U.S. 1 at 711 Eisenhower Drive, (305) 294-3093, where
the city's charter boats dock. Even if you're not going fishing
yourself, stop by about 4 p.m. and see—or buy—some of the day's
catch. Charter rates are about $550 a day for up to six people.

Mosquito Coast Island Outfitters & Kayak Guides, 1107
Duval Street, (305) 294-7178, takes kayakers to Geiger Key or Sugarloaf Key on five-hour natural history tours close to shore.

Rent bikes or scooters from **Adventure Scooter & Bike**, 1102
Key Plaza Shopping Center, (305) 293-9933, and at many other
locations around the island.

FOOD

Food is a little pricey on the island, but you can find plenty of
moderate spots, too. Definitely in the former category, **Café des
Artistes**, 1007 Simonton Street, (305) 294-7100, is one of the top
restaurants in the city and one of the most attractive, with a romantic
dining room where you feast on contemporary French flavors. Other
high-end restaurants include **Martha's**, 3591 Roosevelt Boulevard,
(305) 294-3466, a chic spot overlooking the ocean and specializing in
aged Angus beef and island seafood served to the accompaniment of
piano music; **Louie's Backyard**, 700 Waddell Avenue, (305)
294-1061, which isn't just a backyard, but rather a handsome old
two-story home where you can dine upstairs, downstairs, or in the
backyard overlooking the sea—Caribbean flavors spice award-
winning cuisine; and **Square One Restaurant**, 1075 Duval Street,
(305) 296-4300, which prides itself on new American cuisine made

with local seafood and served in an intimate dining room or outdoor courtyard with a piano tinkling in the background.

For less extravagant dining, try **A & B Lobster House**, 700 Front Street, (305) 294-2536, long a mainstay of the island. The atmosphere is rustic, rustic, and rustic, with nautical decor and a second-story view over the docks. Folks come here not only for ambience but also for hearty platters of moderately priced seafood plucked right from the sea outside the door. **Paradise Café**, 1000 Eaton Street, (305) 296-5001, is a budget spot famed for its "Island Legend" monster sandwiches.

LODGING

Key West is wall-to-wall in Victorian homes, many of them now bed-and-breakfast operations or small inns. Tops among the city's historic properties is **Curry Mansion Inn**, 511 Caroline Street, (305) 294-5349 or (800) 253-3466, built around a magnificent 22-room home constructed in 1899 and lined with drop-dead-gorgeous mahogany woodwork. Next to the mansion, the 15-room inn is furnished with wicker, four-poster beds, and antiques, with a garden and pool. Rates are $200 to $275.

Marriott's Casa Marina Resort, 1500 Reynolds Street, (305) 296-3535 or (800) 228-9290, traces its history back to 1921, when railroad entrepreneur Henry Flagler built this striking hotel at the last stop of his Overseas Railroad. Transformed by a multimillion-dollar makeover, the Mediterranean-style hotel has a massive fireplace, beamed ceiling, French doors, columns, high-backed wicker chairs, chic rooms, water sports, fitness facilities, and restaurants beside the sea. Peak rates are $288 to $325.

Another beautifully restored property is the **Historic Holiday Inn La Concha Hotel**, 430 Duval Street, (305) 296-2991 or (800) HOLIDAY, which went through some rugged days before a renovation turned it back into the showplace it was when it was built in 1926. Now a vision in paddle fans, wicker, and tropical colors, La Concha is a tranquil spot with sunset views that are downright magic. Peak-season rates are $235 to $260.

The **Gardens Hotel**, 526 Angela Street, (305) 294-2661 or (800) 526-2664, was for many years a garden tourist attraction and is today one of the loveliest small inns in the Keys. Beautiful antique and reproduction furnishings adorn rooms nestled among a breathtaking display of rare palms, orchids, and massive old trees. Rates are $225 to $315, higher for suites.

KEY WEST

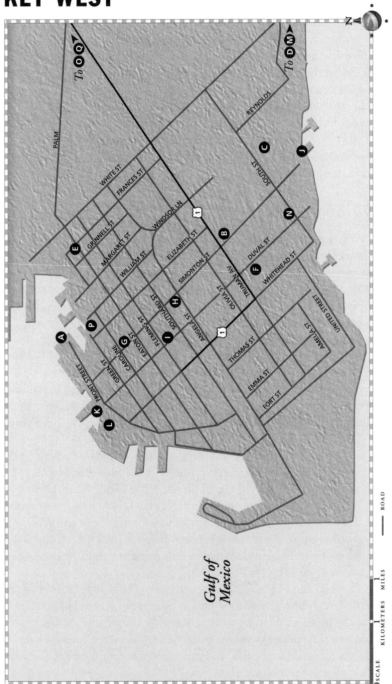

Gulf of
Mexico

0 SCALE

1
KILOMETERS   MILES
1

——— ROAD

Food

Ⓐ A & B Lobster House

Ⓑ Café des Artistes

Ⓒ Louie's Backyard

Ⓓ Martha's

Ⓔ Paradise Café

Ⓕ Square One Restaurant

Lodging

Ⓖ Curry Mansion Inn

Ⓗ Gardens Hotel

Ⓘ Historic Holiday Inn
La Concha Hotel

Ⓙ Marriott's Casa Marina Resort

Ⓚ Ocean Key House
Suite Resort & Marina

Ⓛ Pier House Resort
& Caribbean Spa

Ⓜ Sheraton Suites Key
West Resort

Ⓝ Southernmost Motel

Camping

Ⓞ Boyd's Key West
Campground

Ⓟ Jabour's Trailer Court

Ⓠ Leo's Campground

Ocean Key House Suite Resort & Marina, 0 Duval Street, (305) 296-7701 or (800) 328-9815, occupies enviable acreage right at the foot of Key West's main thoroughfare and smack on the sea. Rates at the hotel, which has a big pool, three lounges, two restaurants, a Gulf fishing pier, and plenty of water sports, are $340 to $440.

Pier House Resort & Caribbean Spa, 1 Duval Street, (305) 296-4600 or (800) 327-8340, was the hotel in which Key West's favorite son, Jimmy Buffett, got his start as a singer in the Old Havana Docks Bar. An award-winning resort, this spot has four restaurants and five bars, lots of wicker and paddle fans, all of it tucked away in typically Keys-ian buildings right on the sea. Rates in peak season are $275 to $450.

Sheraton Suites Key West Resort, 2001 South Roosevelt Boulevard, (305) 292-9800, (800) 45-BEACH, or (800) 325-3535, occupies a tranquil part of town and offers bright, spacious suites togged out in tropical prints, an airy restaurant, a pool, and a lively lounge. Rates are $319 to $419.

Southernmost Motel, 1319 Duval Street, (305) 296-6577 or (800) 354-4455, is a cozy, colorful spot nestled into grounds at—where else?—the southernmost tip of the United States. Bedecked with flowers and tropical touches, Southernmost charges $129 to $195.

Key West is also very popular with gay travelers, so some of the city's many inns cater specifically to gay visitors. A **guide to gay accommodations** is available from the Key West Business Guild, 424 Fleming Street, (305) 294-4603 or (800) 535-7797.

CAMPING

Key West is so jammed with houses, shops, restaurants, and hotels that there's very little room for campgrounds, so you'll probably have to settle in the Lower Keys or on Stock Island, just a few miles away. As close as you can get to Key West without being in it, **Leo's Campground**, 5236 Suncrest Road, Stock Island, (305) 296-5260, charges $24, and **Boyd's Key West Campground**, 6401 Maloney Avenue, MM5, Stock Island, (305) 294-1465, charges $44 to $54. However, if you're determined to be where the action is, right in Key West, try **Jabour's Trailer Court**, 223 Elizabeth Street, (305) 294-5723, which charges $51.

NIGHTLIFE

Key West has countless bars and lounges, catering to every taste in nightlife, so check out local publications to see what's on in town. Listed here are a few of the top spots.

Character and characters in roughly equal parts mark the famous **Sloppy Joe's**, 201 Duval Street. It's a Key West must-do, if for no other reason than to get some insight into what life must have been like when this city was a tiny backwater frequented by die-hard fishermen such as Ernest Hemingway and the occasional life dropout, also such as Hemingway. It's said that the author and Sloppy Joe frequently retired to a locked back room with a case of whiskey, which they put to good use while Joe told sea stories. Hemingway absorbed them, later turning them into novels, the most famous of which were written in Key West.

Some say **Captain Tony's Saloon**, 428 Greene Street, (305) 294-1838, is the real Sloppy Joe's, which, all things considered, might very well be true: Hemingway loved spots like this and so, apparently, do many others—practically everyone in Key West stops by here at least once every evening. Once ranked as one of *Esquire's* Top Ten bars, Captain Tony's is . . . well, you'll see. There's also **Hog's Breath Saloon**, 400 Front Street, 296-4222—need I say more?

SIDETRIP: FORT JEFFERSON

One of the most unusual trips you can take in Florida—or almost anywhere else, for that matter—is to Fort Jefferson, which looms in weirdly surrealistic splendor over the tiny island of **Dry Tortugas**, 70 miles off the coast of Key West. Hands down the nation's least accessible national monument, Fort Jefferson National Park can be reached only by boat or on trips put together by Key West Air Service. A flight on a pontooned seaplane that lands on water is unusual for openers, but nothing compared to flying over waters clear as a teardrop, then landing at a remote island in the shadow of a huge, crumbling fortress that took 30 years to complete and cost $3.5 million.

Fort Jefferson had 140 guns ready for Civil War action, but not one of them ever fired a shot. Instead, the fort became a prison for Dr. Samuel Mudd, who spent two years in this desolate spot, atoning for the sin of setting the broken leg of Abraham Lincoln's assassin, John Wilkes Booth. That medical aid gave rise, in fact, to the expression "your name is mud." Mudd was later pardoned, after his help in a yellow fever epidemic.

Today park rangers watch over the fort, where a visitor center video tells you a little about the challenges of transporting 16 million bricks to this remote location—and finding workers willing to sweat away their days out here in the middle of nowhere. Plaques lead you on a self-guided tour of the fort, where you can picnic, snorkel in beautiful shallow waters, get a close look at some of the 150 bird varieties that nest in this sanctuary, or just stroll the moat wall, accompanied by the ghosts of inhabitants past. **Key West Air Service**, Sunset Marina, 5603 West College Road, Stock Island, (305) 292-5201 or (888) FLT-FORT, has trips at 8 a.m., 10 a.m., 12:30 p.m., and 2:30 p.m. daily for $159 for a half-day trip for adults, $129 children ages 7 to 16, and $89 children ages 2 to 7. Full-day trips are also available.

A 100-foot yacht, *Yankee Freedom*, operates a ferry service to Fort Jefferson. Board at 7:30 a.m. at **Lands End Marina**, 1 Margaret Street, (305) 294-7009 or (800) 634-0939, departing at 8 a.m., returning at 7 p.m. Breakfast is included in the fare, which is $75 adults, $65 students, and $45 children ages 6 to 12. Lunch is available on the ship, along with a full bar and snorkel equipment.

6
THE EVERGLADES

J ust south of the skyscrapers that loom over the flat land of Miami lies
  a vast primeval prairie called the Everglades, which stretches 100
miles from Lake Okeechobee to Florida Bay and covers 1.5 million acres
of South Florida. Actually a huge, very shallow river whose water moves
southward from Lake Okeechobee at the rate of ¼ mile a day, the
Everglades is a secretive and mysterious place, dank and dark, sometimes
fierce, sometimes gentle, always fascinating. Beneath the silence that
mantles this eery marsh is a complex biological chain that begins with
microscopic organisms and ends with humans who are struggling to
protect this wilderness from a creeping tide of commercial development.

To hear the message of the marshland, you must immerse yourself
in the silence and the sounds of this huge river of grass. If you're
patient and attentive, you'll begin to perceive the life hidden here: high
atop a dead tree, a massive osprey nest is filled with tiny chicks
stretching their necks to the sky; rising just inches above black water,
an alligator's rough-and-ready snout looks alarmingly like a log;
hanging on a branch in ungainly splendor, an anhinga dries its wings in
the sun; clinging to a limb, a large lavender tree snail awaits its fate as
the only food of the snail kite, which flies in here just to consume that
delicacy; winding around a tangle of branches, a night-blooming epi-
dendrum orchid's white, fragrant blossoms gleam in the moonlight. ◪

THE EVERGLADES

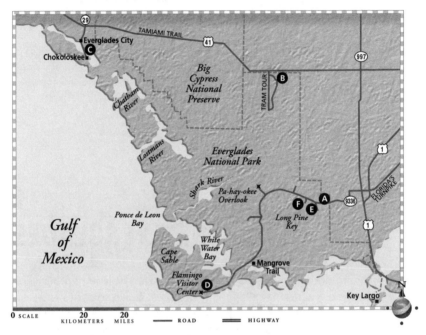

Sights

A Main Entrance/Everglades National Park

B Shark Valley Entrance/ Everglades National Park

C Ten Thousand Islands Entrance/Everglades National Park

Food

D Flamingo Lodge Restaurant

Lodging

D Flamingo Lodge, Marina and Outpost Resort

Camping

E Chekika

D Flamingo

F Long Pine Key

Note: Items with the same letter are located in the same place.

A PERFECT DAY IN THE EVERGLADES

Rise early to hear and see some of the 'glades' birds and animals as they breakfast in the mud flats or along the walking trails. Join a ranger for a morning walk and then board a park boat tour to learn how this complex ecosystem works. After lunch, rent a canoe, skiff, or bicycle for your own Everglades adventure—with some advice from park rangers on routes and equipment. In the late afternoon, animals and birds are visible again on the many easy-walking boardwalks and trails. As twilight nears, head for the Flamingo Lodge's restaurant for dinner—with entertainment provided by spectacular sunsets over the Gulf. Later, stop in for a libation at the Buttonwood Café, or join the rangers for a look at the stars or a lecture on Everglades' night critters. Spend the night at Flamingo Lodge, lulled by grunting frogs and the occasional roar of a bull alligator.

EVERGLADES' ECOLOGY, HISTORY, AND FUTURE

Known as Pahayokee (pronounced paw-HOE-kee), or grassy waters, to the Miccosukee and Seminole tribes who settled here, this vast grassy glade seems to go on forever, thus its name: Everglades. A subtropical wilderness, Everglades National Park is a collection of superlatives: it is the largest continuous stand of sawgrass prairie in North America, a World Heritage Site, the largest designated wilderness east of the Rockies, the most significant breeding grounds for tropical wading birds in North America, and the only subtropical preserve on the continent.

Despite its size and importance, the park is no tourist playground. You won't see dramatic glaciers or rocky outcroppings, cottage-rimmed lakes or yacht-bedecked marinas, game rooms or theme rides, caged animals or greenhouses. Instead, you'll see vast, sweeping acres of sawgrass, a rough-edged sedge that is the mainstay of the Everglades; hardwood hammocks, the raised limestone-island retreats that provide dry land for an amazing array of flora and fauna ranging from deer and mice to raccoons, bobcats, barred owls, hawks, marsh rabbits, and water moccasins; and gumbo-limbo, oak, mahogany, and strangler fig trees.

Air plants and orchids grow in profusion throughout the Everglades, their colors and spiky fronds appearing unexpectedly among tree branches. Giant egrets as graceful and beautiful as swans are often seen, as are the "un-hinged" anhingas, whose feathers have no oil and eventually become waterlogged, forcing the birds to spread their angular wings and hang themselves out to dry. Lavender, green, orange, and blue tree snails can be spotted on tree trunks. Fuchsia roseate spoonbills, with platypus-like bills, peek out from the greenery. Pines that need practically no soil for their roots grow on high ground.

Mangroves spread their roots right into salt water, creating shelter for microorganisms that feed shrimp and turtles, which in turn feed fish that feed birds that feed alligators and crocodiles, and so on. Those same roots also catch leaves and debris, cleansing the water and eventually forming new islands in the stream. Alligators have no natural predators except humans, and they play an unusual role in the Everglades: Before each winter's dry season, they dig deep 'gator holes that trap small fish and mollusks, providing food for birds and water for larger creatures.

Despite these intricate patterns of survival, many of those species are now dying. So fragile and so threatened is the ecosystem of this massive marsh that far too many of the world's endangered species inhabit it, struggling to survive humans and pollution, drought and drowning, natural predators and poachers. For too many, there may be no future.

At the beginning—and the end—of it all is water; from May through October South Florida can get up to 10 inches of rain in a day, much of it around Lake Okeechobee, the second largest inland lake in the world. A century ago, lake water flowed gently south through the porous limestone underpinnings of the state, covering the entire Everglades before the six-month dry season began in November. That seasonal ebb and flow has ruled the plants and creatures of the Everglades from time immemorial, creating their breeding patterns and lifestyles.

But in 1928 a devastating hurricane blew the water right out of huge Lake Okeechobee, inundating the surrounding villages and killing 2,600 residents. To avoid a repeat of that horror, the Army Corps of Engineers built a levee to prevent the lake from running over its banks and added 1,400 miles of levees and canals around the lake. From that time on, water that once ran freely into the Everglades in a slow but certain river flowed only on command, its delivery controlled by powerful business interests.

Farms proliferated, making the region one of the nation's most active winter farming areas, its rich black muck perfect for sugar cane and other crops. But nutrient-rich runoff allowed waterway-clogging plants to flourish, and water-guzzling farms diminished the water available for the Everglades. Into this ever-darkening picture came a

Florida population boom. In South Florida, developers scooped up every inch of available land, turning swampland into suburb and nature's drama into high-density housing. This growth continues to this day, and South Florida's population is expected to continue booming into the twenty-first century.

All these changes have been devastating for the Everglades. With no steady flow of fresh water to stop it, salt water began reaching farther inland, altering the delicate ecological balance of the region. Breeding cycles dependent on alternating extremes of wet and dry seasons were disrupted for such birds as the wood stork, which some predict will not exist beyond the year 2000. According to National Audubon Society estimates, the wading bird population has declined 93 percent since the 1930s, from 265,000 to 18,500. Larger animals, including the sloe-eyed Florida panther, bears, deer, and wading birds, are being pushed out of their habitats by encroaching subdivisions. Bullets and cars add to the dangers these creatures increasingly face. Fish are contaminated by mercury. Maleleuca trees, originally imported here to suck up the swamp water, are proliferating at an awesome rate and wreaking havoc.

Endangered species still visible in the park include a few hundred American crocodiles, which are found only here; about 1,200 Florida manatees, gentle mammals weighing up to 2,000 pounds; just 30 Florida panthers, small, graceful cats that are the only panthers left in the eastern United States; yellow-and-brown swallowtail butterflies; four species of sea turtles, whose habitats are being destroyed by development; and about 100 snail kites, which eat only apple snails and are one of the nation's rarest birds.

But there is hope. In the last decade an impressive array of organizations whose membership cuts across governmental, commercial, tourist, and environmentalist bounds has focused on the future of the Everglades. In 1989 a new law added 107,000 acres to the park and directed the Army Corps of Engineers to disassemble part of the flood-control canal system and restore a vital part of the chain, the Kissimmee River, to its original meandering course. Farming and commercial interests, which consume much of the water that once flowed south into the swampland, are now pledged to participate in a cleanup. Development has become more responsible and responsive. That there must be change—rapid and vast—everyone now admits, and that admission alone is a victory.

In the meantime you can—and should—get a look at this enormous park and perhaps add your voice to that of Everglades-booster and author Marjorie Stoneman Douglas, who wrote about the area in her now-famous book, *The Everglades: River of Grass*:

"There are no other Everglades in the world. They are, they have always been, one of the unique regions of the earth, remote, never wholly known. Nothing anywhere else is like them: their vast glittering openness, wider than the enormous visible round of the horizon, the racing free saltiness and sweetness of their massive winds, under the dazzling blue heights of space. They are unique also in the simplicity, the diversity, the related harmony of the forms of life they enclose. The miracle of the light pours over the green and brown expanse of sawgrass and of water, shining and slow-moving below, the grass and water that is the meaning and the central fact of the Everglades of Florida . . . a river of grass."

SIGHTSEEING HIGHLIGHTS

Everglades National Park has three entrances, the main one about 12 miles south of Homestead on a road that penetrates 40 miles into the wetlands to Flamingo, where you'll find a lodge, restaurant, campground, rental houseboats, canoes, kayaks, and bicycles. Other entrances are at Shark Valley, about 30 miles west of Miami on U.S. 41, which has a 15-mile loop road into the Everglades but no food or lodging facilities; and at Everglades City (see Marco Island and Everglades City, Chapter 7), about 30 miles southeast of Naples, where there are no roads into the Everglades, but rangers offer a boat tour.

Activities mentioned here don't always occur as scheduled. Weather, tides, and other factors frequently cause changes; call ahead for information. All park entrances and activities are very busy in winter, so it's wise to make reservations.

★★★ **Main Entrance/Flamingo Lodge Boat Tours**—In the heart of the park, you can sail on cruises into Florida Bay or the Everglades' backcountry. A two-hour **Pelican-Backcountry Cruise** visits Whitewater Bay and sails into mangrove-lined waterways where you see alligators, herons, and egrets. A 90-minute **Bald Eagle–Florida Bay Cruise** sails into Florida Bay for a look at open, shallow waters where birds and dolphins are often spotted. A three-hour **Dolphin–Whitewater Bay Cruise** offers a more extensive look at the bay and interior. The 57-foot schooner *Windfall* sails silently into the bay on 90-minute trips to see birds at rest and play. Details: Flamingo Marina; (941) 695-3101; Pelican-Backcountry Cruise sails daily at 10:15 a.m., 1 p.m., and 3:30 p.m.; Bald

Eagle–Florida Bay Cruise operates daily at 10 a.m., 12:30 p.m., 2 p.m., and at 5:30 p.m. for a sunset trip; Dolphin-Whitewater Bay cruises operate Thursday through Tuesday at 8:30 a.m. and 1:30 p.m.; and *Windfall* operates daily at 2 p.m. and sunset from November to April only. Fares for the Pelican-Backcountry cruises are $16 adults, $8 children ages 6 to 12; for Bald Eagle cruises $10 adults, $5 children; for Dolphin–Whitewater Bay trips $32 adults or children; and for *Windfall* cruises $16 adults, $10 children, $16 per person for sunset cruises. (2–4 hours)

★★★ **Main Entrance/Flamingo Ranger Trips**—Throughout the year, rangers offer a variety of tours that usually include morning, afternoon, and evening easy walking or biking trips by day, stargazing and park history lectures by night. A local "bird man" who's been guiding bird-watching events for nearly 50 years takes visitors on birding events in winter. "Swamp slogs," in which you wade through shallow water with glass-bottom barrels for viewing sea creatures, are also favorites. A daily three-hour canoe trip with a ranger-guide is so popular that participants are chosen by lottery the day before departure. Details: Flamingo Visitor Center; (941) 695-3101; days and hours vary seasonally; early bird-watching tours are at sunrise on weekends; canoe trips are usually Sunday, Tuesday, and Wednesday at 2 p.m.; lectures are at 4 p.m. daily except Thursday; evening programs daily at 7:30 p.m. (2 hours)

★★ **Gulf Coast/Everglades City Entrance Boat Tours**—Aboard an open, flat-bottomed boat, you chug deep into the mangrove wilderness of the Ten Thousand Islands for a look at wildlife on land and in the sea. A **Mangrove Wilderness** tour sails up Turner River past ancient Calusa Indian shell mounds and through shady tunnels of red mangroves where egrets, white ibises, mangrove squirrels, cuckoos, blue herons, anhingas, and alligators can be spotted. A **Ten Thousand Island Cruise** visits islands where ospreys, snowy egrets, ibises, roseate spoonbills, pelicans, gulls, dolphins, bald eagles, and manatees gather. **Kingston Key** cruises add a visit to a sandy island awash in shells. From January to April, a **Sunset Tour** views the Gulf Coast's spectacular sunsets. Details: off U.S. 41 at Route 29, Park Docks, Chokoloskee Causeway, Everglades City; (941) 695-2591 or (800) 445-7724; open daily 8:30 a.m. to 5 p.m. Admission $13 adults, $6.50 children ages 6 to 12; canoe rentals $21 per day. (2 hours)

★★ Main Entrance/Walking Trails—Information and publications are available at the park's main entrance. Four miles into the park, at the Royal Palm Visitor Center, you'll find some interesting artists' depictions of the 'glades and two good trails for viewing wildlife: **Anhinga Trail**, a half-mile loop that offers a close look at alligators and birds; and **Gumbo Limbo Trail**, another half-mile loop that winds through a tropical hardwood hammock radically reshaped by Hurricane Andrew.

Six miles from the main entrance is **Long Pine Key**, where you see the Everglades' diversity on a nature trail that wanders past a small lake, old agricultural areas, hardwood hammocks, pinelands, and a sawgrass prairie. Hikers will find rocky trails and easier hiking paths as well as a 22-mile-round-trip paved road, Old Ingraham Highway, which is accessible year-round for hiking and biking.

Along the remainder of the Main Park Road leading to Flamingo Visitor Center are the quarter-mile **Pinelands Trail** through a sub-tropical pine forest that is the most diverse habitat in South Florida; **Pa-hay-okee Overlook**, a quarter-mile boardwalk leading to an observation tower; the quarter-mile **Mahogany Hammock** boardwalk loop that crosses the 'glades to a subtropical tree island with massive mahogany trees; and the half-mile **West Lake Trail** boardwalk deep in a mangrove forest.

At Flamingo, 38 miles from the park entrance, you can see alligators at the marina, birds on the mudflats near the visitor center, and many creatures at the **Eco Pond** viewing platform, one of the busiest wildlife spots in the park. Details: 40001 State Road 9336, Homestead; (305) 242-7700; park entrance open daily 24 hours, Main Visitor Center open 8 a.m. to 5 p.m., Royal Palm Visitor Center open daily 8 a.m. to 4:15 p.m., Flamingo Visitor Center open daily 9 a.m. to 5 p.m. Admission $10 per vehicle for a seven-day pass usable at any entrance. (4–8 hours)

★★ Shark Valley Entrance—Creatures that inhabit this northern sector of the park share a freshwater ecosystem of sawgrass marsh and tree islands. A 15-mile road is closed to private vehicles, but you can walk or rent a bicycle to explore short trails and parts of the tram road (see Shark Valley Tram Tours, below), where you may spot a snail kite or alligator, and walk the spiraling loop that leads up to the 50-foot observation tower. When the road was built, holes were dug to provide stone for the surface, creating artificial 'gator holes that, in the dry winter season, are gathering spots for a variety of animals, including alligators.

There are two walking trails: **Bobcat Boardwalk**, a quarter-mile walk through sawgrass marsh and a bayhead; and **Otter Cave**, a 1-mile walk through a tropical hardwood hammock. A 15-mile bicycle trail along the loop road offers views of marsh and slough animals. Details: 30 miles west of Miami on U.S. 41; (941) 221-8455; open daily 8:30 a.m. to 6 p.m., closing at 5:15 p.m. May to October. Admission $8 per car; $4 for bicyclists and pedestrians. (2–3 hours)

★★ **Shark Valley Tram Tours**—National Park Service rangers narrate 15-mile tours aboard open-sided trams convenient for photography. Along the way you stop at sweeping, circular, Shark Valley Tower, which rises 50 feet over the Everglades for a hawk's-eye view across the wilderness. You can rent a bike from 8:30 a.m. to 3 p.m. for $3.25 per hour. Details: 30 miles west of Miami on U.S. 41; (305) 221-8455 or (305) 221-8776; tours May to November at 9:30 a.m., 11 a.m., 1 p.m., and 3 p.m., hourly in other months. Admission $8 adults, $4 children ages 3 to 12. (2 hours)

FITNESS AND RECREATION

Outdoor pursuits in the park vary by season—and by mosquito population. November to May, the most popular time to visit, is the dry season, when mosquitoes are fewer and temperatures are moderate. Torrential downpours are common from May through October, when temperatures and humidity are high, but the rains usually don't last more than an hour or so. In spring and summer, loggerhead sea turtles lumber onto the beach to lay their eggs, and alligators build nests of marsh vegetation. Tropical trees bear fruit, and cypress trees that look dead in winter come to green and feathery life. Swallowtail kites, which court their mates with fancy flying and a meal, can be seen in spring and summer.

Everglades National Park is a most challenging environment that, as one ranger put it, "makes rough, tough guys whimper." If you want to strike out on your own, you *must* consult with park rangers. Utmost respect for the environment is mandatory. Wild creatures should be neither approached nor disturbed, both for your safety and their contentment. Alligators are not normally aggressive but may react viciously if startled or approached. At least four kinds of deadly snakes can be found in the park. Get the picture?

A century ago, when Flamingo was an isolated settlement of shacks on stilts, a visiting naturalist swore he saw an oil lamp extinguished by a cloud of mosquitoes. While development and spraying have reduced the mosquito horde a bit, the insects are still voracious here, particularly from May to October. Repellents are essential; long sleeves and long pants, a wise investment.

If you're up to it, there are three developed campgrounds plus "backcountry" primitive camp sites on beaches, mangrove islands, or thatch-roofed, elevated wooden platforms called "chickees." Backcountry sites are reachable only by canoe, boat, or hike from Flamingo.

Much of the park is accessible only by water. Canoes and motorized skiffs are available for rent at Flamingo or at the ranger station in Everglades City for $8 an hour, $27 a day for canoes; $20 an hour, $80 a day for a motorized skiff; $40 to $50 a day for kayaks. You can paddle off from Flamingo or Everglades City along a 99-mile **Wilderness Waterway** canoe trail that's for experienced canoeists only. A free backcountry camping permit is required, and rangers can provide you with charts that are vital to this pursuit.

You can also take day trips that last from an hour to a full day at Flamingo or Everglades City visitor centers. Flamingo has nine trails, including **Nine Mile Pond**, a 5.2-mile loop through a shallow saw-grass marsh containing alligators, wading birds, and eagles; **Noble Hammock**, a 2-mile loop through a maze of mangrove-lined creeks with sharp corners and narrow passageways; **Hells Bay**, a 3- to 5-mile trip that's billed as "hell to get into and hell to get out of," with trails marked with numbered poles; **Florida Bay**, where you will see fish, scenery, and birds at Snake Bight; **Bear Lake Canal**, a 1.6- to 23-mile trip along an historic canal; **Mud Lake Loop**, a 6.8-mile loop between Coot Bay and Bear Lake where many birds dwell; and **West Lake**, a 15-mile round-trip through a series of lakes connected by narrow creeks where alligators and crocodiles slumber.

Flamingo has eight hiking trails (distances are round-trip): **Snake Bight**, 3.2 miles through a tropical hardwood hammock; **Rowdy Bend**, 5.2 miles along an overgrown old roadbed and coastal salt prairie; **Christian Point**, 3.6 miles past buttonwood trees full of air plants; **Bear Lake**, 3.2 miles through a dense hardwood hammock where woodland birds live; **Eco Pond**, a half-mile loop around a freshwater pond where songbirds warble and alligators play; **Guy Bradley**, a 1-mile ramble along Florida Bay past birds and butterflies; **Bayshore Loop**, a 2-mile loop past the remnants of an historic fishing village; and **Coastal Prairie**, a 15-mile trek along an old road once used by wild-cotton pickers and fishermen.

Snapper, sea bass, sea trout, bass, tarpon, and snook await fishing fans, who can have their catch cooked in the restaurant at Flamingo. Charter fishing trips can be arranged at the Flamingo Marina.

Forget swimming, except in the Flamingo Lodge pool.

FOOD

The **Flamingo Lodge Restaurant** is open daily; hours change with the season. The adjoining **Buttonwood Lounge and Café** serves pizza, salads, and sandwiches from December through April.

LODGING

Flamingo Lodge, Marina and Outpost Resort, 1 Flamingo Lodge Highway, Flamingo, (941) 695-3101 or (800) 600-3813, is 38 miles from the Main Entrance and is the only dining and lodging spot in Everglades National Park. Here you'll find 103 attractive rooms and 24 cottages with kitchen facilities, a swimming pool that overlooks Florida Bay, a marina, and a grocery store. Rates are $95 for lodge rooms, $145 for suites, and $135 for cabins from December 15 through March; $79, $110, and $99 in April and from November 1 to December 15; and $65, $99, and $89 from May to November.

Houseboats are a popular lodging alternative. A 37-foot fiberglass boat with a 100-horsepower outboard motor, air conditioning, diesel generator, electric stove, refrigerator, sundeck, bathroom and shower, propane grill, water tank, and room for six costs from $575 (two nights) to $1,375 (six nights) from November to May, $50 to $150 less in other months. A 40-foot aluminum pontoon boat with 12-volt electric offers a little more space but no air conditioning and ranges from $475 for two nights to $1,115 for six nights from November to May, $135 to $315 less in other months.

CAMPING

Everglades National Park has 44 backcountry campsites: chickees, which are elevated 10-by-12-foot platforms with thatched roofs and self-contained toilets, located along interior rivers and bays where no dry land exists; ground sites, which are mounds of earth a few feet higher than the surrounding land; and beach sites located on shell beaches with no toilets. Lengths of stay are limited from one to seven nights. Backwater camping permits are $10 and can be obtained in person at Flamingo Center, (941) 695-2945, and Gulf Coast Visitor Center, (941) 695-3311.

Permits for the **Long Pine Key** and **Chekika** camping areas are available only from the Main Visitor Center/Entrance Station. **Flamingo** area permits are available in Flamingo. None of the sites within the park has hookups. Long Pine Key has 108 sites, restrooms, a sewer dump station, fishing pond, amphitheater, and picnic area. Chekika has 20 sites, a pond, restrooms, dump station, and hot showers. Flamingo has 129 sites (some on the water), cold showers, dump stations, picnic area, grills, and an amphitheater. Reservations and information are available at (941) 695-4579 or (800) 365-2267.

7
MARCO ISLAND AND EVERGLADES CITY

S econds before developers moved in about 20 years ago, a University of Miami historian dubbed Marco Island "Florida's Last Frontier." Now wall-to-wall in condominiums and hotels, Marco bears no resemblance to its once-sleepy days as a getaway spot for wealthy hunters and anglers—it's a resort island par excellence, with lots of sun and sand.

As for Everglades City, don't let the word "city" throw you: you won't find a single high-rise here. It is, in fact, about as far from a city as you can get and just remote enough to have long appealed to smugglers, pirates, and rumrunners. Those less-than-lawful folks operated here for a century, right up to the 1980s, when police swept in to arrest 200 "square mullet" fishermen for trafficking waterproofed bricks of marijuana. Despite the *Miami Vice*–ish high jinks, Everglades City is still a sleepy spot, where you can catch a glimpse of how nearly all of Florida looked not long ago.

Now a gateway to the western edge of the Everglades, these two villages are also the entrance to a watery world known as the Ten Thousand Islands. How they know that 10,000 exist is anybody's guess; just don't expect to see 10,000 sand-rimmed, palm-treed, Robinson Crusoe islets—every little cluster of mangroves is counted as an "island." Remote as they are, the Ten Thousand are fabulous fishing and bird-watching spots, where you can easily snag a fat grouper, meet a manatee, or get a close look at a squawking osprey chick. ◼

MARCO ISLAND AND EVERGLADES CITY

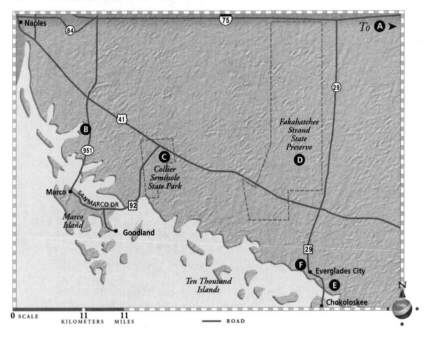

Sights

A Big Cypress National Preserve/Oasis Visitor Center

B Briggs Nature Center

C Collier-Seminole State Park

D Fakahatchee Strand State Preserve

E Majestic Everglades Excursions

F Historic Smallwoods Store Museum/Indian Trading Post

A PERFECT DAY AROUND MARCO ISLAND AND EVERGLADES CITY

Start the day at Faxahatchee Strand State Preserve, where you'll get an idea of how the state's water table rolls across the underlying limestone, creating the rivers that gave the Everglades marsh its "River of Grass" moniker. Then visit nearby Collier-Seminole State Park to stroll a 6½-mile boardwalk, paddle a 13-mile canoe trail, or hop on a ranger-operated boat trip to see endangered species often visible near sunrise and sunset. Head for Everglades City to lunch at historic Everglades Rod & Gun Club, once visited by wealthy hunters and anglers who got away from it all here. Many others have gotten away from *something* here, most often the law, as you will learn at Smallwoods Trading Post, where the man who shot pistol-packin' outlaw Belle Starr—and a few other folks—met a similar end. Sunset over the gulf is a ritual here, so settle into a seat on Marco or rustic Goodlands to watch the big event.

SIGHTSEEING HIGHLIGHTS

★★★ **Collier-Seminole State Park**—In Florida, hammocks are more than something you nap in—they're dry spots in the swampland that support an amazing variety of plant and animal life. Get a close look at one in this 6,423-acre park where salt marshes and pine flatwoods are home to many threatened and endangered species, including brown pelicans, wood storks, bald eagles, black bears, and the American crocodile. In the winter, when the insect population declines, you can paddle a 13-mile canoe trail, walk a 6½-mile hiking trail, or travel by boat through the park's waterway. Details: 20200 East Tamiami Trail, Naples; (941) 394-3397 or (800) 842-8898; open daily 8 a.m. to sunset. Admission $3.25 a carload; boat tour is $8.50 adults, $5.50 children ages 6 to 12; canoe rentals are $3 an hour, $15 a day. (3–4 hours)

★★★ **Historic Smallwoods Store Museum/Indian Trading Post**— Not much has changed for decades at this fascinating spot that is one of the oldest general stores in the nation. Built on stilts to escape floodwaters, this amazing anachronism got its start in 1906, when Seminoles sailed here in dugout canoes to trade pelts and beads for supplies. You can still see alligator hides handing from the beams and the Seminoles' bank box where Smallwood kept the silver bullion tribal elders trusted more than paper money. Today the store and its historic contents are on the National Register of Historic Places. Details: 360 Mamie Street, Chokoloskee; (941) 695-2989; open daily December through May, 10 a.m. to 5 p.m., closing at 4 p.m. in other months. Admission $2.50 adults, children under age 12 free. (1 hour)

★★ **Big Cypress National Preserve/Oasis Visitor Center**—This huge park sprawls over 716,000 acres and is an open preserve with scenic marshlands and hardwood forests that host alligators, herons, bald eagles, deer, and endangered Florida panthers. See it on a drive through the sanctuary's 26-mile scenic loop route and along the 17-mile Turner River and Bridon River Roads, and stop at the Oasis Visitors Center in the heart of the preserve for information about the swamp. Details: U.S. 41, 35 miles south of Naples; (941) 695-4111; open 8:30 a.m. to 4:30 p.m. Admission free. (3 hours)

★★ **Briggs Nature Center**—Butterflies flutter about a garden designed just for them, and snakes do what comes naturally here, where you can also see some of the region's underwater creatures in a 3,000-gallon aquarium. A half-mile boardwalk into the heart of Rookery Bay is an easy and interesting walk, and you can also sail on guided pontoon boat tours or rent a canoe or kayak. Details: 401 Shell Island Road, off SR 951; (941) 775-8569; open Monday through Friday 9 a.m. to 4:30 p.m. year-round, Saturday 9 a.m. to 4:30 p.m. October through June, and Sunday 1 to 5 p.m. January through April. Admission is $3 adults, $1 children under age 18 for the boardwalk, $20 for the boat tour. (3 hours)

★★ **Fakahatchee Strand State Preserve**—Strands are slow-moving rivers, actually a drainage slough cut naturally into the limestone by the slow flow of water into the Gulf of Mexico. Around the "river," which has no discernible shoreline, rise tall, dense, elongated swamp forests. Take a look at this one on a drive along Janes Memorial Scenic Drive, a limestone road that cuts a diagonal swath across the strand. Here you'll see a forest of bald cypress and North America's largest stands of native royal palms and epiphytic orchids. Early morning and sunset hours are the best times to spot swamp wildlife.

On the third Saturday of each month from November through April, rangers conduct "swamp tromps" deep into the marsh, but bring courage: you may sometimes be up to your waist in water, and snakes are often part of the scenery. If you'd rather keep your feet dry, try the Big Cypress Bend Boardwalk on U.S. 41, about 9 miles east of the Collier-

Seminole State Park. Details: headquarters on Janes Memorial Scenic Drive, off SR 29 just west of Copeland, about 3 miles east of the boardwalk and north on SR 29; (941) 695-4593; open daily sunrise to sunset. Admission free. (1–2 hours)

★★ **Majestic Everglades Excursions**—Aboard a 24-foot boat, you travel through the Ten Thousand Islands and Everglades National Park accompanied by Virginian Frank Garrett and his wife, Georgia, who came here from Alaska. Together the duo dumped the corporate life to become the only small company permitted to operate in the national park. They'll take you to secret spots in this vast wilderness and introduce you to dolphins, manatees, 'gators, and birds. Details: pickup is at Glades Haven Store, SR 29, but there's no office so reservations are mandatory; (941) 695-2777; open daily, with trips at 8:45 a.m. and 1:15 p.m.; closed June and July; morning trips only in August and September. Admission $65 adults, $35 children under age 13, including light lunch or "low" tea in the Everglades. (4 hours)

GREAT BEACHES

Marco Island is, after all, an island, virtually surrounded by sand. The best spots are in front of the island's three largest hotels, the **Marriott Marco Island**, the **Marco Island Hilton**, and **Radisson Suites**. **Tigertail Beach,** on Hernando Drive at the south end of the island, is pretty too.

FITNESS AND RECREATION

When the first hotels were built here, golf courses came with them. None of the courses are actually on the island, but three are 5 to 10 miles away. Tops among those is the Marriott Hotel's **Marriott Golf Club at Marco**, 3433 Marriott Club Drive, Naples, (941) 793-6060, a 6,925-yard, 18-hole course with waterways, bogs, water hazards, and a thriller 16th, where the green is across 120 yards of water. Two other nearby mainland courses are **Lely Flamingo Golf and Country Club** and **Marco Shores Country Club**.

Big Cypress National Preserve, U.S. 41, 35 miles south of Naples in Ochopee, (941) 695-4111, is one of the few places in South Florida in which you can go hunting. Deer and wild boar are the favored targets. Rangers on duty 8:30 a.m. to 4:30 p.m. daily can fill you in on the rules.

Folks at **North American Canoe Tours**, 107 Camellia Street, Everglades City, (941) 695-4666 or (203) 739-0791, can get you out into the area on self-guided or guided canoeing, kayaking, hiking, bicycling, shelling, and bird-watching trips November through mid-April.

Champion canoer Maks Zupan will have you paddling your own canoe or kayak on trips organized by his **Huron Kayak & Canoe**, 901 North Copeland Avenue, SR 29, Everglades City, (941) 695-3666, which has day- and week-long tours and instruction—even energy-boosting seminars!

Marco Island Sea Excursions, 1079 Bald Eagle Drive, Marco Island, (941) 642-6400, also books shelling, sightseeing, sailing, and fishing trips in the area. Shelling is wonderful in this region, especially at Sand Dollar Point and Cape Romano, among others.

FOOD

Dining on Marco remains the only way left to get a sense of the island's old days, when just a few wealthy escapists spent most of the winter in the island's one tiny, long-gone hotel. At **Old Marco Inn**, 100 Palm Avenue, (941) 394-3131, Austrian and German flavors dominate the moderately priced cuisine in a romantic restaurant in which you dine under the crystal chandeliers of a lovely 1883 island home.

To see what a simple fishing-and-shelling village like Marco used to look like, drive over to the nearby island of Goodland. Stop at **Old Marco Lodge Crab House**, 401 Papaya Street, (941) 642-7227, a rustic spot whose weathered gray walls have seen much change since they went up in 1869. They still stand around this restaurant serving seafood, steaks, pastas, and homemade barbecue for lunch and dinner daily. **Vito's**, 1079 Bald Eagle Drive (941) 394-7722, occupies enviable acreage with a view of the river. You can dine on the casual deck or inside in a slightly more formal atmosphere.

LODGING

Marco has three large hotels and more than enough condominiums, many of them for rent through local real estate companies such as **Marco Island Central Reservations**, 599 South Collier Boulevard, (941) 394-8150 or (800) 821-7368.

Marriott's Marco Island Resort and Golf Club, 400 South Collier Boulevard, (941) 394-2511 or (800) 438-4373, was the island's

MARCO ISLAND AND EVERGLADES CITY

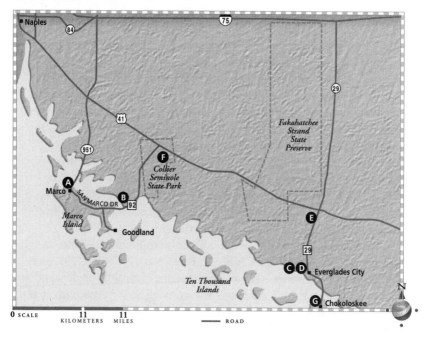

Food

- **A** Old Marco Inn
- **B** Old Marco Lodge Crab House
- **A** Vito's

Lodging

- **C** Everglades Rod and Gun Club
- **D** Ivey House Bed & Breakfast
- **A** Marco Island Hilton Beach Resort
- **A** Marriott's Marco Island Resort and Golf Club
- **A** Radisson Suite Beach Resort

Camping

- **E** Barron River RV Park & Marina
- **F** Collier-Seminole State Park
- **G** Outdoor Resorts of America

Note: Items with the same letter are located in the same town or area.

first high-rise hotel and has won accolades for its decor, service, and business center. Peak-season rates at the resort, which has three swimming pools, whirlpools, seven restaurants, lounges, extensive water sports, and a few cottages and lanai rooms that open onto the beach, are $279 to $324, including breakfast.

Marco Island Hilton Beach Resort, 560 South Collier Boulevard, (941) 394-5000 or (800) 443-4550, has 298 attractive rooms in an 11-story building on the sand. A swimming pool with a palm-bedecked island is a focal point of this resort, which has several lounges and restaurants, water sports, a fitness center, and three clay tennis courts. Winter rates are $249 to $309. Another place where life revolves around the pear-shaped swimming pool is **Radisson Suite Beach Resort**, 600 South Collier Boulevard, (941) 394-4100, (800) 814-0633, or (800) 333-3333, which has 58 rooms and more than 200 family suites. Radisson charges $239 in peak season.

In Everglades City, settle into a chair on the veranda of the **Everglades Rod and Gun Club**, 200 Broadway, (941) 695-2101, and you'll see why this lodge has lured generations of wealthy anglers and hunters. Built nearly 150 years ago as a stopping spot for fur traders, the lodge became the center of the city during the region's 1920s boom days. Barron Collier, a millionaire who once owned a 1.1-million-acre empire here, turned it into an exclusive hunting and fishing club that has welcomed four U.S. presidents and actors John Wayne and Burl Ives, among others. Rates at the rustic 17-room inn are $85 in winter.

Ivey House Bed & Breakfast, 107 Camellia Street, (941) 695-3299, is a rustic budget spot with ten rooms and two shared bathrooms. Built in 1923 as a recreation center—it once had a bowling alley and pool hall—for workers building the Tamiami Trail road between Tampa and Miami, the place was run as a boarding house after the road was finished in 1928. Rates are $40 to $50.

CAMPING

Collier-Seminole State Park, 20200 East Tamiami Trail, Naples, (941) 394-3397, has 130 RV sites, all with water, some with electric. Rates are $13 December to May, $8 in summer. Other area campgrounds include **Outdoor Resorts of America**, SR 29, Chokoloskee, (941) 695-2881, which also has some motel rooms; and **Barron River RV Park & Marina**, 803 Collier Avenue, Everglades City, (941) 695-3591 or (800) 535-4961, both charging under $30.

8
NAPLES

A viator Charles Lindbergh once used what is now Naples' main street, toney Fifth Avenue, as a runway when he flew in here for winter vacations on nearby Sanibel Island. Lindbergh could still land near here today, but he'd certainly see a town quite different from the boggy wilderness of old. Now the quiet back streets and waterfronts are home to million-dollar mansions—winter getaways for an impressive number of Fortune 500 entrepreneurs—and manicured lawns have replaced swamp grass. In the oldest part of town, buildings from the 1920s boom days house chic shops filled with designer dressers, glowing jewels, and gourmet chocolates.

A refined, quiet enclave where nightlife ends early and daylight hours center on the region's beautiful—and fiercely protected—beaches, Naples is one of the best places in South Florida to get a close view of the flora and fauna that have been diminished or eradicated elsewhere by unceasing urban sprawl. Popular among South Floridians as a getaway spot, Naples has managed to retain a *mañana* approach to life. Its village atmosphere weaves a relaxing web. Its beaches are uncrowded, its diversions beguilingly traquil. Naples is where you go to loaf and like it, to revel in doing nothing—and doing it well. ◼

NAPLES

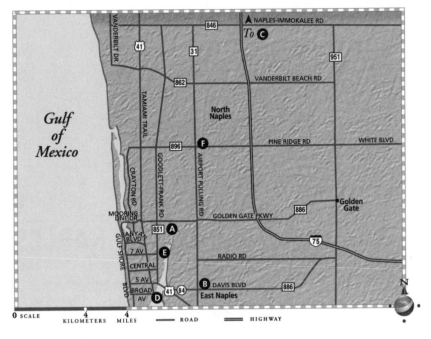

Sights

- **A** Caribbean Gardens, Home of Jungle Larry's Zoological Park
- **B** Collier County Museum
- **C** Corkscrew Swamp Sanctuary
- **D** Everglades Excursions
- **E** Naples Nature Center
- **D** *Naples Princess*
- **D** Naples Trolley Tours
- **F** Teddy Bear Museum of Naples

Note: Items with the same letter are located in the same area.

A PERFECT DAY IN NAPLES

Learn a little about the history of this growing coastline aboard the Naples Trolley Tour. Then tour the region's showpiece, fascinating Corkscrew Swamp Sanctuary. Often eerily quiet, this primeval forest of 500-year-old cypress trees is teeming with creatures under the canopy of the stark grey trees at the sanctuary's center. For a change of pace, stop by Caribbean Gardens, where animals are part of the entertainment, and an amazing array of tropical plants are exotically displayed. After lunch, see some of the wildlife rescued and recuperating at the Naples Nature Center before you explore the pastel streets of Old Naples. Drop in for tea served among the 3,000 bears of the Teddy Bear Museum. As sunset nears, head for a waterside spot to view a spectacularly dramatic sunset over the Gulf of Mexico. By night, there's always something happening at Tin City or in Naples' new Philharmonic Center for the Arts.

SIGHTSEEING HIGHLIGHTS

✯✯✯ **Caribbean Gardens, Home of Jungle Larry's Zoological Park**—In 1919 a plant-lover settled in Naples and planted the more than 3,000 species that, in 1954, became Caribbean Gardens. Then "Jungle Larry" Tetzlaff and his wife, "Safari Jane," worked with wild animals to create entertaining lecture/shows highlighting everything from an albino python to lions, tigers, and a bevy of mischievous monkeys, lemurs, and apes. A Primate Expedition Cruise introduce you to island-dwelling monkeys and a Scales and Tails show lets you get personal with some unusual critters. Exotic cats and their caretakers interact in the Big Cats show, and you can cuddle up to a baby 'gator at the Alligator Lecture and Feeding show. Details: 1590 Goodlette-Frank Road; (941) 262-5409; open daily 9:30 a.m. to 5:30 p.m. Admission $12.95 adults, $8.95 children ages 4 to 15. (3–4 hours)

✯✯✯ **Corkscrew Swamp Sanctuary**—A primeval wilderness, this swampland operated by the National Audubon Society is home to the largest remaining stand of bald cypress trees in the world. As you walk the boardwalk trail, these ancient trees—some 500 years old, with massive trunks—tower overhead, creating a wilderness cathedral that shelters more than 200 species of birds, deer, alligators, bobcats, and small swamp creatures. In summer the trees are thick and green; in winter they're stark and leafless; at any time they're quite a sight. Details:

Route 6, 20 miles north of Naples; (941) 657-3771; open daily December through April 7 a.m. to 5 p.m.; May through November 8 a.m. to 5 p.m. Admission $6.50 adults, $5 students, $3 children ages 6 to 18. (2–3 hours)

★★ **Collier County Museum**—A handsome old 1920s home, a 1910 steam locomotive, and a re-creation of a Seminole village chronicle the history of this seaside city. An adjoining garden is filled with plants native to this part of South Florida. Details: 3301 Tamiami Trail East; (941) 774-8476; open Monday through Saturday 9 a.m. to 5 p.m., Sunday noon to 5 p.m. Admission free. (2 hours)

★★ **Everglades Excursions**—An all-day adventure begins in the heart of the Everglades, where you board a jungle cruise and chug through the sawgrass prairies and mangrove wilderness that are home to birds, alligators, and manatees. In Everglades City, a tiny settlement at the edge of the 'glades, you get a look at Smallwoods Store, the oldest operating general store in the nation. At lunch you're treated to an appetizer of 'gator nuggets, blue-crab claws, conch fritters, and hush puppies before you board an airboat to zip through the Ten Thousand Islands and visit a 'Gator Exhibit wildlife show. Stops at Fakahatchee Strand State Preserve and a Seminole village conclude the wilderness expedition. Details: pickup at major hotels and at Trolley Barn, 1100 6th Avenue South, Suite 227A; (941) 598-1050 or (800) 592-0848; open daily 8 a.m. to 5 p.m. Admission $79 adults, $64 children ages 6 to 12, including lunch. (6 hours)

★★ **Teddy Bear Museum of Naples**—Tucked away in a stand of pine trees is Winnie the Pooh's dream cottage—a bear-y interesting place filled with more than 3,000 teddy bears. There are almost-wedded teddys and their bridal parties, lady bears in satin and lace, dapper gentlemen bears, a bear wedding, a teddy bear-d of directors deep in a meeting, a li-beary, a teddy bear tea party, and, of course, a Teddy Bear Picnic. Details: 2511 Pine Ridge Road; (941) 598-2711; open Wednesday through Saturday 10 a.m. to 5 p.m., Sunday 1 to 5 p.m., February through April also Monday 1 a.m. to 5 p.m. Admission $6 adults, $2 children ages 4 to 12. (1 hour)

★ **Naples Nature Center**—A wildlife rehabilitation clinic is the star of this center operated by the Nature Conservancy, but there are plenty of other things to see, including bald eagles, hawks, and owls who are permanent residents here. Guided trail walks and boat tours fill you in on resident wildlife, or you can rent a kayak or canoe and tour on your own. Occasionally there's a night walk to meet the creatures of the tidal lagoon that borders this attraction. Details: 1450 Merrihue Drive; (941) 262-0304; open Monday through Saturday 9 a.m. to 4:30 p.m., January through March also Sunday 1 to 5 p.m., with boat rides 9:30 a.m. to noon. Admission and boat rides free. (2–3 hours)

☆ *Naples Princess*—You can spend time on the water that has played such a vital part in the growth of this city aboard this small cruiser that sails the Gulf on lunch, dinner, cocktail, and sunset cruises. Details: 1001 10th Street; (941) 649-2275; sailing daily at varying times usually including noon, 2 p.m., and 5: 30 p.m., with a Saturday dinner cruise at 5:30 p.m. and Sunday breakfast cruise at 9 a.m. Admission $22.95 adults, $16.95 children ages 5 to 11 for lunch and sunset cruises; $17.95 adults, $13.95 children for sightseeing cruises; $37.95 adults, $29.95 children for dinner cruises; and $27.95 adults, $21.95 children for breakfast cruises. (2 hours)

© Ken Laffal

Village of Venetian Bay

☆ **Naples Trolley Tours**—Aboard an old-time trolley, you learn a little of this city's history which stretches back thousands of years to the first native inhabitants who hunted and fished alongside the sea and in the nearby Everglades. A narrated tour covers more than 100 points of interest, ranging from the city's antique Palm Cottage built in 1895 to the new multimillion-dollar palaces that are winter homes to the wealthy. You can get off the trolley anywhere you like to lunch or shop, then reboard to continue the tour. Details: Trolley Barn, 1010 6th Avenue South, with 27 trolley stops, including many hotels; (941) 262-7300; Monday through Saturday 8:30 a.m. to 3:30 p.m., Sunday 10:30 a.m. to 3:30 p.m. Admission $11 adults, $5 children under age 13. (2 hours)

GREAT BEACHES

Two beaches in the Naples area have won national acclaim for their scenic sands. You'll find them at **Delanor-Wiggins Recreation Area**, off Vanderbilt Drive in North Naples, and at **Clam Pass Park** on Seagate Drive.

SHOPPING

In Naples, shopping is also a trip into history—much of the city's oldest sector is now occupied by boutiques and cafés. Historic Old Naples, now on the National Register of Historic Places, is one of the few areas along the Gulf Coast that has managed to retain buildings constructed during its 1920s heyday. Called **Third Street South**, Old Naples is bordered by Broad Avenue on the north and 14th Avenue South on the south from 2nd to 4th Street South. Centerpieces of the district are the 1919 **Mercantile Building** at 1177 3rd Street South and the 1922 **Old Naples Building** at 1148 3rd Street South. **Tin City**, 1200 5th Avenue, (941) 262-4200, still retains the planked floors and distinctive tin roof from its clam-shelling plant days. Today its rustic environs house gift shops and casual bistros.

FITNESS AND RECREATION

Naples has more than 40 golf courses, including **Ironwood Golf Club**, an 18-hole public executive course at 205 Charity Court, (941) 775-2584, and **Marco Shores Country Club**, a public club at 1450 Mainsail Drive, (941) 394-2581. Tennis courts are available at several area parks, including **Veterans Park**, 1900 Immokalee Road, (941) 566-2367, and **Golden Gate Park**, 3300 Santa Barbara Boulevard, (941) 353-0404.

Fishing and water sports are the big lures along this coastline, so there are many folks here who can lead you to the big catch or a lively day of Jet Skiing, parasailing, canoeing, or kayaking. In Naples, try **Fish Finders**, (941) 597-2063, for full- or half-day party-boat trips; or head for the **Naples City Dock**, 880 12th Avenue South, (941) 434-4693, to find a charter boat. You can drop a line in the water at any time of day or night at **Naples Pier**, 12th Avenue at Gulf Shore Boulevard South, (941) 434-4696.

King Richard's Fun Park, 6780 North Airport Road, (941) 598-1666, and **Naples Go-Cart Rides**, 11402 U.S. 41 East, (941) 774-7776, are family fun spots with go-karts, bumper boats, mini-golf, and video and pinball games, open daily about 11 p.m.

Seminole Gaming Palace, 506 South First Street, Immokalee, (941) 658-1313, plays high-stakes bingo and poker 24 hours a day, every day.

Baseball fans can see the **Boston Red Sox** (941-334-4700) and **Minnesota Twins** (800-28-TWINS) at spring practice games in nearby Fort Myers.

Greyhounds race for championship rankings and there's betting on races simulcast on big screens at **Naples-Fort Myers Greyhound Track**, Old U.S. 41 at Bonita Beach Road, Bonita Springs, (941) 992-2411. From January to May, doors open Monday through Saturday at 6:30 p.m., Sunday 3:30 p.m., and daily except Monday and Thursday for matinees 11:30 a.m. In other months the track schedule varies. Grandstand admission is $2, clubhouse $3.

FOOD

Village of Venetian Bay, 4270 Gulf Shores Boulevard North, is a cluster of colorful neo-Mediterranean architecture nestled along the water. The area is home to many shops and several acclaimed cafés, including the upstairs-downstairs **Bayside, A Seafood Grill and Bar**, (941) 649-5552, serving oak-grilled seafood, steaks, and lamb; **Maxwell's on the Bay**, (941) 263-1662, which won "best" awards for seafood and views; and **Marie Michelle's**, (941) 263-0900, for indoor-outdoor waterside dining on French flavors. All three places open for lunch and dinner.

At **St. George and the Dragon**, 936 5th Avenue South, (941)

NAPLES

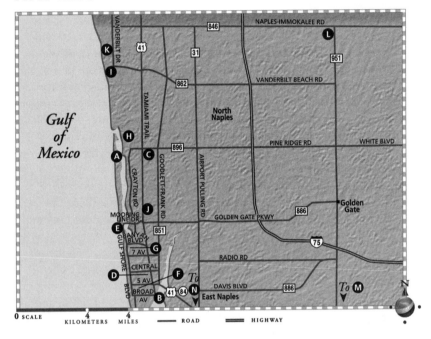

Food

Ⓐ Bayside, A Seafood Grill and Bar

Ⓑ Dock at Crayton Cove

Ⓒ Farino's/Gilda's Casa Italiana

Ⓐ Marie Michelle's

Ⓐ Maxwell's on the Bay

Ⓑ Riverwalk Fish & Ale House

Ⓓ St. George and the Dragon

Lodging

Ⓔ Edgewater Beach Hotel

Ⓕ Inn by the Sea

Lodging (Continued)

Ⓖ Naples Beach Hotel and Golf Club

Ⓗ Registry Resort

Ⓘ Ritz-Carlton

Ⓙ Stoney's Courtyard Inn

Ⓚ Vanderbilt Beach Motel

Camping

Ⓛ Crystal Lake Resort

Ⓜ Kountree Kampin RV Resort

Ⓝ Naples/Marco Island KOA

Note: Items with the same letter are located in the same area.

262-6546, you'll find a pubby atmosphere, beef, and seafood. For earthy Italian flavors, there's no better spot than **Farino's/Gilda's Casa Italiana**, 4000 North Tamiami Trail, (941) 262-2883, operated by a family that's been cooking Neapolitan here for more than 20 years. Two other longtime waterside favorites are the **Dock at Crayton Cove**, 12th Avenue South at the City Dock, (941) 263-9940, and **Riverwalk Fish & Ale House**, Tin City, 1200 5th Street South, (941) 263-2734, both open for reasonably priced lunch and dinner.

LODGING

The granddaddy of hotels in the downtown/Tamiami Trail area is the elegant **Naples Beach Hotel and Golf Club**, 851 Gulf Shore Boulevard North, (941) 261-2222 or (800) 237-7600, a showy Gulfside spot that's been here for more than 50 years and retains a touch of the formality once common at large winter resorts for the wealthy. You'll find a golf course, chic restaurants, tennis, water sports, and 5 miles of sand; rates are $205 to $305.

  Edgewater Beach Hotel, 1901 Gulf Shore Boulevard North, (941) 262-6511 or (800) 821-0196, is a small and luxurious all-suites hotel in a posh neighborhood with beautiful views over the Gulf. Winter rates are $250 to $440 daily for a one-bedroom suite and $370 to $1,250 for two-bedroom suites.

  Inn by the Sea, 287 11th Avenue South, (941) 649-4124, is a friendly bed and breakfast in a 1937 house that's listed on the National Register of Historic Places. Brass beds, pine floors, arts, and flowers adorn just five rooms named after nearby islands. Rates in winter are $130 to $165.

  Stoney's Courtyard Inn, 2630 North Tamiami Trail, (941) 261-3870 or (800) 432-2870, is a simple downtown area spot offering basic, moderately priced motel rooms, a pool, laundry, and friendly service at room rates of $80 to $95, $114 for suites.

  Vanderbilt Beach, a long, beautiful strip of sand north of the city, is lined with hotels in many sizes and prices. King of the roost is the chic **Ritz-Carlton**, 280 Vanderbilt Beach Road, (941) 598-3300 or (800) 241-3333, one of the most beautiful hotels in South Florida, with glittering chandeliers, showy oil paintings, elaborate moldings, pools, restaurants, and a fountain in a central courtyard overlooking the sea. Elegantly decorated rooms are $350 to $545 in winter.

  Registry Resort, 475 Seagate Drive, (941) 597-3232 or (800)

247-9810, is another luxurious spot, with 474 rooms on 200 waterfront acres along the Gulf and a pleasant casual atmosphere, very attractive decor, tennis, restaurant, health club, lounges, and a pool. Winter rates run $305 to $395.

Vanderbilt Beach Motel, 9225 Gulf Shore Drive North, Naples, (941) 597-3144 or (800) 243-9076, sports beamed ceilings and a variety of efficiencies, motel rooms, and one-bedroom apartments in a building that stretches from the Gulf to a lagoon. A pool, tennis courts, pier, and boat ramp complete the offerings. Winter rates are $110 to $144.

CAMPING

Naples/Marco Island KOA, 1700 Barefoot Williams Road, Naples, (941) 774-5455 or (800) 562-7734, has palm-shaded sites and 17 cabins, canoe rentals, and a Gulf-access boat ramp for $37 to $40 in winter. **Kountree Kampin RV Resort**, 5200 CR 951, Naples, (941) 775-4340, is in a tropical forest with shady sites and paved roads for $32. **Crystal Lake Resort**, 160 CR 951, North Naples, (941) 353-4212 or (800) 322-4525, occupies 150 acres with a lake, clubhouses, pools, whirlpools, tennis, and mini-golf for $35 to $45.

9

HOLLYWOOD AND HALLANDALE

Back in the 1920s when the land boom exploded in Florida, a visionary named Joseph Young saw the sunlight and set out to sell homesites to a winter-weary public. He succeeded, perhaps beyond even his dreams. Young made millions and built himself a handsome home in Hollywood, complete with billiard room, on a plot of ground that offered him a view across the sands to the ocean nearly a mile away. Today that home still stands, but Young's view is long gone, obscured by hundreds of homes and a towering pink hotel built during the same boom days.

The tourism explosion that Young touched off continues today in these quiet, seaside cities that have long been favorite vacation spots for French-speaking Canadian travelers. Hollywood is proudest of its Broad—not "board'"—walk, measuring in at 27 feet wide and 2½ miles long. Lined with small shops and cafés, it is anchored by the historic Hollywood Beach Hotel. New trees, old-fashioned streetlamps, and antique clocks have given the city's downtown a much-needed facelift and turned it trendy. Nearby Hallandale, lined with condominiums, is home to one of the nation's most famous thoroughbred racecourses. To the north the small town of Dania, one of the earliest settlements in South Florida, is now renowned for the dozens of antique shops on its Antique Mile. ◨

HOLLYWOOD

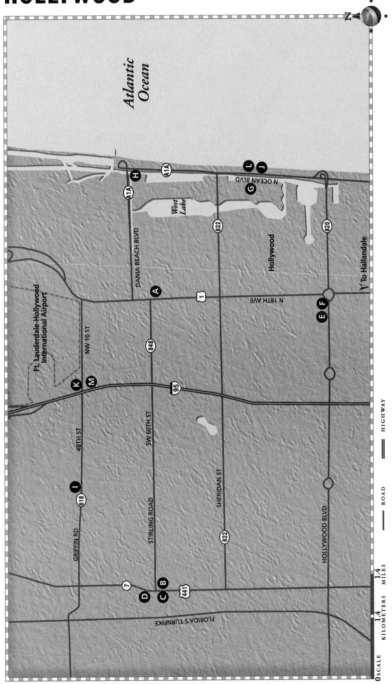

Sights

Ⓐ Gravel Museum of Archaeology & Natural History

Ⓑ Native Indian Village

Ⓒ Seminole Indian Bingo and Poker Casino

Ⓓ Seminole Okalee Village Cultural Center

Food

Ⓔ Brazil Samba

Ⓕ Conca d'Oro

Ⓖ Le Tub

Food (Continued)

Ⓗ Martha's

Ⓘ Tropical Acres Steak House

Lodging

Ⓙ Driftwood on the Ocean

Ⓚ Hilton Airport

Ⓛ Howard Johnson Hollywood Beach Resort Inn

Ⓜ Wyndham Fort Lauderdale Airport

Ⓛ Surf 'n' Spray Motel

Note: Items with the same letter are located in the same area.

A PERFECT DAY IN HOLLYWOOD AND HALLANDALE

Start the day by breakfasting with world-famous thoroughbreds and jockeys at flower-bedecked Gulfstream Park in Hallandale, home of the Florida Derby. Then stop by the Seminole Okalee Village Cultural Center to learn a little about the fascinating history of the Seminoles, who still have not signed a treaty with the United States. After lunch, search for buried treasure in the tiny, jam-packed antique shops of nearby Dania, or return to Gulfstream Park for a look at the thoroughbreds in action. As the sun sets, drop in on a jazz concert at the Hollywood Beach Theater or stroll among the cafés and shops along trendy Harrison Street or Hollywood Boulevard. Have a tropical meal at Brazil Samba. Close the day at Dania Jai Alai Fronton, where you can gamble on the talents of skilled handball players who keep a rock-hard *pelota* ball moving at speeds up to 100 miles per hour. Or bet a fiver on the fleet feet of a racing greyhound in hot pursuit of a mechanical bunny at the Hollywood Dog Track. If you like bingo, the Seminole tribe operates a huge bingo parlor and poker casino where $100,000 jackpots draw throngs of hopefuls.

SIGHTSEEING HIGHLIGHTS

★★★ **Seminole Okalee Village Cultural Center**—A branch of the Ah-Tha-Thi-Ki Museum slated to open in late 1997 will include a video detailing the tribe's history, exhibits of Seminole artifacts, and a living museum in which tribal members demonstrate the crafts for which they have become famous, including patchwork quilting, construction of palm-thatched chickee houses, and beaded jewelry. Details: 5845 South State Road 7, Fort Lauderdale; (954) 792-0745; operating hours and admission fees to be announced. (2–4 hours)

★★ **Graves Museum of Archaeology & Natural History**—A massive skeletal cranium crowns this museum where a wide-ranging collection of exhibits roams the ages, from days when the Tequesta Indians lived here to the Egyptian pharaohs' era. The mineral collection is colorful, and the museum has many gold and ceramic relics of the pre-Hispanic Americas as well as a rain-forest environment and shipwreck artifacts. Details: 481 South Federal Highway, Dania; (954) 925-7770; open Tuesday through Saturday 10 a.m. to 4 p.m., Sunday 1 to 5 p.m. Admission $6 adults, $4 children ages 4 to 12. (2 hours)

★★ **Native Indian Village**—Alligators show their toothy grins and snakes slither around at this village that showcases the life and talents of the Seminole Indians. Intrepid types wrestle those 'gators into sub-mission, while tribal ladies create beaded jewelry and intricate patchwork-quilted clothing. Details: 3551 North State Road 7 (U.S. 441), Hollywood; (954) 961-4519; open Monday through Saturday 9 a.m. to 4 p.m., Sunday 11 a.m. to 4 p.m. Admission to a self-tour is $5 adults, $3 for children ages 3 to 12; a guided tour and lecture is $8 adults, $6 children. Alligator-wrestling shows are $10 adults, $8 children. (2 hours)

★★ **Seminole Indian Bingo and Poker Casino**—Florida's Seminoles, who never have signed a treaty with the U.S. government, have become canny entrepreneurs; they were the first Native Americans to open a gaming facility. Among their financial triumphs is a high-stakes bingo game that draws hundreds of players every week. Seven-card stud is played here too. Details: 4150 North State Road 7 (U.S. 441), Hollywood; (954) 961-3220; open daily 24 hours. Free. (2 hours)

GREAT BEACHES

Hollywood's **Broadwalk** marches alongside nearly 2 miles of sand, and Hallandale's beaches are visible at **Hallandale Beach Boulevard**. You'll also find pretty sands shaded by seagrapes along **Route A-1-A**, north of Hollywood Boulevard and just south of Dania Beach Boulevard.

SHOPPING

While you're roaming the Broadwalk, stop in at **Oceanwalk at Hollywood Beach Resort**, 101 North Ocean Drive, Hollywood, (954) 922-3438, a small but significant oceanfront shopping mall with several restaurants, some boutiques, gift shops, and an alluring patio bar. Shops along **Hollywood Boulevard** and **Harrison Street** offering intriguing buys. Hallandale is famous for its **Schmata Row** at Hallandale Beach Boulevard and Dixie Highway, where an enclave of wholesalers sell designer fashions, gifts, and accessories.

RIDIN' AND ROPIN'

Once upon a time, South Florida was covered in cow pastures and spawned many a dairyman millionaire. There's only one small vestige of those days left: the city of Davie, which has steadfastly clung to its ridin', ropin' days and turned those memories into a contemporary tourist attraction. Located just a few miles southwest of Fort Lauderdale and west of Hollywood, Davie plays up its rootin'-tootin' past with feed stores, boot shops, and professional rodeos that lure the rodeo circuit's star riders to the Davie Rodeo Arena. A favorite stomping spot for urban cowpokes, the town has hitching posts outside its shops and even a "ride-through" line at McDonald's. City hall, down the road apiece from the feed store, also has a Western look. Find out what's happening at the Chamber of Commerce, 4185 SW 64th Avenue, Davie, (954) 581-0790.

FITNESS AND RECREATION

Hollywood has several notable golf courses and many public tennis courts, but its greatest prides are a few large parks that offer a wide range of activities for sports fans. For beach enthusiasts it's difficult to beat **John U. Lloyd State Recreation Area**, 6503 North Ocean Drive, (954) 923-2833, which covers 251 oceanfront acres shaded by tall trees. Open 8 a.m. to dusk, the park is a serene spot for an oceanside picnic and also has a marina, fishing jetty, changing areas, snack bar, and 2½ miles of often-deserted beach with a reef about 100 feet offshore.

Topekeegnee Yugnee Park, 3300 North Park Road, (954) 985-1980, known—for obvious reasons—as T-Y Park, has a lake for fishing and swimming, a marked trail for biking and jogging, and a miniature Safety Town village that teaches toddlers safety rules. T-Y is open 8 a.m. to sunset. At **West Lake Park**, 1200 Sheridan Street, (954) 926-2410, the center of attention is the Anne Kolb Nature Center, a 1,400-acre mini-Everglades wetland right in the middle of the city. It's open daily 8 a.m. to sunset. Biking, fishing, tennis, and racquetball are also here, and are all free.

Dania and Hallandale are home to three of the state's top pari-mutuel sports facilities. **Gulfstream Park**, 901 South Federal Highway, Hallandale, (954) 931-7223, features the Florida Derby, where many a Kentucky Derby thoroughbred hopeful races. **Dania Jai Alai**, 301 East Dania Beach Boulevard, Dania, (954) 949-2424, is a fast-paced game played by two or four players who catch a wooden ball in a handbasket and throw it against a concrete wall at speeds of up to 100 mph. From December to April, swift greyhounds chase a metal rabbit around **Hollywood Greyhound Track**, 511 North Federal Highway, Hallandale, (954) 454-9400. All offer betting opportunities.

FOOD

Hungry crowds flock to moderately priced cafés along the Broad-walk, where posted menus help you select the evening's dining experience. If your taste buds are set on sizzle, head for one of the region's oldest restaurants, **Tropical Acres Steak House**, 2500 Griffin Road, Hollywood, (954) 989-2500, where they've been selling sizzle at fair prices for more than 47 years and have plenty of seafood and poultry, too. At **Martha's**, 6024 North Ocean Drive, Hollywood, (954) 923-5444, there's informal dining upstairs overlooking the Intracoastal Waterway and a more formal and more expensive supper club downstairs. A favorite here for many years, the restaurant specializes in continental preparations of beef, seafood, and poultry. Musical entertainment warbles on until midnight or later most nights.

For a touch of the exotically tropical, try **Brazil Samba**, 1902

Hollywood Boulevard, Hollywood, (954) 920-4426, where Saturday's *feijoada* feast of black beans and meats echoes a long-standing Brazilian tradition. If you're on a tight budget, try **Conca d'Oro**, on Young Circle at 1833 Tyler Street, Hollywood, (954) 927-6704, which draws crowds every night with lusty Italian flavors, a cozy, cheerful atmosphere, and pasta dishes; or **Le Tub**, 1109 North Ocean Drive, Hollywood, (954) 921-9425, an amusing spot adorned with—what else?—bathtubs. Shrimp, burgers, and light meals are the fare at this rustic waterside spot.

LODGING

Howard Johnson Hollywood Beach Resort Inn, 2501 North Ocean Drive, (954) 925-1411 or (800) 423-9867, is an attractive 242-room property near the beach. Its rooms feature coffeemakers, and there's an oceanside pool. Rates in peak winter season are $149 to $179.

   Driftwood on the Ocean, 2101 South Surf Road, (954) 923-9528 or (800) 944-3148, has a variety of home-away-from-home options including hotel rooms, efficiencies, and one- and two-bedroom suites on the beach. There's a heated pool, and rates are $70 to $110 in peak season.

   Two hotels near the airport are popular spots if you don't mind a ten- to 15-minute drive to the sand. **Wyndham Fort Lauderdale Airport**, 1825 Griffin Road, Hollywood, (954) 920-3500 or (800) 325-3535, and the **Hilton Airport**, 1870 Griffin Road, Dania, (954) 920-3300 or (800) 221-2424, are both well-equipped and attractive hotels with swimming pools, fitness centers, and restaurants. Both are popular for their proximity to the airport and cruise ships. Winter rates are in the $120 to $180 range. **Surf 'n' Spray Motel**, 1402 North Broadwalk, Hollywood, (954) 922-0088, has a swimming pool and pleasant accommodations right on the Broadwalk and books scuba packages as well. Room rates in peak season are $55 to $60 a day.

CAMPING

Embassy RV Park, 3188 Lake Shore Drive, Pembroke Park, (954) 961-8892, is 3 miles from the beach and has hookups on shaded lots. Rates are $26. **Seminole Park**, 3301 North State Road 7, Hollywood, (954) 987-6961, has 102 full hookups, hot showers, and a laundry but accepts adults only from November though April. Rates are $26.

NIGHTLIFE

Nightlife focuses on the Broadwalk area in Hollywood, where a number of small, casual lounges keep things hopping. Actors at **Hollywood Playhouse**, 2640 Washington Street, (954) 922-0404, have been presenting old-favorite theater productions for more than 40 years. In the **Theater Under the Stars** on the beach at Johnson Street, (954) 921-3404, the city features free musical performances. Those alternate with concerts at **Young Circle Park Bandshell**, Young Circle, U.S. 1 at Hollywood Boulevard, (954) 921-3404. **Hallandale Symphonic Pops Orchestra**, (954) 454-3721, produces a series of pops concerts at various locations. There's often something going on at **Hollywood Art and Culture Center**, 1650 Harrison Street, (954) 921-3275, which occupies one of the city's oldest homes, built in 1924.

A triple-decker casino ship called *SunCruz* is docked at Martha's, 6024 North Ocean Drive, Hollywood, (305) 929-3800, and sails at 11:30 a.m. and 7 p.m. daily. Its four-hour cruises include casino gambling on slot machines, "mini-baccarat," poker, and blackjack. The $10 charge includes a drink and appetizers, with other light fare available on board. **One Night Stand**, 2333 Hollywood Boulevard, (954) 929-1566, is a blues club featuring jazz, comedians, and jam sessions.

10
FORT LAUDERDALE
AND POMPANO BEACH

D espite its soaring skyline, Fort Lauderdale manages to retain a
small-town feeling and an alluringly casual atmosphere. Many a
multimillionaire shows up at meetings in a golf shirt, the mayor
rarely wears a tie, and one city commissioner has led a long crusade
against suits and high heels. Much the same atmosphere prevails in
Pompano Beach, where boat shoes are a fashion staple. The city calls
itself the "Swordfish Capital of the World" because so many record
catches have been pulled from the sea here. It doesn't take long for
visitors to adopt this happy-go-lucky attitude. Miles of palm-shaded
sand, casual seaside cafés, and more waterways than Venice can boast
lure newcomers straight to the beaches.

Nearly a century ago, unfailingly warm temperatures here enticed
founding father Frank Stranahan to these shores, where he traded with
the Seminole tribe. A century later his tiny trading post is dwarfed by
high-rises but remains a centerpiece of Fort Lauderdale's brick
Riverwalk, which winds past an imaginative science museum, a
renewed historic district, and a glittering performing arts center.
Capitalizing on ocean views and miles of sand trimmed with a sleek,
serpentine walkway that undulates past frothy sea oats and swaying
palms, Fort Lauderdale and Pompano Beach are perfect spots to kick
off your sandals, kick up your heels, and kick back to lazy days of sun,
sand, and sea. ◼

FORT LAUDERDALE AND POMPANO BEACH

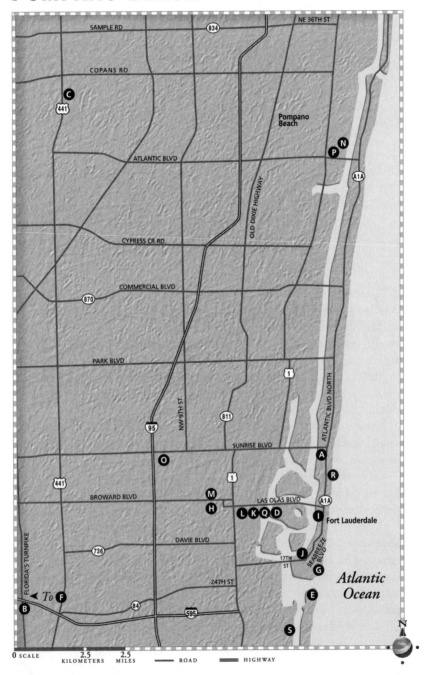

Sights

Ⓐ Bonnet House

Ⓑ Buehler Planetarium

Ⓒ Butterfly World

Ⓓ *Carrie B* Harbor Tours

Ⓔ Discovery Cruise Lines

Ⓕ Everglades Holiday Park

Ⓖ Flamingo Gardens

Ⓖ Glass-Bottom Boat Ride

Ⓗ Himmarshee Historic District/Riverwalk

Ⓘ International Swimming Hall of Fame
Museum & Pool

Ⓙ *Jungle Queen*

Ⓕ Kissimmee Billie Swamp Safari

Ⓚ Las Olas Horse & Carriage Tours

Ⓛ Museum of Art

Ⓜ Museum of Discovery & Science/Blockbuster
IMAX Theater

Ⓝ *Monte Carlo* Casino Cruiser

Ⓞ Old Dillard Museum

Ⓟ Pompano Beach Historical Museum at
Founder's Park

Ⓕ Sawgrass Recreation Park

Ⓔ SeaEscape Cruises

Ⓠ Stranahan House

Ⓡ Trolley City Tour

Ⓢ *Vegas Express*

Note: Items with the same letter are located in the same area.

A PERFECT DAY IN FORT LAUDERDALE AND POMPANO BEACH

Head for one of the cafés along the ocean for breakfast. Then take a look at the Fort Lauderdale of old at Bonnet House or Flamingo Gardens, where nothing seems to have changed for a century. Lunch in the city's tiny historic district, then visit the rainbow-hued denizens of Butterfly World. Try waterskiing without a boat at Pompano's Quiet Waters Park or go fishing for one of the fabled catches snagged offshore here. Settle into a Fort Lauderdale beachfront café to watch the sunset cast golden shadows over the sea. Later, sail on the legendary *Jungle Queen* for a look at some of the city's celebrity homes or pick a winner at Pompano Park's harness races. Wind up the evening with a seaside stroll in the moonlight or a rip-roaring evening at one of the local dance spots.

SIGHTSEEING HIGHLIGHTS

★★★ **Bonnet House**—Hidden away in a jungled wonderland, handsome Bonnet House was built in 1921 as a winter home for the daughter of Fort Lauderdale's most lauded investor, Hugh Taylor Birch, who donated land across the street for what is now Birch State Park. Nestled into a woodland beside a tiny lake, these 35 acres portray South Florida in pre-development days. Monkeys swing through the trees, and swans float on the lake beside this casual winter home. Details: 900 North Birch Road, Fort Lauderdale; (954) 563-5393; open Wednesday through Friday 10 a.m. to 2 p.m.; Saturday and Sunday noon to 3 p.m. Admission $9 adults, $8 students ages 6 to 18. (2 hours)

★★★ **Butterfly World**—Thousands of rainbow-hued creatures flutter by in a kaleidoscope of color as waterfalls burble, orchids tumble from the trees, and fish and birds go about their colorful business. You can learn how to create a butterfly garden here and visit a butterfly breeding lab, botanical gardens, insectarium, museum, and café. Details: 3600 West Sample Road, Tradewinds Park South, Coconut Creek; (954) 977-4400; open Monday through Saturday 9 a.m. to 5 p.m., Sunday 1 to 5 p.m. (except Christmas and Thanksgiving); gate closes at 4 p.m. Admission $10.95 adults, $6 children ages 4 to 12. (3 hours)

★★★ **Flamingo Gardens**—Enter this 160-acre botanical garden and drop back into the South Florida of yesteryear. Massive oaks shade clusters of palms. Birds gurgle and shriek, their colorful feathers adding a pointillist touch to the jungle greenery. A tiny tram chugs along a 1½-mile trail through the citrus grove, and wildlife stars in daily lectures. Details: 3750 Flamingo Road, Davie; (954) 473-2955; open daily 10 a.m. to 6 p.m. Admission $5. (3–4 hours)

★★★ **Himmarshee Historic District/Riverwalk**—In the early days of Fort Lauderdale, New River was the city's center. Here the first hotel, New River Inn, was built in 1896 to welcome automobile kingpin Henry Ford and railroad entrepreneur Henry Flagler. Next door is tiny King-Cromartie House, built in 1907 of rock-hard pine and wood recovered from sunken ships. A few steps away are the twin Bryan Homes, built in 1905 and now a restaurant. A small enclave of antique shops and cafés has become a trendy gathering spot close to the city's glittering performing arts center and Riverwalk. Details: 219 SW 2nd Avenue, Fort Lauderdale; (954) 463-4431; open Tuesday through Friday 10 a.m. to 4 p.m. Admission free. (2 hours)

★★★ *Jungle Queen*—A popular diversion for more than 50 years, this double-decked paddle wheeler comes complete with vaudeville show, singalong, and narrated tour of local celebrity homes and historic spots. Cruises through winding waterways include alligator-wrestling and lunch by day, an all-you-can-eat barbecued feast by night. Details: 801 Seabreeze Boulevard (FL A1A), Fort Lauderdale; (954) 462-5596; cruises daily at 10 a.m., 2 p.m., and 7 p.m.; on Wednesday and Saturday 9:15 a.m. cruise to Bayside Shopping Center in Miami. Admission $10.95 adults, $7.50 children ages 2 to 12 for day cruises; $14.95 adults, $10 children for Bayside Mall cruises; $23.95 adults, $12 children for dinner cruises. Reservations are important on this very busy boat. (4–6 hours)

★★★ **Kissimmee Billie Swamp Safari**—Drop back into another era, deep in the Everglades, where you can sleep in a palm-thatched chickee, lulled to sleep by the guttural roar of a bull alligator. Combining a touch of Seminole and a smattering of Africa, the safari slogs through the wetlands aboard a broad-wheeled swamp buggy or skims the shallows in an speedy airboat. Dugout canoes and a Seminole campfire storytelling evening are part of the adventure. Details: 12261 SW 251st Street, Big Cypress Seminole Indian Reservation, Alligator Alley (I-75), Exit 14, 23 miles west of Fort Lauderdale, 15 miles into park, Princeton; (954) 257-2134; open daily 8:30 a.m. to 6:30 p.m., with tours at 11 a.m., 1 p.m., 3 p.m., and 5 p.m. Admission $20 adults, $10 children ages 6 to 12 for swamp buggy tours; $10 adults and children for airboat tours; overnight stays are $35, or $101 including day and night swamp buggy safaris. (3–5 hours or overnight)

★★★ **Museum of Art**—A $6-million permanent collection of arts and artifacts ranging from pre-Columbian and African work to twentieth-century paintings stars here. Major traveling exhibits, which have included such diverse options as the works of pop artist Andy Warhol and the French Impressionists, add to the glitter. Details: 1 East Las Olas Boulevard, Fort Lauderdale; (954) 763-6464; open Tuesday through Thursday 10 a.m. to 5 p.m., Friday 10 a.m. to 8 p.m., Saturday 10 a.m. to 5 p.m., and Sunday noon to 5 p.m. Admission $6 adults, $4 students ages 19 to 25, $1 children ages 5 to 18. (2 hours)

★★★ **Museum of Discovery & Science/Blockbuster IMAX Theater**—Fun and education unite in gizmos that whirr, buzz, and clank to provide lots of hands-on action. A toddlers-only area is full of bouncing balls, water to splash, and things to pummel without parental admonitions. In the IMAX theater, a five-story-high movie screen and huge sound system add high drama to a changing array of dramatic film footage. Details: 401 SW 2nd Street, Fort Lauderdale; (954) 467-6637 (museum), (954) 463-4629 (theater); museum open Monday through Friday 10 a.m. to 5 p.m., Saturday 10 a.m. to 8:30 p.m., Sunday noon to 5 p.m.; IMAX open varying days and times. Admission to museum $6 adults, $5 children ages 3 to 12; theater $9 adults, $7 children; combination ticket $12.50 adults, $10.50 children. (3 hours)

★★ *Monte Carlo* **Casino Cruiser**—This big yacht sails on casino cruises with live entertainment, light dining, and plenty of gaming. Details: Sands Harbor, 125 North Riverside Drive (on the Intracoastal just north of Atlantic Boulevard), Pompano Beach; (954) 781-7810; sails Wednesday through Sunday noon to 4:30, daily 7:30 p.m. to midnight. Admission $14.95 for day cruises, $19.95 evenings; minimum age 21. (4–6 hours)

★★ **Old Dillard Museum**—Once known as the Colored School, this handsome 1924 building was the region's only school for African American children. Today it's on the National Register of Historic Places and houses displays tracing the spread of Africa's Yoruba culture. You can don colorful tribal masks and clothing, play musical instruments from all over the world, try tie-dying and basketweaving, or crawl into a thatched African hut to hear a storyteller spin tales. Details: 1001 NW 4th Street, Fort Lauderdale; (954) 765-6952; open Tuesday through Saturday noon to 4 p.m., Wednesday until 8 p.m. Admission free. (2 hours)

★★ **SeaEscape Cruises**—Sail away on trips to nowhere or to the Bahamas, complete with lots of food, casino gambling, bingo, nonstop dancing, games, and kids programs. Details: 140 South Federal Highway, Dania; (954) 925-9700; Bahamas cruises are Sunday, Monday, and Wednesday at 8 a.m. and Friday at 7 a.m.; day trips Tuesday, Thursday, and Saturday at 10 a.m.; evening trips Tuesday and Thursday at 7:30 p.m., Friday at 10:30 p.m., and Saturday at 8 p.m. Day trips $29.95 to $39.95 per person, $129 for Bahamas cruises. (4–6 hours)

★★ **Stranahan House**—In 1893, on this once-lonely spot alongside New River, pioneer Frank Stranahan began trading with Seminoles who poled their dugouts downriver to exchange otter pelts, egret feathers, and alligator hides. Local teacher Ivy Cromartie became the lady of this two-story National Register house, built in 1901 with porches on both floors to accommodate Seminoles, who often slept here before returning upriver. Details: 335 SE 6th Avenue, Fort Lauderdale; (954) 524-4736; open mid-September through July, Wednesday through Saturday 10 a.m. to 4 p.m., Sunday 1 to 4 p.m. Admission $5 adults, $2 children under age 12. (1 hour)

★★ *Vegas Express*—This casino ship cruises out beyond the 3-mile limit while the gambling wheels spin. Musical entertainment, a dinner-cruise show, and a day-sailing breakfast buffet add to the fun. Details: Tugboat Annie's, Harbourtown Marina, docked at 815 NE 3rd Street, Dania; (954) 927-8473; cruises daily except Tuesday 11 a.m. to 4 p.m. and 7 p.m. to 12:30 a.m., Friday and Saturday to 1 a.m. Tickets $13 with reservations, $18 at the gate. (5–6 hours)

★ **Buehler Planetarium**—Attention, Trekkies! Members of the *Star Trek* team give special presentations at the planetarium, and laser light shows feature music by Pink Floyd, Pearl Jam, and Nine Inch Nails. Night skies and meteor showers come to life in narrated tours. Details: 3501 SW Davie Road, Davie; (954) 475-6680; open Friday, Saturday, and Sunday, varying hours. Admission $4 to $5. (3 hours)

✷ *Carrie B* **Harbor Tours**—This double-decker craft sails past bustling Port Everglades' cruise ships, Navy vessels, and huge waterway homes into the serene waters of the New River, with onboard dining. Details: Riverwalk at SE 5th Avenue, Fort Lauderdale; (954) 768-9920; cruises daily at 11 a.m., 1 p.m., and 3 p.m. from December to May, closed Tuesday in other months. Admission $10.95 adults, $5 children under age 12. (2 hours)

✷ **Discovery Cruise Lines**—Dining, dancing, Calypso bands, a swimming pool, cabaret revues, and casino gambling combine on this cruiser that sails several times a day, occasionally to the Bahamas. Details: Port Everglades; (305) 525-7800 or (800) 93-SHIPS; sailing Tuesday, Thursday, and Saturday at 10 a.m. and 7:15 p.m., Friday at 11 p.m., Saturday at 1:15 a.m. All-day Bahamas cruises depart Monday, Wednesday, Friday, and Sunday 7:45 a.m. to 11 p.m. Day trips $29.99 to $51.99 per person, $99.99 for Bahamas cruises. (5–6 hours)

✷ **Everglades Holiday Park**—Spot alligators, rare birds, and a host of other critters that live in this park as you skim over the shallow swamp waters in a jet engine–powered airboat. At a re-creation of a Seminole encampment, there's an arts and crafts display and an alligator gets "wrassled." Details: 21940 Griffin Road, Fort Lauderdale; (954) 434-8111; open daily 9 a.m. to 5 p.m. Admission to airboat rides $12.50 adults, $6.25 children ages 3 to 11. (3 hours)

✷ **Glass-Bottom Boat Ride**—Get a close look at down-under without getting wet, or join divers who hand-feed colorful reef dwellers. Details: Bahia Mar Yacht Basin (FL A1A), Fort Lauderdale; (954) 467-6030; trips Tuesday through Saturday 9:30 a.m., Sunday 2 p.m. Admission $15 adults, $10 children under age 11. (2 hours)

✷ **Las Olas Horse & Carriage Tours**—Gaslights flicker as you clip-clop along the brick-trimmed streets of handsome Las Olas Boulevard aboard a surrey with fringe on top. Details: SE 8th Avenue and East Las Olas Boulevard, Fort Lauderdale; (305) 763-7393 or (305) 357-1950 (beeper to reach driver); Thursday, Friday, and Saturday 8 p.m. to 12:30 a.m. Rides $10 per person. (1 hour)

✷ **Pompano Beach Historical Museum at Founder's Park**—
Pompano Beach traces its history at this museum, which displays two

historic cottages with furnishings, books, and clothing of earlier eras. Details: 222 NE 3rd Avenue, Pompano Beach; (954) 762-3015; open Wednesday and Saturday 11 a.m. to 3 p.m. Free. (1 hour)

☆ **Sawgrass Recreation Park**—Whiz around on an airboat, then return to base for a 'Gator Expedition, a look at a Seminole village, and a visit with the Everglades' birds of prey. Details: 5400 North U.S. 27, Weston; (954) 426-2474 or (800) 457-0788; open daily 9 a.m. to 5 p.m., 24 hours for RV camping. Admission $13.85 adults, $6.75 children ages 4 to 12. (2 hours)

International Swimming Hall of Fame Museum & Pool—Remember Johnny "Tarzan" Weissmuller, Mark Spitz, Esther Williams, and Greg Louganis? This museum chronicles the watery feats of these and other swimming stars and offers five pools for splashing. Details: 1 Hall of Fame Drive, Fort Lauderdale; (305) 462-6536; open daily 9 a.m. to 7 p.m., varying hours in summer. Admission $2. (1 hour)

Trolley City Tour—Learn a little about local history and high points as you ride an old-time trolley. Details: pickup at area hotels by reservation; (954) 429-3100; open daily with tours at 10:20 a.m., 11:20 a.m., 12:35 p.m., 1:50 p.m., 2:50 p.m., and 3:50 p.m. Admission $12 adults, children under age 12 free. (1 hour)

GREAT BEACHES

You can't miss Fort Lauderdale's best beach—it rolls right alongside you as you drive **Route A-1-A** from Las Olas to Sunrise Boulevard and beyond. Tree-shaded sands abound at **John U. Lloyd State Park**, a pretty spot that requires a drive south on U.S. 1 to Dania, then east on Dania Beach Boulevard to the park's entrance, which you'll see on your right just as the road takes a sweeping curve to become Route A-1-A. Just outside the park are the beaches of **Dania**, which stretch out along woodsy areas and are usually not crowded.

SHOPPING

With its tiny alleyways, chic shops, outdoor cafés, and ornate architecture, **Las Olas Boulevard** is one of Florida's most beautiful shopping boulevards. Quite the other side of the coin is the **Swap Shop**, a massive indoor-outdoor flea market that spreads 2,000 vendors over 70 acres and includes circus shows and country singers. An indoor version of the same is **Pompano's Festival Flea Market**, 2900 West Sample Road, Pompano Beach, (954) 979-4555. King of the many area shopping centers is **Sawgrass Mills**, 12801 West Sunrise Boulevard, (954) 846-2350, a mile-long alligator-shaped mall billed as the world's largest discount outlet center, with 250 stores. Among traditional malls, **Galleria**, 2414 East Sunrise Boulevard, (954) 564-1015, is convenient to the beach, as is a new oceanside cluster of shops and cafés called **Beach Place**, 17 South Atlantic Boulevard, (954) 760-9570.

FITNESS AND RECREATION

With 3,000 hours of sunshine and unfailingly warm weather, Fort Lauderdale has made play a way of life. Beyond the region's 23 miles of seaside playground, there are more than 200 parks. Try Jet Skis, waterskiing, or sailing with equipment available from **Bill's Sunrise Watersports Rentals**, 2025 East Sunrise Boulevard, Fort Lauderdale, (954) 462-8962.

Fort Lauderdale has dozens of golf courses and tennis courts, topped by Tournament Players Club courses at **TPC at Heron Bay**, 11801 Heron Bay Boulevard, Coral Springs, (954) 796-2000, and **TPC at Eagle Trace**, 1111 Eagle Trace Boulevard, Coral Springs, (905) 753-7222. Among the tennis facilities is the Tennis Center at **Holiday Park**, 730 North Federal Highway, (954) 761-5378, where star Chris Evert Mills learned her lobs.

Blockbuster Golf & Games, NW 136th Avenue, Sunrise, (954) 846-7650, is fun for all ages, with miniature golf and a driving range, bumper boats, batting cages, 1,100 video and virtual reality games, and a play area for toddlers. At **Grand Prix Race-o-Rama**, 1801 NW 1st Street, Dania, (954) 921-1411, both adults and kids whiz around on go-karts and bumper cars, play at miniature golf and batting cages, and ride the wild Skycoaster that swings you out into space.

Dedicated tan fans can play and brown at the same time at **Birch State Park**, 3109 East Sunrise Boulevard, Fort Lauderdale, (954) 564-4521, where 180 acres of oceanfront wilderness are tied to the sea by an under-road tunnel. Nature trails, fishing, canoeing, and irrepressible raccoons captivate visitors, and the park is a favorite spot for watching the glittering Winterfest Boat Parade each December.

It's not every day you find a place where you can learn to water-ski without a boat. But that's just what can happen at **Quiet Waters Park**, 6601 North Powerline Road, Pompano Beach, (954) 360-1315, where a training system called Ski Rixen hooks you to a cable and races you around the course. Open daily 8 a.m. to 7:30 p.m. (earlier closing September through May), the big park also has two lakes, fishing, mini-golf, boat and canoe rentals, and paddleboats.

Baseball fans can watch the **Baltimore Orioles** at spring training from February to May with games at Fort Lauderdale Stadium, 5301 NW 12th Avenue, Fort Lauderdale, (954) 938-4980.

At **Pompano Harness Track**, 1800 SW 3rd Street, Pompano Beach, (954) 972-2000, carefully trained trotting horses pull feather-light carts carrying colorfully clad drivers without losing a beat of their high-stepping pace. One of the top trotter tracks in the country, Pompano opens June to December at 6 p.m. Wednesday through Saturday, with the first race at 7:30 p.m.

GETTING THE ONE THAT DOESN'T GET AWAY

Pompano Beach got its fishy name when an early engineer who loved the pompano he ate here wrote the name on a map, and it stuck. Today the city's annual April seafood festival lures thousands, and a fishing rodeo in May is one of the nation's largest sportfishing events, luring hundreds of anglers determined to snag $100,000 in prize money. Record catches have even jumped onto hooks right off the city's pier. To see if you're clever enough to outsmart a fighting fish, book a sportfishing trip at one of the city's marinas. *Helen S*, 101 North Riverside Drive, Pompano Beach, (954) 941-3209, is a drift-fishing boat that takes you out to the Gulf Stream for $25. Deep-sea fishing boats and drift-fishing boats are docked at **Fish City Pride**, 2625 North Riverside Drive, Pompano Beach, (954) 781-1211; **Cove Marina**, 155 SE 3rd Court, Deerfield Beach, (954) 427-9747; **Hillsboro Inlet Marina**, 2629 North Riverside Drive, Pompano Beach, (954) 943-8222; and **Sands Harbor Marina**, 125 North Riverside Drive, Pompano Beach, (954) 942-9100.

In Fort Lauderdale, dozens of drift-fishing boats and deep-sea charter boats can take you into the fish-filled waters of the warm Gulf Stream. *Dragon*, 425 Seabreeze Boulevard, Fort Lauderdale, (954) 522-3474, is a popular drift-fishing boat, and you'll find the big deep-sea cruisers at **Bahia Mar Marina**, 801 Seabreeze Boulevard, Fort Lauderdale, (954) 764-2233, and **Pier 66 Marina**, 2301 SE 17th Street, Fort Lauderdale, (954) 728-3572.

FOOD

Fort Lauderdale is said to have more restaurants per capita than anywhere else in the nation, with the possible exception of New York City, so come prepared to eat. Award-winning cuisine and authentic Polynesian entertainment combine at one of the city's top showplaces, the **Mai-Kai**, 3599 North Federal Highway, (954) 563-3272. A palm-thatched wonderland complete with thundering drums, fire dancers, swaying hula hips, waterfalls, flaming torches, and a jungle of greenery, the Mai-Kai has been the city's big-night-out spot for more than 30 years. Try *pad Thai* and *tom ka kai* served in the dramatic black decor of **Sukho Thai**, 1930 East Sunrise Boulevard, (954) 764-0148. **Lotus**, 1434 NE 26th Street, (954) 566-5565, is a popular Chinese restaurant where you can down three courses or more for budget prices.

Sip giant margaritas and munch on *chimichangas* at **Carlos 'n' Pepe's Cantina**, 1302 SE 17th Street Causeway, (954) 467-7192. Two other good Mexican spots: **Tequila Sunrise**, 4711 North Dixie Highway, Oakland Park, (954) 938-4475, has lots of budget-wise specials and a 48-ounce margarita; and **La Cantina**, 2870 East Sunrise Boulevard, (954) 565-3839, is a convenient stop when you're looking for a restaurant near the beach.

Long one of the most popular Italian restaurants in Fort Lauderdale, **Paesano's**, 1301 East Las Olas Boulevard, (954) 467-3266, prepares full dinners in its elegant dining rooms and contemporary, light cuisine in its adjoining indoor-outdoor Bar Amici. **Regalo**, 4215 North Federal Highway, Oakland Park, (954) 566-6661, once a gift shop, now prepares gifted Italian cuisine, including a rib-sticking platter of baked ziti.

Gourmets head straight for **Mark's of Las Olas**, 1032 East Las Olas Boulevard, (954) 463-1000, where one of the area's most successful chefs has done it again, creating contemporary haute cuisine. Tops among the seaside cafés that have erupted on Fort Lauderdale Beach are **Mistral**, 201 South Atlantic Boulevard, (954) 463-4900, and **Evangeline**, 213 South Atlantic Boulevard, (954) 522-7001, where the flavors of Cajun country prevail. **Creolina's**, 209 SW 2nd Street, (954) 524-2003, in the historic district, is famed for its moderately priced Creole food. Cruise ships sail by just a few feet from your table at **Burt & Jack's**, Berth 23, Port Everglades, (954) 522-5225, where you dine by candlelight. Burt is actor Burt Reynolds.

Fort Lauderdale offers casual and very casual dining. For the latter, try the thick slabs of Bahamian bread, spicy conch chowder, hot conch salad, and good barbecue options served at **Ernie's**, 1843 South Federal Highway, (954) 523-8636. **Malibu**, 1901 Sunrise Boulevard, (954) 524-7240, is an eclectic spot filled with antiques, stained glass, and even a piano player. **Chuck's Steak House**, 1207 SE 17th Street Causeway, (954) 764-3333, has a good beef-and-salad bar.

A lively crowd keeps things roaring at **Flanigan's Quarterdeck**, 1541 SE 17th Street Causeway, (954) 467-2028, and boaters flock to the **Southport Raw Bar**, just across the street at 1536 SE 17th Street Causeway, (954) 525-2526. Nearby, **Bimini Boatyard**, 1555 SE 17th Street, (954) 525-7400, is a romantic waterside spot with dining under the stars in the shadow of mega-yachts or indoors in a woodsy, contemporary ambience. There's not much atmosphere, but local folks flock to good, inexpensive, home-cookin' 24 hours a day at **The Floridian**, 1410 East Las Olas Boulevard, (954) 463-4041. Find more of the same at **Lester's**, 250 South State Road 84, (954) 525-5641, an authentic 30-year-old, silver-sided diner.

If you're in Pompano Beach in April, join seafood fans who turn out to try some of the city's most renowned seafood at the Pompano Seafood Festival. Seafood is also king at **Cap's Place Island Restaurant**, 2765 NE 28th Court, Lighthouse Point, (954) 941-0418, where you can sample one of the rarest treats in Florida: fresh hearts of palm hacked out of palm tree centers. To get to the restaurant, a relic of rum-smuggling days, follow the signs off U.S. 1 (Federal Highway) in Lighthouse Point, pull up to the dock, flash your headlights, and wait for the *African Queen* to bring you to the small Intercoastal Waterway island. Winston Churchill and Franklin Delano Roosevelt once dined here, as did many celebrities. **Café Arugula**, 3110 North Federal Highway, Lighthouse Point, (954) 785-7732, and **Café Maxx**, 2601 East Atlantic Boulevard, Pompano Beach, (954) 782-0606, are favorite haunts of gourmet diners. **Pelican Pub**, 2635 North Riverside Drive, Pompano Beach, (954) 785-8552, has both a rustic, casual dining room and a white-linen one overlooking the water—the source of the seafood it serves.

LODGING

Fort Lauderdale's popularity peaks December through March, when hotels are packed with sun-seekers, but the city attracts visitors throughout the year. Part of its appeal arises from its innovative Superior Small Hotels program, which accredits small hotels offering low prices and personalized service.

FORT LAUDERDALE AND POMPANO BEACH

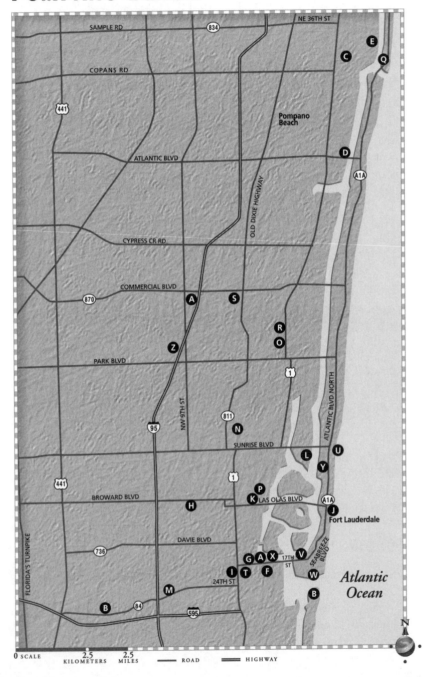

Food

- **A** Bimini Boatyard
- **B** Burt & Jack's
- **C** Café Arugula
- **D** Café Maxx
- **E** Cap's Place Island Restaurant
- **F** Carlos 'n' Pepe's Cantina
- **G** Chuck's Steak House
- **H** Creolina's
- **I** Ernie's
- **J** Evangeline
- **G** Flanigan's Quarterdeck
- **K** The Floridian
- **L** La Cantina
- **M** Lester's
- **N** Lotus
- **O** Mai-Kai
- **L** Malibu
- **K** Mark's Las Olas
- **J** Mistral
- **P** Paesano's
- **Q** Pelican Pub
- **R** Regalo
- **A** Southport Raw Bar
- **L** Sukho Thai
- **S** Tequila Sunrise

Lodging

- **T** Embassy Suites
- **U** Holiday Inn
- **U** Howard Johnson's
- **F** Hyatt Regency Pier 66
- **V** Lago Mar
- **W** Marriott Harbor Beach Resort
- **X** Marriott Hotel & Marina
- **Y** Sea Chateau
- **Y** Sea View

Camping

- **Z** Buglewood RV Resort
- **A** Easterlin Park
- **B** Yacht Haven Park & Marina

Note: Items with the same letter are located in the same area.

Among the popular small beach hotels is **Sea Chateau**, 555 North Birch Road, Fort Lauderdale, (954) 566-8331, where rooms are adorned with antique touches, puffy comforters, and lace. Large efficiencies are ideal for those who want to do a little cooking, and winter rates are $65 to $75. A similar small hotel is the **Sea View**, 550 North Birch Road, (954) 564-3151, which has accommodations in the $75 to $135 range.

Marriott Harbor Beach Resort, 3030 Holiday Drive, Fort Lauderdale, (954) 525-4000, is an oceanfront standout among luxury hotels, with waterfall-fed pool, several restaurants, and a seaside location. Rates are $299 to $339. A sister property, **Marriott Hotel & Marina**, 1881 SE 17th Street, (954) 463-4000, nestles alongside the Intracoastal Waterway and has several dining spots, including one that's a local favorite for Sunday brunch. Rates are $185 to $199.

Award-winning **Hyatt Regency Pier 66**, 2301 SE 17th Street Causeway, (954) 525-6666 or (800) 233-1234, sprawls alongside an Intracoastal marina and is famed for 360-degree views from a revolving tower lounge. Peak-season rates are $249 to $329. **Lago Mar**, 1700 South Ocean Lane, Fort Lauderdale, (954) 523-6511, is one of the city's best-kept secrets, a posh spot that welcomes celebrities without fanfare and snuggles right up to the sand, with rates of $175 to $395.

Holiday Inn, 999 North Atlantic Boulevard, (954) 563-5961, and **Howard Johnson's**, 700 North Atlantic Boulevard, (954) 563-2451, both have properties across the street from the sea. Rates at either are in the $100 to $150 range in peak season. **Embassy Suites**, 1100 SE 17th Street Causeway, Fort Lauderdale, (954) 527-2700 or (800) EMBASSY, wows 'em with waterfalls and palms in the atrium lobby of this all-suites property, which includes breakfast and cocktails in winter rates of $209.

CAMPING

Buglewood RV Resort, 2121 NW 29th Court, Fort Lauderdale, (954) 485-1150, is just 6 miles from the beach and offers billiards and a swimming pool for $33.80 with full hookups. **Easterlin Park**, 1000 NW 38th Street, Oakland Park, (954) 938-0610, is 3 miles from the sea and charges $21 a night. **Yacht Haven Park & Marina**, 2323 SR 84, Fort Lauderdale, (954) 583-2322 or (800) 581-2322, has 250 camping sites, a recreation center, heated pool, and marina for $27 to $34.

NIGHTLIFE

Performing Arts

Fort Lauderdale is proud to have expanded its cultural life with the glittering new **Broward Center for the Performing Arts**, 201 SW 5th Avenue, (954) 462-0222, which hosts a wide variety of music, drama, and dance events. **Fort Lauderdale Opera**, 201 SW 5th Avenue, (954) 728-9700, features top-name opera stars from December through April and top Broadway touring companies, which also appear at handsome **Parker Playhouse** in Holiday Park, 707 NE 8th Street, (954) 763-2444. The **Philharmonic Orchestra of Florida**, (954) 561-2997, performs from September through March in a variety of locations, while some of the best names in contemporary music appear at **Sunrise Musical Theater**, 5555 SW 95th Street, Sunrise, (954) 523-3309. **Off Broadway on 26th Street**, 1444 NE 26th Street, Wilton Manors, (954) 566-0554, presents the latest in avant-garde theater, often focusing on gay issues; and **Vinette Carroll Repertory Theater**, 503 SE 6th Street, (954) 462-2424, housed in a charming old church, offers multiethnic drama.

Clubs and Bars

Fort Lauderdale loves a party, so there's always action somewhere in town until the wee hours of the morning. One rockin' favorite is **Baja Beach Club**, 3200 North Federal Highway, (954) 561-2432, where everyone is wild, from the bartenders to the patrons. For loud music, lots of bars, and nonstop crowds, try **Bermuda Triangle**, 219 South Atlantic Boulevard, (954) 779-2544. If you don't wear black lipstick and don't know what slam-dancing is, then you don't belong at **The Edge**, 109 SW 2nd Avenue, (954) 525-9333. **Copa Cabaret & Disco**, 624 SE 28th Street, (954) 463-1507, is the top gay club in a town that has many gay venues, including **Cathode Ray**, 1105 East Las Olas Boulevard, (954) 462-8611, and **825**, 825 East Sunrise Boulevard, (954) 524-3333. Count on hearing an Irish brogue at **Maguire's Hill 16 Pub**, 535 North Andrews Avenue, (954) 764-4453, where there's usually a dart game and always a $6 shepherd's pie and a glass of Guinness. If nudity's your cuppa, **Pure Platinum**, 3411 North Federal Highway, (954) 360-4342, is renowned. If the Electric Slide is your glide, walk those dancin' boots into **Desperado's**, 2520 South Miami Road, (954) 463-2855.

Scenic Route: Lake Okeechobee

From Fort Lauderdale, Miami, Palm Beach, or any of the cities along the Gold Coast, you can travel through South Florida's fascinating farmlands and sugar country as you circle Lake Okeechobee, the second largest inland lake in the nation and, indeed, the world.

From Fort Lauderdale travel north on U.S. 27, which cuts straight through the heart of fishing, cattle, and farming country. You'll arrive at the edge of the lake upon whose existence most of southern Florida and the vast Everglades depends. Remnant of a prehistoric sea, massive Lake Okeechobee covers 730 square miles, its fresh water rarely deeper than 12 feet and nowhere deeper than 22 feet. Lynchpin of a powerful agri-industrial system that produces fish, vegetables, sugar, and cattle, Lake Okeechobee also plays a vital part in the natural limestone underground pipeline that supports South Florida's complex ecological system.

A devastating 1928 hurricane that blew the water right out of the lake and drowned 2,600 people led to construction of a massive water control project that created a series of lake locks and dikes. A system once ruled by nature was now under human control. One hundred forty miles of 34-foot-high levees were built to encircle the lake and prevent a recurrence of disaster. Today the levee has several parks where you can picnic or rent a boat to travel across this huge lake. You can also drive onto the levee at marked entrances or stroll on a walking trail around many miles of the lake.

Generations of Seminole Indians have lived around this 45-mile-wide lake, which they named "big water." They live here still, occupying the large Brighton Seminole Reservation on the west side. In more recent history, farmers lured by the rich muck soil settled here to raise more than 30 kinds of vegetables, including corn, lettuce, celery, rice, radish, parsley, cabbage, and endive. By far, however, the major crop of the region is sugarcane, which grows in vast fields that are burned during harvesting.

If you're traveling from Palm Beach, you'll arrive first in the city of Belle Glade, where that rich, black, muck soil generated the city's motto: "Her Soil Is Her Fortune." Huge farmsteads surrounding Belle Glade and Pahokee welcome visitors to packing houses, and in early April, the region celebrates its veggie victories at the Black Gold Jubilee, where you can taste some of the harvest. Next door to the city's Chamber of Commerce at 540 South Main Street, (407) 996-2745, is a memorial to the victims of the 1928 hurricane.

Traveling west on U.S. 441 to U.S. 27 through the farm town of South Bay, turn north on U.S 27 to **Clewiston**, the town that sugar built. Home to 300,000 acres of the green cane stalks, Clewiston is also the headquarters of the U.S. Sugar Corp., which operates the handsome old **Clewiston Inn**, 108 Royal Purple Palm Avenue (U.S. 27), (941) 983-8151 or (800) 749-4466. Its tall white pillars, arched windows, and double-doored entrance are backed by beamed ceilings, polished cypress paneling, and a fireplace flanked by wing chairs. A pretty dining room rounds out the offerings of the inn, which charges $59 to $79 year-round.

A Clewiston fixture and don't-miss spot is the **Old South Bar-B-Q**, U.S. 27, (941) 983-6390, where you're greeted by life-size plaster cowboys. Inside, a kitschy collection of Old West memorabilia and antique tools is abetted by a super-spicy sauce doused on pit-barbecued chicken, pork, and beef specialties.

Ah-Tha-Thi-Ki Museum, H.C. 61 (a county road), Clewiston, (941) 902-1113, opened in 1997 to chronicle the stirring saga of the Seminoles, is the only museum of its kind in Florida. Tucked away deep in the Everglades on a 64-acre wooded cypress hammock on

LAKE OKEECHOBEE

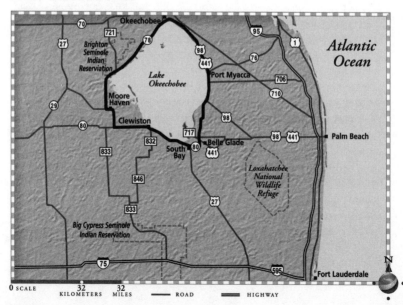

the tribe's **Big Cypress Reservation**, the museum (its name, pronounced Ah-TAW-thick-key, means "time to learn") re-creates turn-of-the-century Seminole life with nature trails and exhibitions of the tribe's amazingly intricate patchwork quilting, open-fire cooking, palm-thatched chickee hut construction, hunting, and fishing. A video outlines the Seminole struggle for survival against the elements—and the U.S. Army. Displays include typical Seminole dress, jewelry, pottery, basketmaking, a dugout canoe, and archeological artifacts, as well as military weapons used during the Seminole Wars. It's open Tuesday through Sunday 9 a.m. to 5 p.m. Admission is $6 for adults, $4 for children ages 6 to 12. (3 hours)

North on U.S. 27 is **Moore Haven**, where you'll see some of the huge, horned, and humpbacked Brahma cattle imported from India to improve the breed's' resistance to insects. Florida is now one of the nation's top five cattle-producing states. An ancient cypress here, believed to be 450 years old, was once a hitching post for swamp boats, but it's now a mile inland, left high and dry by changes in the level of the lake. At the north end of the lake is the region's biggest town, **Okeechobee**, site of a grim Christmas Day battle between the Seminoles and General Zachary Taylor, who went on to become president of the United States. A monument to the battle, won by the Seminoles, is on U.S. 441 south of town.

You can visit any of the locks around the lake and watch boats "locking through" it. Wildlife in and around the lake ranges from alligators, which can now be hunted one month a year with licenses granted by lottery, to manatees, raccoons, muskrats, marsh rabbits, river otters, bobcats, and an enormous variety of birds, including ibises, herons, woodstorks, cormorants, anhingas, eagles, caracaras, ospreys, bald eagles, hawks, and black vultures. Top professional anglers call Lake Okeechobee the best bass-fishing lake in the nation, but you can also snag speckled perch, crappie, shellcracker, slabsided bluegill, bream, and freshwater catfish.

Motels are most prevalent in Okeechobee and Belle Glade, and many campgrounds can be found throughout the region, including the **Okee-Tantie Recreation Area**, 10430 Highway 78 West, Okeechobee, (941) 763-2622, which charges $28.54 for full hookups.

Get a good look at the lake in **Port Myacca**, where you can walk on the levee before returning to Palm Beach by heading north on SR 76, then south on SR 710. ◾

11

BOCA RATON AND DELRAY BEACH

G et the big snobs," flamboyant architect Addison Mizner is reported to have said, "and the little ones will follow." That's certainly what Mizner set out to do, bringing a trainload of the famous here to hype his Cloister Inn, whose 100 rooms were built at a cost of $1.25 million—in 1920s money—and were intended to be the cornerstone of a resort lined with waterways plied by gondolas. To give his plan a boost, he dreamed up an ad campaign that boomed: "I Am the Greatest Resort in the World," adding in small print, "a few years hence." It worked. Sales skyrocketed to $2 million—a week! But the bubble burst with the Depression, and the grand dream died as property-boom scandals earned Boca Raton the moniker "Beaucoup Rotten."

Mizner, however, went down in style. When he appeared in court to defend himself against charges that he'd sold a barren plot of sand with a promise that the buyer could grow nuts on the land, Mizner replied, "Oh no, I said he could *go* nuts on the land." Some went nuts, some went broke, but eventually the Gold Coast recovered, and today Boca Raton, Delray Beach, and a cluster of coastal villages form a community said to be the wealthiest in the nation. ◙

BOCA RATON AND DELRAY BEACH

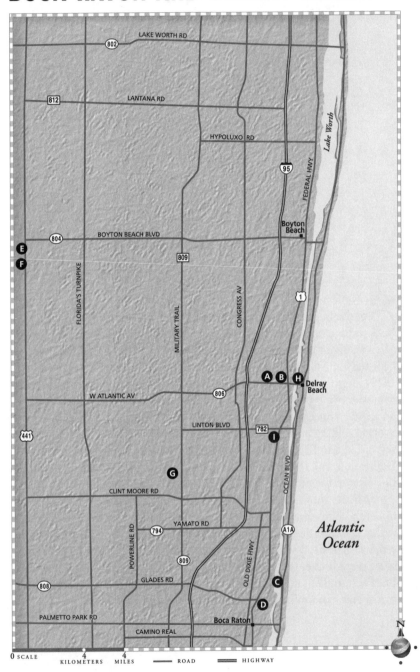

LAKE WORTH RD

802

812 LANTANA RD

HYPOLUXO RD

95

Lake Worth

FEDERAL HWY

Boynton
Beach

804 BOYNTON BEACH BLVD

E

F 809

FLORIDA'S TURNPIKE

MILITARY TRAIL

CONGRESS AV

1

A B H Delray
Beach

W ATLANTIC AV 806

LINTON BLVD 782

I

OCEAN BLVD

441

G

CLINT MOORE RD

POWERLINE RD

YAMATO RD

A1A

Atlantic
Ocean

794

809

OLD DIXIE HWY

GLADES RD

808 C

D

PALMETTO PARK RD

Boca Raton

CAMINO REAL

N

0 SCALE
4
KILOMETERS   4
MILES ━━━ ROAD ═══ HIGHWAY

Sights

- Ⓐ Cason Cottage Museum
- Ⓑ Cornell Museum at Old School Square
- Ⓒ Gumbo Limbo Nature Center
- Ⓓ International Museum of Cartoon Art
- Ⓔ Loxahatchee National Wildlife Refuge
- Ⓕ Loxahatchee Everglades Tour
- Ⓖ Morikami Museum and Japanese Gardens
- Ⓗ *Ramblin' Rose* Riverboat
- Ⓘ Sports Immortals Museum

A PERFECT DAY IN BOCA RATON AND DELRAY BEACH

Start the day with a walk through the winding trails of Loxahatchee
Wildlife Refuge, the northernmost reaches of the Everglades, where
creatures of the swamp are most often visible in early morning. See the
region's impressive mansions from the deck of a tour boat, then head for
Delray Beach to visit a restored Old Florida home, tiny Cason Cottage,
and the cluster of historic buildings that won the city a national award for
its determined restoration efforts. Sample Asian flavors at lunch at the
Morikami Museum and Japanese Gardens and hear how an equally
determined group of Japanese settlers turned sand into pineapple plantations and, generations later, created these tranquil gardens. Head for
Boca Raton for a visit to the International Museum of Cartoon Art,
which displays one of the world's largest collections of cartoon cels and
memorabilia. At sunset, sip something cool beside the sea in Delray and
dine later in one of the region's picturesque restaurants. Wind up the day
at one of the local nightspots or casual sports bars.

SIGHTSEEING HIGHLIGHTS

★★★ **International Museum of Cartoon Art**—Who would ever
have dreamed that comic strips would someday become collectibles?
But here it is, an entire museum devoted to the cartoon, with more
than 150,000 works on paper, 10,000 books, and 1,000 hours of
animated film in Toon Town, Cartoon Hall of Fame, Prehistoric

Cartoon Cave, Cartoonist's Studios, and the Laugh Center. Details: 201 Plaza Real, Boca Raton; (561) 391-2200; open Tuesday through Saturday 11 a.m. to 6 p.m., Sunday noon to 6 p.m. Admission $6 adults, $4 students, $3 children ages 6 to 12. (1 hour)

★★★ **Loxahatchee Everglades Tours**—If you'd like to see the Wildlife Refuge with a tour guide, these folks will take you into these "northern Everglades" on narrated airboat tours that let you in on some of the details of this complex environment. Tours range in length from 45 minutes to two hours. Details: call for instructions to the base site; (561) 482-0880; open daily 9 a.m. to 4:15 p.m. Admission varies, depending on the length of the tour, $20 to $60 adults, half-price for children under age 12. (1–2 hours)

★★★ **Loxahatchee National Wildlife Refuge**—Alligators, herons, the endangered snail kite, herons, ibises, coots, and dozens of other birds and swamp creatures live in this wildlife refuge. You can explore it in a half-mile boardwalk through the cypress swamp or a longer trail through the marshes, where constructed ponds can be controlled to lure birds. Details: 10216 Lee Road, Boynton Beach; (561) 734-8303; open daily sunrise to sunset (6 a.m. to 7 p.m.), with a visitor center open 9 a.m. to 4 p.m. Admission $4 per vehicle. (2 hours)

★★★ **Morikami Museum and Japanese Gardens**—Many Japanese settled here in the early 1900s to create large pineapple plantations and honored their heritage with this tranquil 150-acre site. Included are a 5-acre Japanese garden, bonsai collection, pond, nature trails, café serving Asian luncheons 11 a.m. to 3 p.m., seasonal festivals, and a museum that brings ancient Japanese customs and culture to life. Details: 4000 Morikami Park Road, Delray Beach; (561) 495-0233; open Tuesday through Sunday 10 a.m. to 5 p.m. Admission $4.25 adults, $2 children ages 6 to 18; grounds open sunrise to sunset, free. (2–3 hours)

★★ **Gumbo-Limbo Nature Center**—Gumbo-limbo trees are often called the "tourist tree" for their bright red "sunburned" bark. You'll learn all about them at this nature center, where they are one of the stars of this tropical hardwood forest interlaced with elevated board-walks. An observation tower lets you overlook the hammock and mangroves, where you may spot butterflies, manatees, pelicans, ospreys, and sea turtles. A nature center offers a close view of some of the creatures who live here and in adjoining Red Reef Park. Details: 1801 North Ocean Drive, Boca Raton; (561) 338-1473; open Monday through Saturday 9 a.m. to 4 p.m., Sunday noon to 4 p.m. Free. (2 hours)

★★ *Ramblin' Rose* Riverboat—This 250-passenger triple-decker riverboat rambles through the area's pretty waterways for a spin past million-dollar mansions from Manalapan to Boca Raton. Details: 801 East Atlantic Boulevard, Boca Raton; (561) 243-0686; cruises Monday through Friday 11 a.m., Saturday 1 and 6:30 p.m., and Sunday 1 p.m. Admission $9.95 to $15.95 adults depending on length of the cruise, $3.75 to $4.95 children ages 2 to 12; Saturday dinner cruise $29 adults, $19.95 children ages 7 to 12, $10.95 children ages 2 to 6. (2–3½ hours)

★ Cason Cottage Museum—Delray has worked hard on restoring its historic buildings, including this pretty, turn-of-the-century cottage that now houses the city's historical society and rotating art exhibits. Details: 5 NE 1st Street, Delray Beach; (561) 243-0223; open Tuesday through Friday 10 a.m. to 4 p.m. Free. (1 hour)

★ Cornell Museum at Old School Square—The museum in this cluster of restored antique buildings has an impressive collection of toy soldiers and presents a changing array of art and sculptural exhibits. Details: 51 North Swinton Avenue, Delray Beach; (561) 243-7922; open Tuesday through Saturday 11 a.m. to 4 p.m., Sunday 1 to 4 p.m. Admission $3 adults, children under age 12 free. (1 hour)

★ Sports Immortals Museum—Collected by a sports fan supremo, this enormous collection of sports memorabilia claims to be the world's largest—and who's disputing that? You can see the world's rarest baseball card—it's a Honus Wagner, one of only two in the world in mint condition—lots of autographed pieces, Muhammad Ali's belt, Jim Thorpe memorabilia, and scads more in this packed museum. Details: 6830 North Federal Highway, Boca Raton; (561) 997-2575; open Monday through Friday 10 am. to 6 p.m., Saturday 10 a.m. to 5 p.m. Admission $5 adults, $3 children under age 12. (1–2 hours)

GREAT BEACHES

Two miles north of Palmetto Park Road is **Spanish River Park**, whose beaches are all the rave in Boca. In Delray, you can't miss the beach—on **Route A-1-A** you'll be driving right alongside its dunes and sea oats.

FITNESS AND RECREATION

Tennis is a big game in these parts, with some of the top names playing at the **Delray Beach Tennis Center**. Golf courses abound throughout the region, and both Boca Raton and Delray have municipal courses as well.

Polo players stream in each year for chukkers at the **Royal Palm Polo Club**, 6300 Clint Moore Road, Boca Raton, (561) 994-1876, where competitions occur most weekends between December and May for ticket prices in the $6 to $12 range; and at the nearby **Gulfstream Polo Grounds**, 4550 Polo Club Road, Lake Worth, (561) 965-2057.

Canoe Outfitters of Florida, 8900 Indiantown Road, Jupiter, (561) 746-7053, can get you into a rental canoe for an 18-mile paddle down the Loxahatchee. Along the way you can visit an early river settlement and spot exotic birds and perhaps an alligator. You set off between 8 and 11 a.m., paddle downstream, and return to the base by bus. Rates are $15 per person, plus $1 admission to the park.

Thump around in bumper boats or speed on the Indy-carts racetrack at **Boomer's Family Recreation Center**, 3100 Airport Road, Boca Raton, (561) 347-1888, where you can play on two miniature-golf courses and in a two-story video arcade. It's open Monday through Thursday noon to 11 p.m., Friday and Saturday 10 a.m. to 1 a.m., and Sunday 10 a.m. to 11 p.m.

Rise above it all in a vintage biplane at **Glider Rides of America**, 2633 Lantana Road, Lantana (561) 965-9101, which charges $79.90 to $159.95 for two with mile-high flights and a 300-degree view over reefs and barrier islands. If only one person is flying, they'll let you take the controls for $99.95.

FOOD

La Vieille Maison, 770 East Palmetto Park Road, Boca Raton, (561) 391-6701, means "old house," but that description doesn't do justice to this beautiful old Mizner creation. Each of several dining rooms is beautifully decorated with lots of crystal and gilt, and its culinary triumphs have won many an award; à la carte entrees and three-course and six-course fixed-price dinners available.

Maxaluna, 5050 Town Center Circle in Crocker Center, Boca Raton, (561) 391-7177, and **Max's Grille**, 404 Plaza Real in Mizner Park, Boca Raton, (561) 368-0080, are the creation of a restaurateur with enough magic to have produced a whole herd of award-winning restaurants in the region. Both are upscale spots with a casual atmosphere and nouvelle cuisine focusing on such selections as angel hair pasta with light sauces, roasted chicken with garlic mashed potatoes, and seared tuna.

In a chic, sumptuous atmosphere of mahogany, wrought iron, and brick, **Maxwell's Chophouse**, Palmetto Park Road at the Intracoastal Waterway, Boca Raton, (561) 347-7077, produces top steaks, seafood, and chops, with nightly entertainment and a piano bar.

Crowds throng to **The Firehouse**, 6751 North Federal Highway, Boca Raton, (561) 997-6006, to devour the modestly priced steaks and prime rib, served among memorabilia of firefighters and famous blazes. **Busch's**, 840 East Atlantic Avenue, Delray Beach, (561) 278-7600, has been wonderful since the beginning of time and continues to find creative new ways to serve seafood at high but fair prices.

Tom's Place, 7251 North Federal Highway, Boca Raton, (561) 997-0920, has grown from a simple barbecue place to a crowded-every-night simple barbecue place that's won national attention. You can taste what all the fuss is about and still come out with change from a $20 bill. **Two Georges Harbour Hut Restaurant & Raw Bar**, Two Georges Marina, Boynton Beach, (561) 736-2717, is a favorite dropping-in spot for local restaurateurs—which says something about the moderately priced jumbo shrimp, conch fritters, fresh filets of whatever's just been caught, tuna steak, and shrimp kebabs seared on an outdoor grill at this waterside spot. **Banana Boat**, 730 East Ocean Avenue, Boynton Beach, (561) 732-9400, is another reasonably priced waterside watering hole that draws a casual crowd to outdoor dining overlooking the marina or indoor rustic surroundings. Seafood's the specialty here, but there are plenty of other options, including entertainment.

Sports fans swear by the **Pete Rose Ballpark Café**, 8144 West Glades Road, Boca Raton, (561) 488-7383, where baseball triumphs are well-documented, and 50 television screens keep you up to score on every game. Weekdays, Rose records his radio show live from the café,

BOCA RATON AND DELRAY BEACH

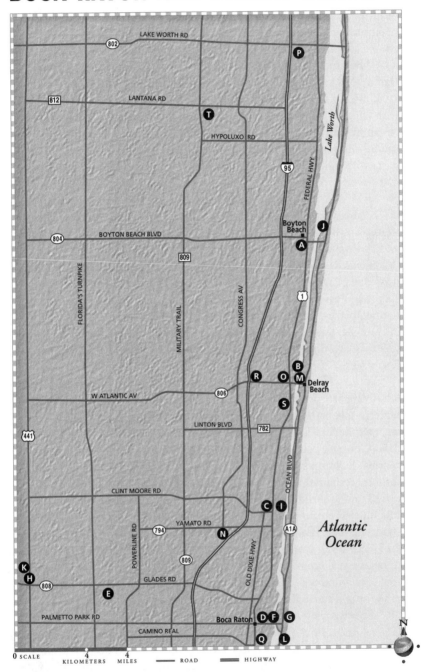

Food

- Ⓐ Banana Boat
- Ⓑ Busch's
- Ⓒ The Firehouse
- Ⓓ La Vielle Maison
- Ⓔ Maxaluna
- Ⓕ Max's Grille
- Ⓖ Maxwell's Chophouse
- Ⓗ Pete Rose Ballpark Café
- Ⓘ Tom's Place
- Ⓙ Two Georges Harbour Hut Restaurant & Raw Bar
- Ⓚ Wilt Chamberlain's

Lodging

- Ⓛ Boca Raton Hotel & Club
- Ⓜ Colony Hotel
- Ⓝ Embassy Suites
- Ⓞ Holiday Inn Camino Real
- Ⓟ Hummingbird Hotel
- Ⓠ Radisson Bridge Resort of Boca Raton
- Ⓡ Spanish River Resort

Camping

- Ⓢ Del-Raton Travel Trailer Park
- Ⓣ Palm Beach Traveler Park

which serves burgers, pastas, steaks, and seafood at low prices. Find more of the same at **Wilt Chamberlain's**, 8903 Glades Road, Boca Raton, (561) 488-8881, where the Stilt is honored at a casual sports bar with 45 televisions, a kids' game room, and a basketball court; stop in for moderately priced, classy oak-grilled beef, burgers, and Asian-inspired seafood fare.

LODGING

Legend has it that architect Addison Mizner, who built about half of Palm Beach and Boca, used to stroll the hallways of his **Boca Raton Hotel & Club**, 501 East Camino Real, Boca Raton, (561) 395-3000 or (800) 327-0101, in his pj's, accompanied by a pet monkey and a squawking toucan. In the huge, impressive halls of this towering old hotel, it's easy to believe most anything. Here, in the house that Mizner built for more than a million bucks 70 years ago, is the best that money can buy. Marble pillars soar, water burbles into fanciful fountains, crystal gleams, and brass glitters. An amazing complex that encompasses the original hotel, called **The Cloisters**, plus the ocean-front **Boca Raton Beach Club** and **The Towers**, these three hotels are among the best in the nation, winning awards for everything from decor to dining. Besides 11 restaurants, you'll find golfing, tennis, croquet, pools, water sports, and a marina. Peak season rates range $240 to $575.

    Spanish River Resort, 1111 East Atlantic Avenue, Delray Beach, (561) 243-7946 or (800) 543-7946, offers a variety of accommodations in a high-rise condominium overlooking the beach and the Intracoastal Waterway. Rates are $75 to $310 in winter.

    Delray's **Colony Hotel**, 525 West Atlantic Avenue, Delray Beach, (561) 276-4123, is an historic spot with a private beach club. Open November through April, the 1926 hotel charges $145.

    Holiday Inn Camino Real, 1229 East Atlantic Avenue, Delray Beach, (561) 278-0882 or (800) 234-6835, is a trim spot right on the beach in this quiet city, with 150 rooms—many of them two-bedroom suites—equipped with refrigerators and cable television. Peak rates are $99 to $250.

    Radisson Bridge Resort of Boca Raton, 999 East Camino Real, Boca Raton, (561) 358-9500 or (800) 333-3333, has a pool, health club, and rooms with balcony views of the ocean or Intracoastal Waterway. Rates are $169 to $199 in peak winter season.

Hummingbird Hotel, 631 Lucerne Avenue, Lake Worth, (561) 533-0833 or (800) 588-4297, a pleasant budget spot, offers cable television, shuttle to town, and complimentary continental breakfast at a small resort about ten minutes from the beach. Peak-season rates are $65 to $85.

Embassy Suites, 661 NW 53rd Street, Boca Raton, (561) 994-8200 or (800) EMBASSY, is a popular hotel chain that offers one-bedroom suites equipped with refrigerators, coffeemakers, and separate sitting rooms, with complimentary cocktails and breakfast daily. Winter rates at the resort are $189 to $209.

CAMPING

Del-Raton Travel Trailer Park, 2998 South Federal Highway, Delray Beach, (561) 278-4633, is about a mile from the beach and near attractions and entertainment. Winter rates are $25. **Palm Beach Traveler Park**, 6159 Lawrence Road, Lantana, (561) 967-3139, has plenty of activity, from bingo to horseshoes, and is about 3 miles from the beach. Winter rates are $23.

NIGHTLIFE

Performing Arts

One of four Florida state theaters, the **Caldwell Theater Company**, Boca Raton, has been around for more than 20 years, presenting professional contemporary and classic plays, comedy, and musical revues year-round in its 305-seat facility.

Jan McArt's Royal Palm Dinner Theater, Cabaret, 303 SE Mizner Boulevard, Boca Raton, (561) 392-3755, is an award-winning dinner theater that is the creation of local actress Jan McArt, winner of many an award for her musical and comedy productions. Dinner is at 6 p.m., show at 8 p.m. Tuesday through Saturday, two hours earlier on Sunday. Prices are $43 to $52; children under age 12 half-price.

Musicana Dinner Theater, 2200 NW 2nd Avenue, Boca Raton, (561) 361-9704, creates a musical evening with two revues and dancing during intermission. Dinner prices, including entertainment, are $22 to $32 for evening performances Tuesday through Saturday at 6 p.m. and Sunday at 4 p.m., $30 for Wednesday and Saturday noon matinees. Children under age 12 pay $14.

Clubs and Bars

Reggae and steel bands play at **Boston's On the Beach**, 40 South Ocean Boulevard, Delray Beach, (561) 278-3364, where there's live entertainment every night in a lounge overlooking the ocean. **Club Boca**, 7000 West Palmetto Park Road, Boca Raton, (561) 368-3333, is a high-energy nightclub with a different theme every night. **Ale House**, 1221 North Congress Avenue, Boca Raton, (561) 735-0591, serves plenty of what the name suggests in a casual sports bar and restaurant.

Scenic Route: Route A-1-A

To see South Florida in both its pristine and developed state, take a ride on Route A-1-A from Boynton Beach or Delray Beach to Boca Raton, and beyond to pretty Hillsboro Beach, home of a scenic lighthouse. Route A-1-A meanders along between the ocean and the Intracoastal Waterway through a number of small towns with low speed limits, so plan a drive of an hour or so.

As you travel south, you'll pass a small settlement called **Ocean Ridge**, where many millionaires dwell, and arrive in **Delray**, where sea oats and grasses trim the sand. Because you're driving along on a dune in Delray, you'll see the sea glittering a few feet below. Next you'll pass through a community called **Gulf Stream**, also home to many of the world's wealthiest, and a tiny town—population 1,600— with the alluring name of **Briny Breezes**.

You'll then find yourself in **Boca Raton**, which has four attractive beachfront parks, including **South Beach Park**, where you might stop for a swim. It's an undeveloped beach with no lifeguard, but it's a good getaway spot. Along this drive, you'll pass at least six public oceanfront

ROUTE A-1-A

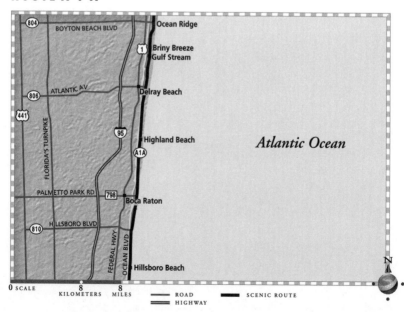

parks, most with lifeguards and other facilities; consider stocking up on the makings of an oceanfront picnic. Beyond Boca Raton is **Highland Beach** and, farther south, lovely **Hillsboro Beach**, where the sands are lined with mansions tucked so deeply into jungled acreage that they're barely visible. No matter: the tree-canopied roadway and glimpses of yachts on the Intracoastal Waterway are alone worth the drive. At the southern edge of Hillsboro Beach, the waters of the Atlantic and the Intracoastal join in a rush at **Hillsboro Inlet**, where you can see the lighthouse rising above the trees. Just south of the inlet is a rustically pretty restaurant, **Pelican Pub**, in which you can dine overlooking still more of South Florida's lovely waterfront. ◼

12
PALM BEACH

If you want to experience the drop-jaw splendor that mega-money can create, this is the place to do it. A postcard-perfect spot, seaside Palm Beach does things just a little differently: there are actually laws that prohibit jogging without a shirt and that ban car washes. As exclusive an enclave as it is, this well-groomed town is a friendly spot that's more egalitarian these days than many of its residents might prefer. The new influx of quite-ordinary-income folks comes on the heels of low summer rates, a plethora of golf courses and outdoor activities, and a list of year-round diverting special events. Good restaurants and beautiful hotels add to the allure.

Architect Addison Mizner, the man whose grandiose architecture has been dubbed Bastard–Spanish–Moorish–Romanesque–Gothic–Renaissance–Bull-Market–Damn-the-Expense style, started it all here with the Everglades Club, which still lords it over Worth Avenue. This famous, high-chic shopping street caters to the city's pampered pooches with a tile-trimmed watering hole, and to their pampered owners with limosine-sized parking spots. And so it goes in quirky Palm Beach. We are drawn to it, in fact, because it allows us to experience, if only vicariously, the awesome otherworld-liness of immense wealth. Any way you look at it, Palm Beach is an enriching experience. ◼

PALM BEACH

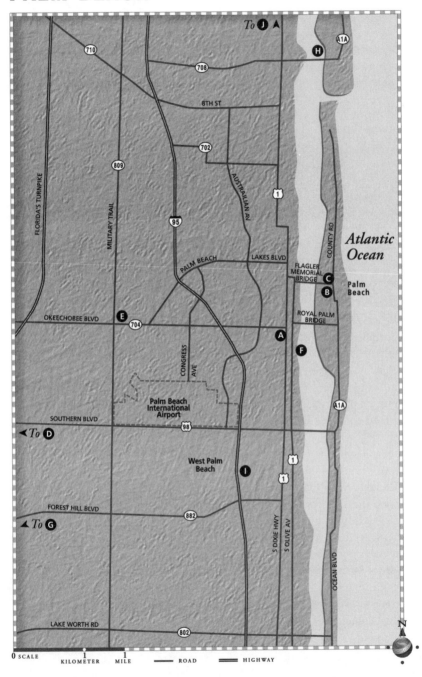

Sights

Ⓐ Ann Norton Sculpture Gardens

Ⓑ Henry Morrison Flagler Museum

Ⓒ Hibel Museum of Art

Ⓓ Lion Country Safari

Ⓔ Mounts Botanical Garden

Ⓕ Norton Museum of Art

Ⓖ Okeeheelee Nature Center

Ⓗ Palm Beach Water Taxi

Ⓘ Palm Beach Zoo

Ⓘ South Florida Science Museum and Planetarium

Ⓗ *Star of Palm Beach*

Ⓙ *Viking Queen* Cruises

Ⓙ Water Taxi

Note: Items with the same letter are located in the same area.

A PERFECT DAY IN PALM BEACH

A mandatory activity in Palm Beach is a "You've got to be kidding!" look at the town's gargantuan mansions. To see what one looks like inside, stop in at the showplace Flagler Museum, built by South Florida's founding father, railroader Henry Flagler—who didn't mess around, architecturally speaking. To get a waterside view of some of those show-places, hop on one of the town's tour boats, where all the latest gossip is part of the fun. Have lunch at the Breakers to keep the mood going, then switch gears for a visit to Lion Country Safari, where the animals roam free and you stay caged in your car. Shopping on Worth Avenue is also a required course here, not only for the amazing study in consumerism but also for the picture-perfect streets and fascinating "via" alleyways—complete with a fancy, tiled, ground-level drinking spot for pampered pooches. Wind up a day of embarrassing riches with dinner in one of the restaurants around Worth before you stop in for a sip at a local nightspot to catch up on town scandals, of which there are always plenty.

SIGHTSEEING HIGHLIGHTS

★★★ **Henry Morrison Flagler Museum**—A legend in his own time and long thereafter, Henry Flagler was not only the man who put Florida on the map—and the railroad—but he was also a power broker of note who knew how to get what he wanted. When he wanted a divorce, a thing virtually impossible in his day, he simply had legislators change the law—for one day. When he wanted a house befitting his status, he built this magnificent estate, hailed in 1902 as the Taj Mahal of North America. You will see why as you roam through acres of marble floors and columns, huge high-ceilinged rooms with elaborate moldings, glittering chandeliers, and glowing furniture. Flagler had his own railroad car, The Wanderer, and it's here beside the Flagler home. Details: Cocoanut Row and Whitehall Way; (561) 655-2833; open Tuesday through Saturday 10 a.m. to 5 p.m., Sunday noon to 5 p.m.; closed Christmas and New Year's Day. Admission $7 adults, $3 children ages 6 to 12. (2 hours)

★★★ **Lion Country Safari**—Golden-eyed lions pad across your path, giraffes lope about, and zebras streak through the fields. Safe in your car, you drive among them in this most unusual 500-acre facility where 1,300 animals roam free. In Safari World you can take a free boat trip, visit a petting zoo, ride paddle boats and a merry-go-round, see dinosaur and reptile exhibits, and play miniature golf. Details: Southern Boulevard, 15 miles west of West Palm Beach; (561) 793-1084; open daily 9:30 a.m. to 5:30 p.m., last car admitted at 4:30. Admission $14.95 adults, $9.95 children ages 3 to 16. (2 hours)

★★★ **Norton Museum of Art**—An extensive collection of Oriental art and more than 4,500 paintings by French Impressionist and post-Impressionist artists are on display in this museum, which is one of the best of its kind in the nation. Details: 1451 South Olive Avenue, West Palm Beach; (561) 832-5196 or 832-5194; open Tuesday through Saturday 10 a.m. to 5 p.m., Wednesday until 8 p.m., Sunday 1 to 5 p.m.; closed holidays. Admission $5 adults, $2 students ages 14 to 21, others free. (2 hours)

★★★ *Star of Palm Beach*—In Florida, many of the most magnificent homes are barely visible from the street but open up to the water, as you will see on a cruise aboard this paddle-wheeler that has been chugging along the Palm Beach Intracoastal Waterway, past massive mansions and the busy Port of Palm Beach for many years. You can go out just to see the sights—narrated by a captain who knows all the local lore and gossip—or take buffet lunch, dinner, or Sunday brunch cruises. Details: Phil Foster Park, 900 East Blue Heron Boulevard, Singer Island; (561) 848-7827; sightseeing cruises daily at noon and 2:30 p.m.; lunch cruises daily at noon; dinner cruises Thursday through Sunday at 7 p.m. Admission $10.87 adults, $8.68 children ages 3 to 15; lunch cruises $20.69 adults, $15.23 children; dinner $32.70 adults, $25.06 children; brunch $25.06 adults, $19.60 children. (2 hours)

✯✯ **Mounts Botanical Garden**—Garden enthusiasts will love this spot, which offers tours through an impressive array of gardens devoted to tropical plants, roses, herbs, hibiscus, and citrus—even a rain-forest environment. Details: 531 North Military Trail, West Palm Beach; (561) 233-1749; open Monday through Saturday 8:30 a.m. to 4:30 p.m., Sunday 11 a.m. to 5 p.m., guided tours Saturday at 11 a.m. and Sunday at 2:30 p.m. Admission $2 adults, children under 12 free. (2 hours)

✯✯ **Okeeheelee Nature Center**—Birds squawk and flutter, and the wind whistles through the trees at this nature center, where you can walk 5 miles of trails through 100 acres of native pine flatwoods and soggy wetlands. In the visitor center you'll see turtles, reptiles, birds, and butterflies, and you may occasionally spot a deer on the grounds. Details: 7715 Forest Hill Boulevard, West Palm Beach; (561) 233-1400; open Tuesday through Friday 1 p.m. to 4:45 p.m., Saturday and Sunday 8:15 a.m. to 4:45 p.m., with guided tours Saturday at 10 a.m. and 3 p.m.; closed Sunday from approximately May 15 to Sept. 15. Admission free. (2–3 hours)

✯✯ **Palm Beach Zoo**—There are few sounds more chilling than the roar of a jaguar, as you may discover at this huge zoo that sprawls over 23 acres and now has jaguars padding menacingly about, cuddly koalas breakfasting on eucalyptus leaves, and white Bengal cubs cuddling up to mom. Details: 1301 Summit Boulevard, West Palm Beach; (561) 547-WILD; open daily 9 a.m. to 5 p.m. Admission $6 adults, $4 children ages 3 to 12. (2–3 hours)

✯✯ **South Florida Science Museum and Planetarium**—Things clank, swing, rock, and roll at this museum, which teaches you why the world acts the way it does. Dinosaurs and other changing exhibits add new things to see. Details: 4801 Dreher Trail North, West Palm Beach; (561) 832-1988; open Sunday through Thursday 10 a.m. to 5 p.m., Friday and Saturday 10 a.m. to 10 p.m. Admission $5 adults, $3 children ages 4 to 12. (2 hours)

★ **Ann Norton Sculpture Gardens**—Not only are these 3-acre tropical gardens home to a collection of sculptor Ann Norton's monumental creations, but they also house one of the South's most notable palm collections amid more than 200 other species of plants. The gardens are not related to the Norton Museum of Art. Details: 253 Barcelona Road, West Palm Beach; (561) 832-5328; open Tuesday through Saturday 10 a.m. to 4 p.m. Admission $4 adults, $3 children ages 12 to 18, under 12 free. (2 hours)

★ **Hibel Museum of Art**—Lithographs, sculptures, paintings, and porcelains by artist Edna Hibel are the stars of this museum. Details: 150 Royal Poinciana Plaza, Palm Beach; (561) 833-6870; open Tuesday through Saturday 10 a.m. to 5 p.m., Sunday 1 p.m. to 5 p.m. Admission free. (1 hour)

★ **Palm Beach Water Taxi**—This 16-passenger launch gives you the lowdown on the mansions and yachts of Palm Beach—and a little gossip, too—on a narrated tour through the city's beautiful waterways. Details: Sailfish Marina, 98 Lake Drive, Singer Island; (561) 844-1724 or 930-8294; cruises at 11 a.m., 1 p.m., and 5 p.m. Admission $15 adults, $8 children for day cruises; $10 adults, $5 children for the shorter 5 p.m. trip. (1–1½ hours)

★ *Viking Queen* **Cruises**—This cruise ship carries 700 passengers on trips to the Bahamas and on a variety of day and evening trips, even a Sunday brunch sojourn. Gambling is the primary focus, but there's also dining, dancing, and entertainment. Details: Port of Palm Beach, U.S. 1 and Port Road, Riviera Beach; (561) 845-7447 or (800) 841-7447; sails Monday, Wednesday, Friday, and Saturday 10 a.m. to 4 p.m., Monday through Thursday 7:30 p.m. to midnight, Friday and Saturday 7:30 p.m. to 1 a.m., Sunday 11 a.m. to 5 p.m., and monthly cruises to the Freeport in the Bahamas 8 a.m. to midnight. Fares are $25 to $29.50 for all on Monday through Thursday, $44 Friday night, $39 Saturday night; $34 Sunday brunch cruises; $95 Bahamas cruises. (6–16 hours)

★ **Water Taxi**—Aboard this craft you'll visit the northern end of the county and learn a little about the area's famous and infamous people and events. Details: docked at Intracoastal Waterway Bridge at Panama Hattie's Restaurant, 11511 Ellison Wilson Road at PGA Boulevard, North Palm Beach; (561) 930-8294 or 775-2628; cruises daily at noon, 2 p.m., and 4 p.m. Admission $15 adults, $10 children ages 2 to 10. (2 hours)

SHOPPING

Worth Avenue is one of the state's—and the nation's—most famous shopping streets, a venerated boulevard that was home to Florida's first Tiffany & Company and is now also graced by Ferragamo, Gucci, Cartier, Laura Ashley, Ralph Lauren, Hermès, St. John, Chanel, Escada, Jourdan, Pierre Deux, and Georgette Klinger. Stop by—it's Worth it.

FITNESS AND RECREATION

Palm Beach has no fewer than 145 golf courses and is home to the **Professional Golfers Association**. Best-known courses include two at the Breakers Hotel and the PGA National Resort & Spa links. Plenty of tennis courts and water sports exist too.

Break into PB society slowly with a lively game of oh-so-civilized croquet, overseen by the **U.S. Croquet Association**, 11585 Polo Club Road, Wellington, (561) 753-9141, which can tell you where the tournaments are played during the October-to-May season. You can usually find a game in progress on the Breakers Hotel lawn (see Lodging).

Celebrity-watching is more important than the game at **Palm Beach Polo & Country Club**, 13198 Forest Hill Boulevard, Wellington, (561) 798-7000 or 793-1440, where HRH Prince Charles often plays during the January to mid-April season; and at **Gulfstream Polo Grounds**, 4550 Polo Club Road, Lake Worth, (561) 965-2057. Tickets are $10 to $35, excluding champagne.

Wellington, a city west of Palm Beach, is home to the **Palm Beach Polo Equestrian Club**, 13198 Forest Hill Boulevard, Wellington, (561) 793-5867, which hosts Olympic riders at a 125-acre complex that hosts the annual Florida Winter Equestrian Festival.

Race cars roar at **Moroso Motorsports Park**, 17047 Bee Line Highway (SR 710), Palm Beach Garden, (561) 622-1400, with drag racing Wednesday, Friday, and Saturday nights for $10 adults, children under 12 free. Special events including an annual Skip Barber Racing School happen year-round on its three race courses.

Fleet greyhounds race after the mechanical bunny at **Palm Beach Kennel Club**, 1111 North Congress Avenue, West Palm Beach, (561) 683-2222, where tickets are 50 cents or $1 for grandstand seats. There's also a poker club and simulcasting. Races are at 12:30 p.m. Monday, Wednesday, Thursday, and Saturday, and 7:30 p.m. Wednesday through Saturday. There's another simulcast location at 1415 West 45th Street, West Palm Beach, (561) 844-2444, open at 11:30 a.m. Wednesday through Monday from January to May.

Sharpshooters can try their eye at **Palm Beach Trap & Skeet Club**, 2950 Pierson Road, (561) 793-8787, which is open 10 a.m. to 5 p.m. Saturday and Sunday and charges $7.75.

You can rent a bicycle at **Palm Beach Bicycle Trails**, 223 Sunrise Avenue, (561) 659-4583; and **Canoe Outfitters**, (561) 746-7053, rents canoes for Loxahatchee River outings.

Rental powerboats are available from **Club Nautico Power Boat Rentals**, PGA Boulevard, Palm Beach Gardens, (561) 744-5752; and fishing fans can organize outings on charter boats docked at **Sailfish Marina**, 98 Lake Drive, Singer Island, Palm Beach Shores, (561) 844-1724 or (800) 446-4577, one of many marinas here. West Palm Beach Fishing Club, Box 468, West Palm Beach, FL 33402, publishes a $10 *Fish Finder*, with information on tides, reef, marinas, camps, charters, and tournaments.

Even diving has a touch of class here—a favorite reef has grown around a vintage Rolls-Royce Silver Shadow submerged in 1985! See it with **Dixie Divers**, 1401 South Military Trail, West Palm Beach, (561) 969-6688 or (800) 456-3188, with trips at 10 a.m. weekdays and 8 a.m. and 1 p.m. weekends for $40, or with any of a dozen dive centers operating here.

FOOD

To recover from ostentation overload, slip into the cool confines of **Café L'Europe**, 150 Worth Avenue, (561) 655-4020, a sleek and chic award-winner in the Esplanade shops; it's pricey but a great place to see and be seen. For a big-event evening, the **Florentine Room** at the Breakers (see Lodging) is a don't-miss, with a massive beamed ceiling and handsome furnishings. Prices are steep, but the atmosphere's worth every dime.

Café Protégé, 2500 Metrocentre Boulevard, West Palm Beach, (561) 687-2433, is another upscale spot, owned by the Florida Culinary Institute. Master chefs whip up memorable meals served in elegant surroundings, aided occasionally by FCI students, who help create such options as potato-crusted salmon, wood-grilled specialties, and unusual pasta combos. **Jo's**, 375 South County Road, (561) 659-6776, has been getting rave reviews for its mid-priced continental cuisine.

Charley's Crab, 456 South Ocean Boulevard, (561) 659-1500, focuses on seafood right off the boat served at a raw bar in a pubby atmosphere. Unpretentious reverse chic reigns at **Chuck & Harold's**, 207 Royal Poinciana Way, (561) 659-1440, where creative pastas, interesting seafood, and beef selections draw crowds. Lighter late-night menus are available to midnight weekdays, 1 a.m. on weekends. From the kitchen at **Nando's**, 221 Royal Palm Way, (561) 655-3031, pours *saltimbocca alla romana*, scampi, and lots of great pasta, served in a brick-lined garden atmosphere for moderate to high prices. **Testa's**, 221 Royal Poinciana Way, (561) 832-0992, is a charming café that's served lots of moderately priced Italian food here for more than 70 years. Cozy **Ta-Boó**, 221 Worth Avenue, (561) 835-3500, an Avenue mainstay for decades, is a reasonably priced and atmospheric spot with chic decor, good dining, enjoyable music, and a long-time reputation as a gathering spot for socialites. **Hamburger Heaven**, 314 South County Road, (561) 655-5277, lures princes and paupers alike to great beef ground right here; sandwiches and salads are available.

LODGING

Palm Beach has some of the most elegant hotels in Florida, crowned by the breathtaking **Breakers**, 1 County Road, (561) 655-6611 or (800) 833-3141. A downright amazing place, the Breakers is now more than 100 years old and is one of the nation's hotel treasures. In and around its towering architecture are ornate woodwork, sixteenth-century tapestries, art treasures, its own resident historian, a circular room with domed ceiling on which painted cherubs frolic, and an elegant restaurant whose massive architectural details were inspired by a Florentine palazzo. In short, it's a top award-winning hotel with the best of everything for prices ranging from $295 to $490 in peak winter season.

Four Seasons Resort, 2800 South Ocean Boulevard, (561)

PALM BEACH

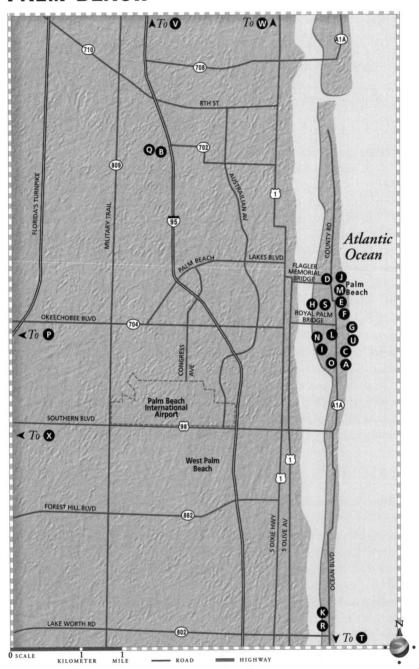

Food

- Ⓐ Café L'Europe
- Ⓑ Café Protégé
- Ⓒ Charley's Crab
- Ⓓ Chuck & Harold's
- Ⓔ Florentine Room
- Ⓕ Hamburger Heaven
- Ⓖ Jo's
- Ⓗ Nando's
- Ⓘ Ta–Boó
- Ⓙ Testa's

Lodging

- Ⓚ Beachcomber Apartment Motel
- Ⓛ Brazilian Court

Lodging (Continued)

- Ⓜ Breakers
- Ⓝ The Chesterfield
- Ⓞ The Colony
- Ⓟ Comfort Inn
- Ⓠ Courtyard by Marriott
- Ⓡ Four Seasons Resort
- Ⓢ Heart of Palm Beach
- Ⓣ Palm Beach Hawaiian Ocean Inn
- Ⓤ Palm Beach Historic Inn
- Ⓥ PGA National Resort and Spa

Camping

- Ⓦ Jonathon Dickinson State Park
- Ⓧ Lion Country Safari KOA

582-2800 or (800) 432-2335, is a drop-dead-gorgeous spot with prices to match. For its elegant furnishings, two sublimely chic, award-winning restaurants, and a beachfront location you'll pay $325 to $525 in peak season.

Blessed with 1920s Mediterranean architecture featuring fountains, columns, and flower-bedecked archways, the beautiful **Brazilian Court**, 301 Australian Avenue, (561) 655-7740 or (800) 351-5656, is beloved by many of the monied. Rates for studio kitchenettes or suites range $295 to $600 in winter.

The Colony, 155 Hammon Road, (561) 655-5430 or (800) 521-5525, is a longtime favorite here for its handsome furnishings, regal Cotillion Room dining, understated elegance, and genteel atmosphere, just a Rolls-Royce length from Worth Avenue. Peak-season rates are $245 to $325.

PGA National Resort and Spa, 400 Avenue of Champions, Palm Beach Gardens, (561) 627-2000 or (800) 633-9150, is home to the Professional Golfers Association and sports five 18-hole golf courses, tennis courts, nine pools, a spa, a sailing lake, six restaurants and lounges, and attractive rooms at $300 to $325 peak-season rates.

Palm Beach Historic Inn, 365 South County Road, (561) 832-4009, is a cozy spot with lots of chintz and lace, tucked away in an old building just steps from some of the city's most historic buildings and Worth Avenue. Its rooms are up the stairs, and winter rates including breakfast are $125 to $225.

An old-timer in town, **The Chesterfield**, 363 Cocoanut Row, (561) 659-5800 or (800) 243-7871, is a fascinating place, with a leopard-trimmed supper club, cigar room, afternoon tea, and a look of the '60s. There could hardly be a better location for a PB hotel, just steps away from Worth Avenue on a quiet side street. Peak-season rates are $245 to $310.

Heart of Palm Beach, 160 Royal Palm Way, (561) 655-5600 or (800) 523-5377, is tucked away on a pretty neighborhood street with manicured lawns just a block or so from the sea. A quiet spot with a tiny restaurant and casual atmosphere, the hotel has pleasant, although not elaborately decorated, rooms in a great location near restaurants and Flagler's elegant home. Rates are $199 in peak season.

Palm Beach Hawaiian Ocean Inn, 3550 South Ocean Boulevard, (561) 582-5631 or (800) 457-5631, is an oceanside resort about 8 miles south of Worth Avenue, with a pool and restaurant, for peak-season rates of $125.

Cuddled up to 300 feet of sand and just steps away from a fishing pier, **Beachcomber Apartment Motel**, 3024 South Ocean Boulevard (FL A-1-A), (561) 585-4646 or (800) 833-7122, lives up to its name. You'll find a variety of accommodations here for rates of $55 to $120.

Comfort Inn, 5981 Okeechobee Boulevard, West Palm Beach, (561) 697-3388 or (800) 221-2222, is a comfortable spot near the airport about 8 miles west of downtown Palm Beach with a pool and basic accommodations for $99.95 in peak season. **Courtyard by Marriott**, 600 Northpoint Parkway, West Palm Beach, (561) 640-9000 or (800) 321-2211, is a well-maintained spot with an outdoor pool and indoor hydrotherapy splasher. Peak rates are $89 to $130.

CAMPING

Jonathon Dickinson State Park, 16450 SE Federal Highway, Hobe Sound, (561) 546-2771 or (800) 746-1466, is one of the largest parks in

South Florida and one of the region's favorite campgrounds, often booked far in advance. Covering 11,000 acres, the park surrounds the Loxahatchee River, Florida's only designated Wild and Scenic River. Cabin rentals are $65 to $85 and full-facility campsites are $18 to $20. **Lion Country Safari KOA**, Southern Boulevard, West Palm Beach, (561) 793-9797, charges $24 for hookups and $21 for tents, and has a general store and heated pool.

NIGHTLIFE

Performing Arts

Stars of song and dance from country-and-western to opera and ballet appear at the city's sparkling concert hall, the **Kravis Center for the Performing Arts**, 701 Okeechobee Boulevard, West Palm Beach, (561) 832-7469. Touring Broadway productions take to the boards at **Royal Poinciana Playhouse**, 70 Royal Poinciana Plaza, Palm Beach, (561) 659-3310. The **Burt Reynolds Institute for Theatre Training**, 201 Clematis Street, West Palm Beach, (561) 833-9190 or 833-8669, is an apprenticeship program for young actors who work alongside guest artists in comedies, dramas, and musicals. **Society of the Four Arts**, 2 Four Arts Plaza, (561) 655-7226, is an architectural showpiece in the city, housing a museum, library, gardens, and theater. For updated info on arts activities, try the **ArtsLine**, (561) 471-2901 or (800) 882-ARTS.

Clubs and Bars

Tops among night spots are two restaurants that hold their own for late-night action: **Ta-Boó** and **Chuck & Harold's** (see Food listings), both very popular. Add to that **E. R. Bradley's Saloon**, 111 Bradley Place, Palm Beach, (561) 833-3520, a 1920s gambling casino turned 1990s watering hole, packed day and night. **Au Bar**, the infamous nightspot in which a Kennedy nephew once met a woman and trouble, is now called **François**, 336 Royal Poinciana Way, (561) 832-4800.

Scenic Route: Mansion Row

Quite shattering quantities of money are required to put a roof over one's coiffure and a garden under one's Guccis in Palm Beach, as you will see on a driving tour of the city's awesome mansions. Millionaires move at the drop of a dollar, so the mansions mentioned may have new owners by the time you read this.

Begin on Florida's route A-1-A, known as **South Ocean Boulevard**, south of Palm Beach in Manalapan, where the hottest rumors have it that **Rush Limbaugh**, the voice—some say the Mouth—of capitalism, has just established a beachhead. House numbers get lower as you go north, then rise north of Worth Avenue. On the other end of the city, Southern Boulevard is just about as far south of Palm Beach as you can live and still retain redeeming social value.

Look for 1768 South Ocean, where **John O. Picket Jr.**, owner of the New York Islanders hockey team, occasionally occupies his 13,233-square-foot home, built in 1937 for E. F. Hutton. Right around the bend, at 1500, **Jan Annenberg Hooker**, whose family publishes *TV Guide*, put a $27.5-million price tag on her house. At 1482 lives **Malcolm Blazer**, who plunked down $2.5 million for 12,272 square feet of homestead. Blazer parted with almost 100 times as much when he bought the Tampa Bay Buccaneers football team for $192 million. At 1435 South Ocean, **Rod Stewart** and wife, model **Rachel Hunter**, own a marble-clad oceanside home with a showy staircase and a price tag of $7.2 million. Rod and Rachel bought these digs from **Barbara Massey Rogers**, whose daddy, Jack, turned a passel of poultry into a Kentucky Fried Chicken empire. When Barb sold her house to the Stewarts, she moved into the yellow oceanside house at 1125. **Casa Apava**, at 1300 South Ocean, is owned by Revlon financier **Ron Perelman**, who paid $11.6 million for the manse and socked another $12 million into renovations to the 1932 home.

Stay to the right at Southern Boulevard, where the big bend is home to the **Bath & Tennis Club**, a beloved play place for rich kids. On your left at 1100 is the most famous house in Palm Beach: majestic **Mar-A-Lago**, built in 1927 for Post cereal heiress **Marjorie Meriweather Post**, who loved to square-dance in the 55,700-square-foot house that covers 17 acres stretching between Lake Worth and the Atlantic. Post sold it to the government, which sold it to **Donald Trump** for a mere $10 million. He turned it into a club with a $75,000 initiation fee that allows you to trundle off to one of the house's 58 bedrooms, 33 bathrooms, three bomb shelters, theater, ballroom, and nine-hole golf course.

At 780 South Ocean is a home that proves what a million American consumers can buy: it's owned by **Bud Paxson**, of Home Shopping Network, who paid $12 million for this house with five master suites. The former owner was **Woolworth Donahue**, of five-and-dime fame. Beatle **John Lennon** and wife **Yoko Ono** once owned the house at 720 South Ocean, which was formerly held by socialite **Brownie McLean**, who married into the family that owned the Hope Diamond. Yoko bought the spot for $725,000, remodeled it, and sold it for $3.15 million.

Turn left at Jungle Road to get a look at the cozy little spread owned by **Ivana**, the former Mrs. Donald Trump, who uttered PB's Quote of the Year: "Don't get mad . . . get everything." Following her own advice, she secured a $4-million charmer at 126 Jungle Road. Back on South Ocean Boulevard, see the house a cheeseburger in paradise bought: singer **Jimmy Buffett**, of "Margaritaville" fame, owns 540 South Ocean at Via Marina. Just north of Via

MANSION ROW

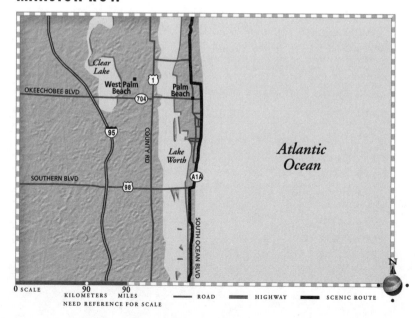

Marina, turn west on Gulfstream Road and north on Middle Road to the end, where billionaire **John Kluge**—very high on the list of the world's richest men—lives.

At 126 Ocean Drive is a white Georgian manse long owned by cosmetics queen **Estee Lauder**. There, the road turns left, and you pass the ethereally beautiful architecture of **Bethesda-by-the-Sea Church**. Turn right at the light and head north on **County Road** to see grandiose architecture at its finest at **The Breakers**, a century-old, world-famous hotel. Drop in at the **Alcazar Bar** for ocean views and barman Pierre's memories of PB life.

At 513 North County Road is the largest house in Palm Beach, a 64,000-square-foot monster built in 1989 for nursing home magnate **Abe Gosman**. He paid nearly $13 million for the property formerly held by The Limited chain owner **Leslie Wexner**, whose shops were deemed unworthy of Worth Avenue.

At 548 North County Road is **Montsorrel**, where junk-bond kingpin **Nelson Peltz** paid $13.5 million for a mansion whose name means "Mountain of Sorrow," a reference to a former owner who shot himself there after a stock-market dive. Finally, 1095 North County Road is the place everyone wants to see: the **Kennedy** compound, where the clan played for more than 30 years. President **John F. Kennedy** made the 9,300-square-foot house his winter White House; the family sold it in 1995 for $4.9 million to buyout specialist **John Castle**. ◼

13
ORLANDO

Just 25 years ago Orlando was a small rural town, a sleepy backwater with no idea what was in store for it. Then a mouse roared into the wilderness, turning cow pastures to city and many of the meek into millionaires. Now pigs dance and elephants fly here, ducks quack jokes and reality is on permanent vacation. Today's Orlando is a tourism megalopolis, the most popular visitor destination in the world. Every day thousands stream through its theme park turnstiles to suspend reality and let inner (and outer) children play.

Orlando's impact stretches from Walt Disney World's 30,000 acres all the way east to the Kennedy Space Center at Port Canaveral, west to Tampa, north to Ocala, and south the Lake Wales and beyond. And the growth shows no sign of slowing down. The region already has more than 70 attractions vieing for attention, over 100,000 hotel rooms, and thousands of restaurants, and yet much more of everything is on the drawing boards.

Sometimes crowded, occasionally too hot, too cold, or too wet, Orlando is nonetheless always magical. Here you'll find a land that loves children, a place that welcomes you with genuine hospitality and warms you with plenty of smiles—a magic kingdom indeed. ◼

ORLANDO

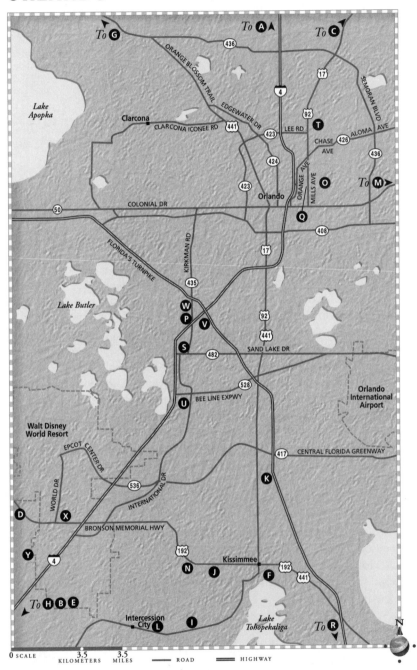

Sights

- Ⓐ Big Tree Park
- Ⓑ Bok Tower Gardens
- Ⓒ Central Florida Zoological Park
- Ⓓ Chinatown/Splendid China
- Ⓔ Cypress Gardens
- Ⓕ Cypress Island
- Ⓖ Don Garlits Museum of Drag Racing
- Ⓗ Fantasy of Flight
- Ⓘ Fighter Pilots U.S.A. 62nd Fighter Squadron
- Ⓙ Flying Tigers Warbird Air Museum
- Ⓚ Gatorland
- Ⓛ Green Meadow Petting Farm
- Ⓜ Jungle Adventures
- Ⓝ Jungleland Wildlife Park
- Ⓞ Leu Gardens
- Ⓟ Mystery Fun House/ Starbase Omega
- Ⓠ Orlando Science Center
- Ⓡ Reptile World Serpentarium
- Ⓢ Ripley's Believe It or Not!
- Ⓣ Scenic Boat Tour
- Ⓤ Sea World of Florida
- Ⓥ Trainland
- Ⓦ Universal Studios
- Ⓧ Walt Disney World
- Ⓨ A World of Orchids

A PERFECT DAY IN ORLANDO

If you have just one day in Orlando, spend it at one of the big three attractions—Walt Disney World, Universal Studios, or Sea World. Finish the day with a visit to one of Epcot's French restaurants, followed by late-night carousing at Pleasure Island. But one day is unlikely to be enough. Schedule several days in Orlando to visit the parks you missed on the first day, and spend the evenings dining and laughing at Church Street Station. If you have even more time, visit Cypress Gardens, Bok Tower, Chinatown/Splendid China, Leu Gardens, or Gatorland, and don't miss the region's entertaining themed dinner evenings. Head to the lovely village of Winter Park for elegant shopping and dining—or just for a look at its shady streets and elegant mansions—and spend the evening sailing the St. Johns River on a moonlight *Rivership Romance* cruise. Work in a visit to the village of Cassadega, where dozens of psychics live in a spooky little village, or to the antique stores of the pretty New England–style village of Mount Dora. Go tubing on the Little Wekiva River or fishing in one of the hundreds of lakes that nestle into the region's rolling hills.

SIGHTSEEING HIGHLIGHTS

★★★ **Cypress Gardens**—Here, in an ancient cypress swamp, is one of the state's most serene and beautiful botanical gardens, home to a wonderland of blossoms peppered with a colorful rainbow of hoop-skirted hostesses. An amazing array of topiaries is among the newest attractions at these famous gardens, which also feature champion waterskiers, a butterfly conservatory, a reptile discovery program, ice skaters, a shopping village, children's rides, and a whole bouquet of seasonal floral festivals. The latest addition is the Biblical Gardens, featuring plants mentioned in the Bible. Details: State Road 540 West, Winter Haven; (941) 324-2111 or (800) 282-2123; open daily 9:30 a.m. to 7 p.m., later in winter months. Admission $29.50 adults including one child, $19.50 each additional child. (4–6 hours)

★★★ **Sea World of Florida**—Killer whales that cuddle up for a kiss, penguins that paddle around their own snowy world, and sharks that glide eerily over your head are just part of the wonders of Sea World, one of Orlando's top three attractions and the world's largest marine-life theme park. Star of the show is Shamu, a massive killer whale who streaks around a huge pool with his trainer perched on his back. Shamu and baby are joined by a bevy of talented dolphins who whirl, twirl, and toss their tails in a dazzling daily display of deep-sea terpsichorean talents. My vote for the most chilling sight in Florida is not the glacial Penguin Encounter but the eerily silent acrylic tunnel through which you glide aboard a moving sidewalk as giant sharks streak through the water around you and over your head. Errrrrg. You can also see a tidal pool, a coral reef, pearl diving, a Key West village, and many entertaining animal shows. Sea World's Education Department offers three 60-minute tours with in-depth visits to polar bears and penguins, birds or sharks. Several restaurants and a nightly luau dinner party add to the fun. Details: 7007 Sea World Drive; (407) 363-2613, (800) 327-2424, or (800) 432-1178; open daily 9 a.m. to 10 p.m. Admission $40.95 adults, $33.90 children ages 3 to 9. (8 hours)

★★★ **Universal Studios**—You gotta love Universal Studios. King Kong's banana-breath on your neck as he tries to getcha. Jaws' fearsome dental work bearing down on you. A wild ride Back to the Future, and—watch it!—the Terminator's on the prowl! Universal's rides are fun; its central square, where cameras can shoot a different backdrop in every direction, is amazingly realistic. Its restaurants are pleasant, its scenery is tranquil, and its star lookalikes strolling the streets are amusing. There's something for everyone here and special treasures for movie fanatics, who can travel through the ages of film. Universal's on the grow again, soon to open an Island of Adventure theme park and four themed hotels.

Even the youngest among us will find their favorites at **Nickelodeon Studios**, which films its popular programs in park facilities. Film buffs might consider booking Universal's four-hour VIP guided tour of street sets and production facilities, which gives you an in-depth look at the park and backstage admittance, letting you avoid the lines. Details: 1000 Universal Studios Plaza; (407) 363-8000; open daily with varying hours that generally run 9 a.m. to 7 p.m., but call for exact times. Admission $39.75 adults, $32 children ages 3 to 9; two-day passes $59.75 adults, $49.75 children; $94.95 adults, $77.95 children for a three-park, five-day Vacation Pass that includes admission to Universal Studios, Sea World, and Wet 'n' Wild; $125.95 adults, $99.95 children for a four-park, seven-day pass that includes admission to Busch Gardens; $75 adults, $69 children for annual passes. $100 per person for a four-hour VIP tour; an eight-hour tour is $975 for groups of 15 people. (2–8 hours)

★★★ **Walt Disney World**—What began as a one-day adventure in cartoonist Walt Disney's imaginative wonderland is today so huge that it takes many days to see and do it all. Growing and changing even as you read, this renowned theme park is the most popular attraction in the world, attended by thousands every day and millions in the 25 years since it opened. Today it's really three parks rolled into one: **Magic Kingdom**, which is divided into "lands"—Tomorrowland, Adventureland, Frontierland, Fantasyland, and Mickey's Toontown Fair; **Epcot**, the Experimental Prototype Community of Tomorrow, in which some of the nation's major corporations sponsor exhibits that take entertaining looks at the past and the future, and 11 nations are showcased; and **Disney-MGM**, which explores the cinematic world with wild rides and lots of interactive fun.

All three parks have plenty of thriller rides and wild experiences, dozens of shops brimming with fun gifts, and entertaining restaurants.

Mickey, Minnie, Pluto, and their buddies turn up everywhere you look throughout the parks, and there's some kind of entertainment going on nearly every hour of the day and night.

Here are some highlights from each of the three parks:

In the Magic Kingdom, **Main Street U.S.A.**, the 18-story Cinderella Castle is a "wow" and has a delightful dining room. It's fun to see Main Street from a seat aboard a trolley drawn by big, clip-clopping horses. Tops among the many entertainment possibilities here is the daily Main Street Parade, starring Mickey, Minnie, Snow White, Cinderella, and the rest of the legendary gang, togged out in their best duds and cavorting with the audience.

In **Adventureland**, Pirates of the Caribbean is a popular favorite, followed closely by Enchanted Tiki Birds and the Jungle Cruise. **Frontierland**'s Country Bear Jamboree is beloved by many, as is Big Thunder Mountain Railroad, which ends with a splash and is one of the park's most popular rides. Our nation's history comes to life at **Liberty Square**, where the Hall of Presidents features animated, life-size figures that gesture as they talk about the nation they served.

Dumbo, Mickey, and Ms. White (a.k.a Snow) and her odd little followers dwell in **Fantasyland**, where Peter Pan's Flight remains a huge hit with the crowds. It's a Small World takes you on a globetrotting journey accompanied by tiny singing dolls in native costumes. Meanwhile, Captain Nemo takes you twenty thousand leagues under the sea aboard the *Nautilus*. Roller-coaster fans should head straight for **Tomorrowland** to the number-one attraction, Space Mountain, where you rocket off into the blackness on a brief but wild ride.

At Epcot's **World Showcase** the nations of the world display their architectural highlights and distinctive handicrafts; head for Mexico, where a jaguar roars in the darkness of a re-created adobe village. Norway's Viking ship ride is fun, and China's 360-degree film screen, showing you where you're going and where you've been, offers an amazing overview of that land. In the United Kingdom, the Rose & Crown Pub is Brit at its best. France has—no surprise—the best restaurants.

To cool off and treat your aching tootsies, jump aboard one of the launches that takes you across the lake to **Future World**. Its best spots are Universe of Energy, which stars wonderfully quizzical dinosaurs amid strange swampy smells, and The Land, where you sail past cucumbers that grow up to 12 inches a day!

At Disney-MGM Studios take the **Backstage Studio Tour** for a close look at costume design, sound effects, and animation techniques; follow the tour with a journey to **Catastrophe Canyon**, where you're caught in an earthquake and a deluge. Two standouts in this park are the **Tower of Terror**, which drops you 13 floors—twice!—and the **Great Movie Ride**, an exciting journey on which you get all-too-close to some slimy stuff from *Alien*, meet Tarzan swinging through the jungle, and find yourself in the middle of some unexpected events. At the soon-to-be **Animal Kingdom**, scheduled to open in the spring of 1998, you'll walk and talk with the animals, bump and bounce on animal-oriented thrill rides, and wander in exotic landscapes.

To keep its visitors coming back (and back, and back), Walt Disney World has a whole bevy of recreational facilities, from tranquil **Discovery Island**, where rare birds warble and Galapagos tortoises slumber, to **River Country**, Walt Disney World's ol' swimming hole where you play among waterfalls and on flume slides, rafts, and inner tubes. At **Typhoon Lagoon**, you can board a log boat and plummet 18 feet down a most unusual "mountain" or bodysurf a 4-foot wave onto a white-sand beach. On **Blizzard Beach**, the latest in Walt Disney World's long list of entertainment facilities, you stumble into a freak Florida snowstorm that melts to become a wintery, watery wonderland with a free-fall speed ride billed as the world's tallest, a family raft ride, and a lazy inner-tube trip, all in heated waters.

For an in-depth experience, sign up for a program at **Disney Institute**, (407) 827-4800, which offers 40 hands-on programs in nine areas: Entertainment Arts, Sports and Fitness, Lifestyles, Story Arts, Culinary Arts, Design Arts, Environment, Youth, and Performing Arts. Details: I-4 Exit 26B, on Highway 192; (407) 824-4321 or 939-7727 for resort reservations; open daily with hours that vary frequently for each park and recreation area—call for daily updates. Admission for a one-day pass to the Magic Kingdom, Epcot, or Disney-MGM $42.14 adults, $33.92 children ages 3 to 9; a four-day value ticket including one day at each of three parks and one more day at any of the three is $142.04 adults, $113.42 children; a four-day Park Hopper, with unlimited admission to any park on any day for four days, is $159 adults, $127.20 children; a five-day multipark Park Hopper with unlimited admission to the three parks for five days and seven-day admission to recreation areas including Pleasure Island, Typhoon Lagoon, Blizzard Beach, River Country, and Discovery Island is $217.30 adults, $173.84 children. An annual pass allowing unlimited admission to the parks and recreation facilities is $380.54 adults, $323.30 children. (8 hours for each park/recreation area)

★★ **Bok Tower Gardens**—One of the most tranquil spots in Florida, this stately Gothic tower rises 295 feet over the rolling hills in the stillness of Mountain Lake Sanctuary on Iron Mountain, once a sacred Native American site. Set atop the highest hill in Florida, the pink and gray marble tower houses a 57-bell carillon whose notes ring out every half-hour, adding a 45-minute recital at 3 p.m. daily. Details: 1151 Tower Boulevard, Lake Wales; (941) 676-1408; open daily 8 a.m. to 6 p.m., last entry at 5 p.m. Admission $4 adults, $1 children ages 5 to 12. (2 hours)

★★ **Central Florida Zoological Park**—Home to more than 400 animals, ranging from tigers and lions to monkeys and birds, the zoo sprawls over 21 acres that are part of a 109-acre cypress and oak forest. Details: 3755 Highway 17/92, Lake Monroe; (407) 323-4450; open daily 9 a.m. to 5 (except Thanksgiving and Christmas). Admission $7 adults, $3 children ages 3 to 12. (4 hours)

★★ **Chinatown/Splendid China**—Mysterious China comes to Orlando in this unusual theme park that features replicas—some full-size, some miniaturized—of China's renowned sights, from the Great Wall to Buddhist temples. Chinese cuisine and shopping too. Details: 3000 Splendid China Boulevard, Kissimmee; (407) 396-7111 or (800) 244-6226; open daily 9:30 a.m. to 7 p.m., longer hours in some seasons; restaurants stay open later. Admission $28.88 adults, $18.18 children ages 5 to 12. (4 hours)

★★ **Fighter Pilots U.S.A. 62nd Fighter Squadron**—Now here's a real adventure! Sit in on an hour of ground school training, then climb into an SF260 Marchetti fighter plane, take the controls, and shoosh! You're off into the wild blue yonder, caught in a dogfight at 6,000 feet! Accompanied by a fighter pilot, you're at the controls as you swoop and shoot at the other guy—bring a friend to beat, they suggest. When one of you shoots your laser beam at a crucial spot, you go up in smoke—and it's all videotaped so you can show the folks back home your heroic moment . . . or maybe not. No age limit, but you need to be at least 5 feet 2 inches to reach pedals. Details: 4010 4th Street, Kissimmee; (407) 931-4333 or 800-56-TOP-GUN; flights at 9 a.m. and noon Wednesday through Sunday. Admission $795 per person. (4–5 hours)

★★ **Flying Tigers Warbird Air Museum**—World War II by air comes to life in this museum dedicated to the flying machines of that devastating conflict. Among the 40 aircraft on display or being reassembled before your eyes is the only restored B-24 bomber in the world, along with a squadron of other big bombers and two rooms of artifacts, including uniforms, guns, bombs, and medals. A tour guide fills you in on the war memorabilia. Details: 231 North Hoagland Boulevard, Kissimmee; (407) 933-1942; open daily 9 a.m. to 6 p.m. Admission $6 adults, $5 children ages 5 to 12. (1 hour)

★★ **Gatorland**—If you occasionally consider throwing some annoying person to the alligators, here's your opportunity to practice with a little chicken, a favorite delicacy of the 5,000 alligators who live here. A talented lot, the 'gators have learned to leap for food in the Gator Jumparoo, a quite-uncommon activity for these ground-loving creatures. Enjoy the great gift shop and the opportunity to try smoked and deep-fried 'gator treats. Details: 14501 South Orange Blossom Trail, Orlando; (407) 855-5496; open daily 8 a.m. to sunset. Admission $13.95 adults, $8.95 children ages 10 to 12, $6.48 children ages 3 to 9. (2 hours)

★★ **Leu Gardens**—Florida's largest formal rose garden is the highlight of these sublime acres, where creamy camellias, flamboyant orchids, and thousands of other blossoms glow in the shadow of historic Leu House, the beautifully restored home of the family for whom these gardens were named. Details: 1920 North Forest Avenue, Orlando; (407) 246-2620; open daily 9 a.m. to 5 p.m. (except Christmas), to 8 p.m. in summer. Admission $3 adults, $1 children ages 6 to 16. (2 hours)

★★ **Mystery Fun House/Starbase Omega**—You can roam among 15 chambers of funny mirrors and weird stuff, play laser tag, journey to the Omega dimension with a trip through an asteroid field, interact with humanoids on a "space gravity" playing surface, try your skills at a shooting gallery, or play Jurassic-era mini-golf. Details: 8767 Major Boulevard, Orlando; (407) 351-3355; open daily 10 a.m. to 11 p.m., box office closes at 9. Admission $7.95 all ages. (2–4 hours)

★★ **Orlando Science Center**—This center debuted in 1997 with some unusual offerings, including opportunities to peer into a sinkhole, journey through the body as a particle of food, and play with high-tech computers. Things whirr, whistle, and whang in ten themed exhibit halls that include planetary travel for the "cosmic tourist" and an interactive "show biz science" display detailing tricks of the theater trade. Changing exhibits have included dinosaurs. Details: 777 East Princeton Street, Orlando; (407) 514-2000; open Monday through Thursday 9 am. to 5 p.m., Friday and Saturday to 9 p.m., Sunday noon to 5 p.m. Admission $8 for adults, $14 if you want to attend planetarium show and a film on underwater life, $6.50 or $11.50 for children. (2–3 hours)

★★ Ripley's Believe It or Not!—Things weird (a shrinking head, for instance, and pictures of a knife-eating man) and occasionally wonderful, ranging from world disaster exhibits to antiques, are on display at this strange spot that absolutely delights in the oddities of the world. Details: 8201 International Drive, Orlando; (407) 363-4418 or (800) 998-4418; open daily 9 a.m. to 11 p.m. Admission $9.95 adults, $6.95 children ages 4 to 12. (2 hours)

★★ Scenic Boat Tour—Operating in the lakes and canals of postcard-pretty Winter Park for more than 50 years, this boating outing takes you past some of the city's magnificent mansions, lovely Rollins College, and the rainbow hues of Kraft Azalea Gardens. Details: 312 East Morse Boulevard at the water, Winter Park; (407) 644-4056; open daily 10 a.m. to 4 p.m. (except Christmas), with sailings on the hour. Admission $6 adults, $3 children under age 12. (1 hour)

★ Cypress Island—Put on that pith helmet and head for a camera safari at this 200-acre island on pretty Lake Tohopekaliga, where more than 400 exotic animals await, including emus, sheep, llamas, peacocks, deer, ponies, Arabian and Clydesdale horses, and alligators. You can also go Jet Skiing or horseback riding, hike a nature trail, or visit a petting zoo. Details: Dickerman Island at Kissimmee lakefront, 1541 Scotty's Road, Kissimmee; (407) 935-0087; open Wednesday through Sunday 10 a.m. to 5 p.m. Admission (for boat trip and island visit) $10 adults, $5 children ages 3 to 12. (3 hours)

★ Don Garlits Museum of Drag Racing—"Big Daddy" Don Garlits, king of the drag racers, spotlights the American mania for speed machines here in two museums, one devoted to antique cars, including The Fonz's beloved 1950 Merc from TV's *Happy Days*; the other to Garlits' Swamp Rat racing cars and other notable drag machines, including the

Little Red Wagon, a truck that can race down a track on its back wheels. Details: 13700 SW 16th Avenue, Ocala; (352) 245-8661; open daily 9 a.m. to 5 p.m., (except Christmas). Admission $7.50 adults for the drag racing museum, $5 to see the antique cars, and $10 for both; $3 children ages 3 to 12. (2 hours)

★ **Fantasy of Flight**—Those with their feet squarely off the ground will love this attraction that features 20 vintage aircraft, a World War II diorama starring a B-17 Flying Fortress, and do-it-yourself flight simulators—even a 1930s art deco diner. Details: 1400 Broadway Boulevard, Polk City; (941) 984-3500; open daily 9 a.m. to 5 p.m. Admission $10.95 adults, $7.95 children ages 5 to 12. (2 hours)

★ **Green Meadow Petting Farm**—Peanuts, the abandoned baby buffalo bottle-fed into a lovable big bruiser who's cuddly as a kitten, is the star of the show at this 40-acre farm, where you can get up-close and personal with goats, sheep, pigs, ducks, llamas, and an ostrich. Milk a cow, ride a pony, or jump on the hay wagon and rumble off across the fields. Details: 1368 South Poinciana Boulevard, Kissimmee; (407) 846-0770; open daily 9:30 a.m. to 4 p.m., farm open to 5:30 p.m. Admission $13 adults and children over age 2. (2 hours)

★ **Jungle Adventures**—Cruise through the eerie waters of a swamp and take a close look at some of Florida's weird native creatures: the endangered Florida panther, alligators, snakes, and the like. Four daily wildlife shows explain these creatures and their part in the tropical environment they inhabit. Details: 26205 East Highway 50, Christmas; (407) 568-2885; open daily 9 a.m. to 6 p.m. Admission $9.75 adults, $7.50 children ages 3 to 11. (2 hours)

★ **Jungleland Wildlife Park**—Lions, leopards, tigers, bears, monkeys, wallabies, deer, goats, birds, and alligators are part of the scenery at this wildlife park that features daily 'gator-wrestling shows. Details: 4580 West Highway 192, Kissimmee; (407) 396-1012; open daily 9 a.m. to 6 p.m. Admission $9.95 adults, $6.95 children ages 3 to 11. (2 hours)

★ **Reptile World Serpentarium**—Things that slither and snap are the stars of the show at this serpentarium, where you can watch some very brave folks "milk" snakes for their venom. Details: 5705 West U.S. 192, St. Cloud; (407) 892-6905; open Tuesday through Sunday 9 a.m. to 5:30 p.m. Admission $4.25 adults, $3.25 students ages 6 to 17, and $2.25 children ages 3 to 5. (1 hour)

★ **Trainland**—Who can resist the Little Engine That Could, scooting around a track through miniature villages? Irresistible holiday trains toot off every day here, but the star of the show is a big G-gauge train layout that's part of a scavenger hunt—you might win one of the train layouts awarded each month. A display of antique toy trains is a favorite with the crowds, and for those who want to do it themselves, there's a 1-mile outdoor train ride. Details: 8255 International Drive, Orlando; (407) 363-9002; open Monday through Saturday 10 a.m. to 6:30 p.m., Sunday 10 a.m. to 6:30 p.m. Admission $8.95 adults, $5.95 children ages 3 to 12. (2 hours)

★ **A World of Orchids**—These delicate blossoms bloom their hearts out in this huge greenhouse that's been turned into a tropical rainforest attraction devoted to the care and breeding of the famous flowers. Details: 2501 North Old Lake Wilson Road, Kissimmee; (407) 396-1887; open daily 9 a.m. to 5:30 p.m. Admission $8.95 adults, free for children under age 15. (1 hour)

Big Tree Park—This park is worth a stop to see the 3,500-year-old bald cypress tree named "The Senator." It measures 138 feet around! Details: General Hutchinson's Parkway, Longwood; (407) 788-0405; open daily 8 a.m. to 6 p.m. Admission free. (1 hour)

CULTURAL ACTIVITIES

Here's something new in Orlando: **CultureQuest**, (407) 855-6434 or (800) 327-5254, a narrated city tour and shuttle service to more than 15 art, science, and historical attractions. You can get on and off whenever you like for $18 adults, $15 children ages 4 to 17.

    Morse Museum of American Art, 445 Park Avenue North, Winter Park, (407) 645-5311, has the world's largest collection of Louis Comfort Tiffany's glowing stained-glass art pieces and works of other American artists. They're displayed Tuesday through Saturday 9:30 a.m. to 4 p.m. and Sunday 1 p.m. to 4 p.m., for $3 adults, $1 students ages 12 to 17. The **Orlando Museum of Art**, Loch Haven Park, 2416 North

Mills Avenue, Orlando, (407) 896-4231, doubled its size in 1997 to house its permanent collection of American art, African and pre-Columbian artifacts, and such major shows as the Imperial Tombs of China. It's open Tuesday through Saturday 9 a.m. to 5 p.m., Sunday noon to 5 p.m. for $4 adults, $2 children ages 3 to 11. **Maitland Art Center**, 231 West Packwood Avenue, Maitland, (407) 539-2181, was built in 1937 as part of an artists' colony, and its architecture, adorned with Aztec-Mayan stone carvings, is now on the National Register of Historic Sites. It's open Monday through Thursday 9 a.m. to 5:30 p.m., Saturday and Sunday noon to 4:30 p.m. Free.

Osceola County Historical Society, 750 North Bass Road, Kissimmee, (407) 396-8644, features a "Cracker" house, a term that refers to early cow-punching residents who cracked long whips to keep cattle in line. You'll also see a country store, nature preserve, antique fire trucks, and a Victorian parlor; open Tuesday through Friday 10 a.m. to 4 p.m.

SHOPPING

Shopping has been elevated to an Olympic sport in Orlando, where each of the big three theme parks—Universal, Walt Disney World, and Sea World—focuses sharply on the huge income derived from gift sales. You'll find hundreds of shops at those three attractions and, in fact, at every attraction in the region. Further shopping opportunities exist at **Crossroads of Lake Buena Vista**, at SR 535 and I-4 just outside WDW, (407) 827-7300; and on **International Drive**, which is avenue-to-boulevard in shops of all variety. **Church Street**, home of Church Street Station, also has dozens of shops.

Longtime king of the Orlando discount shop/factory outlet is **Belz Factory World Outlet**, 5401 West Oakridge Road, Orlando, (407) 352-9611, where more than 160 stores—including Bugle Boy, Cannon, Anne and Calvin Klein, Harvé Bernard, and Bass Shoes—offer the best of the rest at discount prices. A similar spot is **International Designer Outlet**, 5211 International Drive, Orlando, (407) 352-3632, with outlets for Saks Fifth Avenue, Jones New York, Ann Taylor, and Donna Karan, among many others. More discount deals are offered at **Kissimmee Manufacturers Outlet**, 4673 West Highway 192, Kissimmee, (407) 396-8900, where Nike, American Tourister, Fieldcrest, and others hold court; and at **Lake Buena Vista Factory Stores**, 15201 South Apopka-Vineland Road,

Orlando, (407) 239-5429, where more than 30 factory-direct outlets are gathered.

Shopping centers with a continuing round of free entertainment and plenty of restaurants and pubs include **Old Town Shopping, Dining & Entertainment Attraction**, 5770 Highway 192, Kissimmee, (407) 396-4888 or (800) 843-4202, and **Mercado**, 8445 International Drive, Orlando, (407) 345-9337.

Hands down, the most beautiful place to shop in Central Florida is shady **Park Avenue** in nearby Winter Park. Considered one of the three loveliest shopping boulevards in the state, right up there with Fort Lauderdale's Las Olas Boulevard and Palm Beach's Worth Avenue, Park Avenue is enchanting. Don't miss it. Shops are open daily 10 a.m. to 6 p.m.

Flea World, 4311 Highway 17-92, Sanford, (407) 330-1792, claims to be the largest market in the nation under one roof, with more than 1,700 dealers plus lots of regular folks offloading their stuff. Hours are 9 a.m. to 6 p.m. Friday though Sunday.

FITNESS AND RECREATION

Golfers will find more than 125 courses in the region, including six 18-hole courses at Walt Disney World, (407) 939-GOLF, where greens fees are in the $45 to $70 range. Walt Disney World also has a little nine-hole walking course that's great for young duffers or adults ($12 for kids, $24 adults) and Fantasia Fairways, a miniaturized course for youngsters.

If you've ever wondered what it must be like to drive a car at 150 m.p.h., here's your chance to find out. In 1997 Walt Disney World added something new: the **Richard Petty Driving Experience**. Here you can try the $100 Riding Experience, which includes a three-lap ride around the 1-mile oval in a two-seater stock car; a three-hour, $400 Rookie Experience, which includes eight laps of driving thrills and training; and a $1,300 Experience of a Lifetime: three ten-lap training sessions in which you work on establishing a comfortable driving line and building your speed.

Orlando has 800 tennis courts in hotels and parks, and 300 lakes provide fishing and swimming.

You can even go ice skating in Orlando! **Rock on Ice**, 7500 Canada Avenue, Orlando, (407) 352-9878, has an Olympic-size rink open daily with DJ music and wild lighting. Hyatt Regency Grand Cypress Hotel operates the **Grand Cypress Equestrian Center**, 1

Grand Cypress Boulevard, Orlando, (407) 239-1234, for horseback-riding lessons and trail rides. If you'd like to try waterskiing, head for **Buena Vista Water Sports/Dave's Ski School**, 13245 Lake Bryan Drive, Orlando, (407) 239-6939, open 8 a.m. to dusk daily for water-skiing lessons and rides, Jet Ski rentals, and tube rides, as well as daylight beach parties and even luau and sunset cruises.

Orlando Arena, 600 Amelia Avenue, Orlando, is home to the **Orlando Magic**, the city's National Basketball Association team, (407) 649-3200, which has tickets for $20 to $115; and a minor league hockey team, the **Orlando Solar Bears**, (407) 428-6600, which plays from September though April for ticket prices in the $6 to $26 range. If baseball's your game, the **Houston Astros** train at Osceola County Stadium & Sports Complex, 1000 Bill Beck Boulevard, Kissimmee, (407) 933-5400, in February and March; tickets are $6 to $10. In 1997 Walt Disney World went into sports in a big way when it opened the huge Walt Disney World International Sports Complex, which features a 7,500-seat baseball stadium that's now the spring training ground for the **Atlanta Braves**, (407) 363-6600 or (407) 939-7727. Rodeo has long been a favorite recreation in Kissimmee's cow country. You can see rodeo stars at **Kissimmee Rodeo & Sports Arena**, 1010 Sulls Lane, Kissimmee, (407) 933-0020, where there are rodeos at 8 p.m. every Friday for $10 adults, $5 children under age 12.

Parimutuel sports fans can go to the dogs at **Seminole Greyhound Park**, 2000 Seminole Boulevard, Casselberry, (407) 699-4510, open May through October with racing Monday through Saturday at 7:30 p.m. and matinees at 12:30 p.m. Monday, Wednesday, and Saturday. Other parimutuel events are simulcast here too. Grandstand admission is free, clubhouse $2. More dog racing is at **Sanford-Orlando Kennel Club**, 301 Dogtrack Road, Longwood, (407) 831-1600, where events take place from November to May on the same schedule for $1 general admission, $2 for the clubhouse. Jai alai fans can watch the speeding ball at **Orlando-Seminole Jai Alai**, 6405 South Highway 17/92, Fern Park, (407) 339-6221, which has games year-round at 7 p.m. Wednesday through Saturday and charges $1 grandstand admission, $2 clubhouse.

When you've seen enough make-believe creatures and want to get a look at the real thing, you can skim shallow wetlands with **Boggy Creek Airboat Rides**, 3702 Big Bass Road, Kissimmee, (407) 344-9550, open daily 9 a.m. to sunset. Boats roar off on 30-minute, 10-mile rides for $16 adults, $8 children under 8. Fishing fans can drop a line with the **Fishing Connection**, 1016 Emeralda Road, Orlando, (407) 296-0083 or (800) 583-2278, which organizes freshwater or saltwater fishing expeditions.

Katie's Wekiva River Landing, 190 Katie's Cove, Exit 51 at I-4, Sanford, (407) 628-1482, can outfit you with a rental canoe for a tranquil paddle on the pristine Little Wekiva River, the St. Johns River, and Rock Springs Run. A full-day trip is $15 per person including equipment and a ride upriver.

Mini-golf and go-kart racing take place at **Finish Line Racing Adventures**, 3113 South Ridgewood Avenue, Edgewater, (904) 427-8522, (888) RACE-FUN, or (800) 722-3752. At **Malibu Grand Prix Castle**, 5901 American Way, Orlando, (407) 351-4132, you can roar around an Indy-style track in Formula 1 race cars and try go-karts, mini-golf, and baseball batting. More mini-golf, videos, and such are at **Pirate's Cove Adventure Golf**, 8591 International Drive, Orlando, (407) 345-0585 or (800) 345-0595, open 9 a.m. to 11:30 p.m. daily. **Paintball World**, 2701 Holiday Trail (at Olde Towne Shopping Center), Kissimmee, (407) 396-4199, offers ten play areas on 60 acres, where you track down your prey and smack 'em with paintballs for $25 including equipment, $10 if you bring your own toys.

Granddaddy of the watery entertainment world is **Wet 'n' Wild**, 6200 International Drive, Orlando, (407) 351-1800 or (800) 992-9453, where a Fuji Flyer water toboggan ride down 450 feet of hairpin curves recently became yet another of the park's wild water slides and flume rides. Wet 'n' Wild's open year-round 9 a.m. to 7 p.m. and charges $24.95 adults, $19.95 children ages 3 to 9, half-price after 4 p.m. It also sells a five-day Vacation Value Pass that includes admission to Universal Studios and Sea World for $94.95 adults, $74.95 children. For more splashy fun, try **Water Mania**, 6073 Highway 192, Kissimmee, (407) 396-2626 or (800) 527-3092, and its 36 acres of thrills and chills complete with water slides, a wave pool, surfing, and kiddie pools. It's open 10 a.m. to 5 p.m., later in summer, and admission is $23.95 adults, $17.95 children ages 3 to 12, half-price after 4 p.m.

FOOD

Orlando has hundreds of restaurants awaiting you. Some of them are quite extravagant, but lots of moderately priced dining spots exist as well.

For exquisite food in spectacular surroundings, it's difficult to outclass **Maison & Jardin**, 430 South Wymore Road, Altamonte Springs, (407) 862-4410, known locally as "the Mason Jar." Occupying an antique mansion set in oak-shaded formal gardens, the restaurant remains the number-one special-occasion restaurant in Orlando. Prices are high, but the atmosphere's fab. Another pretty spot is **Historic Townsend Plantation**, 604 East Main Street, Apopka, (407) 880-1313, where you dine in a Victorian mansion overlooking farmland. Seafood, beef, poultry, and pastas at modest prices are offered here.

Chalet Suzanne Country Inn and Restaurant, 3800 Chalet Suzanne Road, U.S. 27/17, Lake Wales, (941) 676-6011, is one of the state's funkiest inns, a hodgepodge of collector's items acquired by founder Bertha Hinshaw. Her son operates this award-winning restaurant, renowned for its superior cuisine and eclectic charm but particularly for its romaine soup—which traveled to the moon with the astronauts! The restaurant serves four-course lunches and six-course dinners Tuesday through Sunday. Chalet Suzanne is expensive, no question about it, but it's one of the best and most interesting dining rooms in the region.

Ming Court Restaurant, 9188 International Drive, (407) 351-9988, specializes in Chinese cuisine with lots of seafood at low prices and, at lunch, dim sum served from a cart. **Forbidden City**, 948 North Mills Avenue, (407) 894-5005, is one of my favorites, occupying humble quarters but turning out great Chinese specialties at low fares. **Ran-Getsu**, Plaza International, 8400 International Drive, (407) 345-0044, wraps up moderately priced sushi rolls and sizzles its teriyaki and tempura grills daily.

Morton's of Chicago, The Steakhouse, 7600 Doctor Phillips Boulevard, (407) 248-3485, has brought its butchering knowledge to Orlando, where it serves up sensational steaks—including a 24-ounce porterhouse! Two other good, reasonably priced steak spots: **B.T. Bones**, 11370 South Orange Blossom Trail, (407) 859-7225, for prime rib, steak, and seafood; and **La Cantina**, 4721 East Colonial Drive, (407) 894-4491, which has been plattering huge steaks—including a 2½-pound giant T-bone and a 22-ounce strip—for many years.

For budget meals, try **Morrison's Cafeteria**, 7440 International Drive, (407) 351-0051; and the 24-hour **Steak 'n' Shake**, a Midwestern chain with several restaurants here, including one at 2820 East Colonial Drive, (407) 896-0827, where you can chow down on great burgers, fries, and a spaghetti-chili combo called Chili Mac for under $5.

ORLANDO

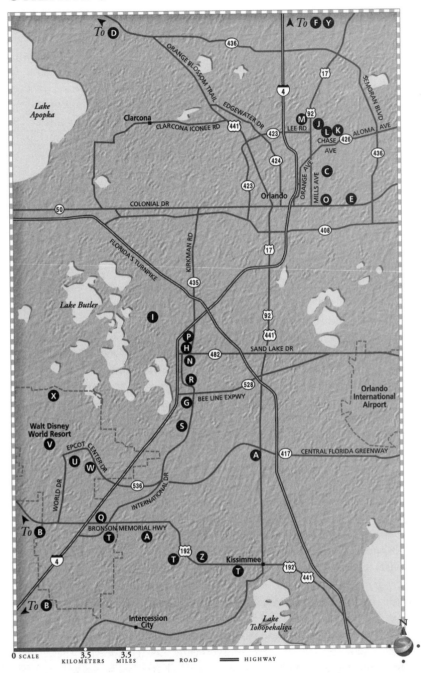

Food

Ⓐ B.T. Bones

Ⓑ Chalet Suzanne Country Inn and Restaurant

Ⓒ Forbidden City

Ⓓ Historic Townsend Plantation

Ⓔ La Cantina

Ⓕ Maison & Jardin

Ⓖ Ming Court Restaurant

Ⓗ Morrison's Cafeteria

Ⓘ Morton's of Chicago, The Steakhouse

Ⓙ Nicole St. Pierre

Ⓚ Park Avenue Grill

Ⓛ Park Plaza Gardens

Ⓜ Pete's Bubble Room

Ⓝ Ran–Getsu

Ⓞ Steak 'n' Shake

Lodging

Ⓟ Holiday Inn Sun Spree

Ⓠ La Suite Inn & Suites

Ⓡ Peabody Hotel

Ⓢ Renaissance Orlando Resort

Ⓣ U.S. 192 Hotel/Motel Row

Ⓤ Walt Disney World Dolphin

Ⓥ Walt Disney World Hotels

Ⓤ Walt Disney World Swan

Ⓦ Walt Disney World Village Resort Area

Camping

Ⓧ Fort Wilderness Resort

Ⓨ Katie's Wekiva River Landing

Ⓩ Orange Grove Campground

Ⓐ Port O' Call Campground

Ⓑ Yogi Bear's Jellystone Park Campground

Note: Items with the same letter are located in the same area.

Orlando's now a big city, so here's a look at some restaurants in nearby suburbs. Two Winter Park favorites: At **Park Plaza Gardens**, 319 Park Avenue South, (407) 645-2475, you dine amid greenery under a glass roof in elegant surroundings on a carefully orchestrated menu; **Park Avenue Grill**, 358 Park Avenue, (407) 647-4556, is a more casual spot, with seafood and beef specialties. Le Cordon Bleu, a long-revered mainstay of Winter Park, moved to 1300 South Orlando Avenue, Maitland, and became the **Nicole St. Pierre,** in salute to the chef/owner's two children. Set amid ancient oak trees, the restaurant serves outstanding continental specialties at fair prices; the handsome decor features impressive stained glass. No matter how hard you look, you won't see it all at **Pete's Bubble Room**, 1351 South Orlando Avenue, Maitland, (407) 628-3331, which is packed to the rafters with antiques and bibelots. An all-American spot serving pastas, seafood, poultry, steaks, prime rib, and the like, the Bubble is open daily.

LODGING

Orlando now has more hotel rooms than any other city in the nation, so you have plenty of options. You'll pay the highest prices at Walt Disney World and for large hotels nearby, with rates dropping as you move farther from the magic. Disney's largest hotels have the convenience of monorail or quick shuttle-bus service to the parks. Other areas with clusters of hotels include nearby International Drive, about a ten-minute drive away, and U.S. 192, which travels right past Walt Disney World's main entrance and is home to the area's largest collection of budget hotels.

Walt Disney World, (407) W-DISNEY or (800) 647-7900, has a huge roster of hotels, including the Victorian gingerbread of the **Grand Floridian Beach Resort**, the thatched roof of the **Polynesian**, the sleek architecture of the **Contemporary Hotel**, the turn-of-the-century beachy atmosphere of the **Yacht & Beach Club** hotels, the showy ambience of the **Boardwalk Inn/Boardwalk Villas**, geysers-and-waterfalls surroundings of the **Wilderness Lodge**, or the two-story **Treehouse Villas** on stilts under the pines. All are Disney-owned and located on Disney property; several are monorail stops. Prices vary by season and room size, topping out at $215 to $530 in February and March. You'll find the highest prices at Grand Floridian and Treehouse Villas, the lowest at Wilderness Lodge.

In recent years the attraction has added a bevy of themed, moderately priced accommodations, including **All Star Sports** and **All Star Music Resorts**, where top winter rates are $84 to $89; and **Dixie Landings, Port Orleans, Caribbean Beach Resort**, and **Coronado Springs**, where winter rates are $134 to $149.

Very close by and connected to the attraction by express buses is **Walt Disney World Village Resort Area**, where a handsomely landscaped road is lined with hotels, including the **Best Western Grosvenor Resort**, (407) 828-4444 or (800) 624-4109; **Buena Vista Palace**, (407) 827-2727 or (800) 327-2990; **Courtyard by Marriott**, (407) 828-8888 or (800) 223-9930; **Hilton**, (407) 827-4000 or (800) 782-4414; **Hyatt Regency Grand Cypress**, (407) 239-1234 or (800)

233-1234; **Doubletree Guest Suites**, (407) 934-1000 or (800) 222-TREE; **Hotel Royal Plaza**, (407) 828-2828 or (800) 248-7890; and **Travelodge**, (407) 828-2525 or (800) 348-3765. Rates vary by hotel and change by season and whim, ranging from a peak-season low of about $135 at Travelodge to highs in the $400 to $500 bracket, but with most charging in the $200 to $300 range.

Two other huge hotels are very close to the park: **Walt Disney World Dolphin** and **Walt Disney World Swan**, (407) 934-3000 or (800) 227-1500, whose respective mascots face each other across a central courtyard. Peak winter season prices are in the $245 to $335 bracket.

International Drive hotels, about a ten-minute drive from Walt Disney World, are on a long boulevard chock-a-block with shops and restaurants. One of my favorites is the **Peabody Hotel**, 9801 International Dr., (407) 352-4000 or (800) 732-2639, an alluringly tranquil spot that twice a day brings its fat little mascot ducks out for a walk and a splash in the fountain, a generations-old tradition that harkens back to the original, historic Peabody in Memphis, Tennessee. Peak rates are in the $240 to $300 range. Another very pretty luxury hotel, built around a towering central courtyard where birds twitter in an aviary, is **Renaissance Orlando Resort**, 6677 Sea Harbor Drive, at Sea World, (407) 351-5555 or (800) 327-6677. Peak-season room rates are in the $205 to $280 bracket. A budget choice on International Drive is **La Suite Inn & Suites**, 5858 International Drive, (407) 351-4410 or (800) 722-7462, with rates of $60 to $85 in top season.

In that same area is an Orlando inn with an interesting twist: **Holiday Inn Sun Spree**, 13351 SR 535, Lake Buena Vista, (407) 239-4500 or (800) FON-MAXX, where kids are king and even have their own suite partitioned off from parents to provide a separate, themed, sleeping/play area. Top winter rates are $153 for kids and parents.

Hotel rooms by the thousands can be found along **U.S. 192 Hotel/Motel Row** heading west or east from Walt Disney World's main entrance in Kissimmee. U.S. 192 has several different names as you head east, including Irlo Bronson Memorial Highway and, as it nears downtown Kissimmee, Vine Street. Generally, the bigger the hotel here, the more it costs, with the largest charging $100 to $200 in peak season; medium-sized properties with 100 or so rooms charging just under $100; and small, unprepossessing motels charging $50 or less. In spring and fall slow seasons, price wars are the rule rather than the exception, and properties charging $25 to $30 can easily be found. A good example of a medium-sized property is **Larson's Lodge**, 6075 U.S. 192, Kissimmee, (407) 396-6100 or (800) 327-9074, a 128-unit hotel, near Walt Disney World's main gate, that's been operated by one family for many years. Peak-season rates range $90 to $100.

Budget hotels offering basic accommodations; sometimes a pool, restaurant, or game facilities; and prices under $50 in peak season include **Best Western Kissimmee**, 2261 U.S. 192, Kissimmee, (407) 846-2221 or (800) 944-0062; **Knights Inn Maingate**, 7475 U.S. 192, Kissimmee, (407) 396-4200 or (800) 944-0062; **Maple Leaf Motel**, 4647 U.S. 192, Kissimmee, (407) 396-0300; **Record Motel**, 4651 U.S. 192, Kissimmee, (407) 396-8400 or (800) 874-4555; **Travelodge Hotel Main Gate East**, 5711 U.S. 192, Kissimmee, (407) 396-4222 or (800) 327-1128; and **Sun Motel**, 5020 U.S. 192, Kissimmee, (407) 396-2673 or (800) 541-2674.

CAMPING

Disney's **Fort Wilderness Resort** sprawls over 600 acres and has camping facilities from full hookups to tenting spots, and even fully equipped trailers that look like log cabins and sleep four or six. Campfires and singalongs are nightly entertainment; rates are $49 to $64 for hookups or tents, $230 in winter for trailers.

Yogi Bear's Jellystone Park Campground, 8555 U.S. 192, Kissimmee, (407) 349-4148, (800) 776-9644, or (800) 558-2954, salutes that famous bear with lakeside or wooded camper sites just 4 miles west of the park, plus mini-golf, boating, fishing, and a restaurant. Full hookups are $31 in winter. There's another Yogi spot at 9200 Turkey Lake Road, Orlando, (407) 351-4394, (800) 776-9644, or (800) 558-2954, about 10 miles from Walt Disney World, with basketball, boating, mini-golf, and hayrides.

Orange Grove Campground, 2425 Old Vineland Road, Kissimmee, (407) 396-6655 or (800) 3-CAMPIN, has been around as long as WDW, is close to all the attraction action, and charges $23 in winter for one of its 200 shady hookups. **Port O' Call Campground**, 5175 Highway 192, Kissimmee, (407) 396-0110, (800) 327-9120, or (800) 432-0766, has shuttle service to Walt Disney World for a small charge and boasts a tropical rock-trimmed swimming pool, game

room, heated pool, and weekend entertainment. Winter rates are $28.
In Sanford, just north of Orlando, is the Wekiva River, a pristine spot
that's famed for its tubing and canoeing. **Katie's Wekiva River
Landing**, 190 Katie's Cove, Sanford, (407) 628-1482, charges $60 for
log cabin rentals including canoeing, $18 for RV or tent sites.

NIGHTLIFE

Performing Arts

Many top stars and groups appear at the **Bob Carr Performing Arts
Centre**, 401 Livingston Street, (407) 849-2020. **Civic Theatre of
Central Florida**, 1001 Princeton Street, Orlando, (407) 896-7365, has
three stages and has been producing plays for nearly 70 years at 8 p.m.
Wednesday through Saturday, with a 2 p.m. Sunday matinee. Tickets
are $15 to $18, $7 for children's theater.

   Florida Symphony Orchestra, 1900 North Mills Avenue, (407)
896-0331, presents concerts from September to June. Many cultural
activities take place at lovely **Rollins College** in Winter Park, (407) 646-
2233. Orlando's **Southern Ballet Theater**, (407) 426-1728, performs at
Bob Carr Performing Arts Centre several times a year, in productions
including *The Nutcracker* at Christmas. **Orlando Opera Company**, 1111
North Orange Avenue, (407) 426-1717 or (800) 336-7372, has brought
arias to Orlando for more than 35 years in winter and spring.

Themed Dining

Themed dinner spots are the rage in Orlando, with everything from
pirates to medieval kings battling for your dollar; Walt Disney World,
Sea World, and Universal Studios all have myriad dining spots within the
parks as well as separate specialty dining experiences. People don't go to
these places so much for the food—which is generally pretty standard,
uninteresting fare—as for the fantasy, a natural extension of the whole
Orlando experience. These attractions are very popular, so make reservations well in advance and plan to devote the entire evening to the event.

   Keep your head while all around you are losing theirs at **King
Henry's Feast**, 8984 International Drive, (407) 351-5151 or (800) 883-
8181, an amusing salute to that hefty monarch who had so much
difficulty with women. Castle doors open at 6:30 p.m. daily. You're
king for a night at **Medieval Times Dinner & Tournament**, 4510

West Highway 192, Kissimmee, (407) 239-0214 or (800) 229-8300, where knights try to roust each other in jousting matches and sword fights. Village artisans bring medieval days to life with exhibitions of weaving, glassblowing, and blacksmithing. Moats are bridged here at 6:30 p.m. or 8:30 p.m., varying daily.

Avast, ye mateys, here comes Blackbeard, scourge of the **Pirate's Dinner Adventure**, 6400 Carrier Drive, (407) 248-0590 or (800) 866-2469, where you dine while pirates battle it out amid special effects and stunts. Later, there's a disco party at this new addition to Orlando's themed evening entertainment, which kicks off at 7:30 p.m. daily except Monday. Wild Bill could shoot a knothole out of a plank at 500 yards and will show you just how it's done at **Wild Bill's Wild West Dinner Extravaganza**, 5260 U.S. 192, (407) 351-5151, which also features high-steppin' cancan gals and Native American dancers. Shooting begins at 7 p.m. **American Gladiators Orlando Live**, 5515 U.S. 192, (407) 390-0000 or (800) 228-8534, fight their way to victory at this dinner show that features some of television's battlin' gladiators. Dinner's at 7:30 p.m. daily.

Orlando Skyline

Orlando/Orange County CVB

At **Aloha! Polynesian Luau at Sea World**, 7007 Sea World Drive, (407) 351-3600 or (800) 227-8048, you can sample that acquired-taste Hawaiian specialty, *poi*, and dine on a four-course family dinner daily complete with Samoan fire- and knife-dances and other Polynesian thrills. Carpets that fly and beautiful white horses that seem to are part of **Arabian Nights**, 6225 U.S. 192, Kissimmee, (407) 239-9223 or (800) 553-6116, which stars the aristocratic Lippizaner stallions—famed for their "airs above the ground" dance routines—as well as many other breeds, from fancy-footwork Andalusians to big-footed Clydesdales, best known as "the Budweiser horses." Your carpet departs at 7:30 p.m. daily.

Chicago's rootin'-tootin' days of flappers and gangland gunfire in the Prohibition Era is the focus of **Capone's Dinner & Show**, 4740 U.S. 192, Kissimmee, (407) 397-2378 or (800) 220-8428, which offers a 15-item Italian/American buffet for show dining. Shootin' and dancin' start at 7:30 p.m. Knock twice and say "Joe sent me."

Chew while you choo-choo aboard **Florida Central Adventure Dinner Train**, 3001 Orange Avenue, Plymouth, (407) 889-7005, which chugs off in heritage railroad dining cars on three-hour trips departing at 6:30 p.m. Thursday through Saturday, noon Saturday, and 12:30 p.m. Sunday for brunch. *Riverboat Romance*, 433 North Palmetto Avenue, Sanford, (407) 321-5091 or (800) 423-7401, sails its pretty Victorian craft daily on lunch sightseeing cruises and moonlight dinner and dancing cruises on the picturesque, historic St. Johns River—which flows north! Occasionally the ship offers overnight cruises.

Mark Two Dinner Theater, 3376 Edgewater Drive, (407) 843-6275 or (800) 726-6275, has prize-winning food and Broadway productions with dancing on Monday. Tickets are $26 to $38, including dinner and play. **Sleuth's Mystery Dinner Theater** is just what the name suggests—dining, theater, and mystery all mixed up together to create a good time as you try to figure out who's acting and whodunit. Showtimes vary but are usually at 6, 7:30, or 9 p.m. daily, at 7508 Republic Drive, (407) 363-1985.

Dining with Disney characters is a very popular pastime at WDW. Cinderella's breakfasts in her castle dining room are often booked 60 days in advance, so reserve as far ahead as possible by contacting **Disney Dining** at (407) WDW-DINE. It helps to know what character you want to see and at what meal. Included among the options are Mickey and Minnie, Pluto, Goofy, Chip 'n' Dale, Winnie the Pooh, Tigger, Eeyore, and characters from *Pocahontas*, *The Hunchback of Notre Dame*, *Aladdin*, and *Mary Poppins*.

Mickey's Tropical Revue takes place at 4:30 p.m. daily at WDW's Polynesian Resort, (407) 939-3463, where Mickey wiggles his tail to hula tunes at a Hawaiian luau, complete with Polynesian dancers and a roast chicken and pork dinner. At 6:45 and 9:30 p.m. Mickey's in bed, but the hula- and fire-dancing continues at this luau extravaganza. **Hoop De Doo Musical Revue** at Disney's Fort Wilderness serves all-you-can-eat country vittles and hoedown entertainment daily at 5, 7:15, and 9:30 p.m. From April through October, WDW invites you to an **All-American Backyard Barbecue** at 6:30 p.m. Monday, Wednesday, and Thursday; you can belly up with the characters for an all-you-can-eat BBQ feast, including beer, wine, and soda.

Clubs and Bars

King of the Orlando nightlife complexes, handsome and entertaining **Church Street Station**, 129 West Church Street, (407) 422-2434, has something for everybody, from a huge twangin' country-and-western lounge to Dixieland jazz and rock 'n' roll. Besides several dining spots of its own, Church Street Station is surrounded by shops, restaurants, and pubs that draw huge crowds every night to what was once a railroad station on the edge of nowhere. There's no charge at Church until 6 p.m., when the fee is $17.95 adults, $10.95 children ages 4 to 12. Hours are 11 a.m. to 1 a.m., closing at 2 a.m. on weekends. Around the corner, **Terror at Church Street**, 135 South Orange Street, (407) 649-FEAR, teams 20 actors with soundtracks and special effects to scare the socks off you. They're, um, dying to have you stop by here in the, um, dead center of Orlando, where they're alive daily from 7 a.m. to midnight, and to 1 a.m. on weekends. Admission is $12 adults, $10 students under 17.

Disney's answer to Church Street Station, **Pleasure Island** at WDW, (407) 934-7781 or 824-4321, celebrates New Year's Eve every night, complete with fireworks and dancing in the streets. Just off the island, you'll find loads of shops and four restaurants: Planet Hollywood, Fireworks Factory, Fulton Street Seafood, and Portobello's Yacht Club. On the island are seven nightclubs, all rocking 7 p.m. to 2 a.m.

When what you want is music and dance and plenty of both, head for **Baja Beach Club**, 8510 West Palm Parkway, Lake Buena Vista, (407) 263-5911 or 239-9629, which joins beach and nightlife in wildly enthusiastic fashion nightly 7 p.m. to 2:30 a.m. for a $3 to $7 cover. A huge, high-energy alternative dance club, **Cairo**, 22 South Magnolia

Street, (407) 422-3595, rocks with three stories of action and a rooftop reggae club filled with sound and light. It's open Wednesday, Friday, Saturday, and Sunday 10 a.m. to 2 a.m., with a $3 to $5 cover.

Latest among Orlando's entertainment complexes is **Embassy Nightclub & Entertainment Complex**, 5100 Adansin Street, (407) 629-4779 or 629-4785, where you'll find a disco, game room, balconied music hall, and 40,000 square feet of entertainment space that even includes what the club calls "quiet areas." Opening hours vary from 7:30 to 9 p.m., closing from 1 a.m. to 3 a.m. Wednesday through Sunday; cover is $2 to $10.

Hard Rock Café, 5800 Kirkland Road, (407) 351-7625, is right next door to Universal Studios and is one of the largest of its namesakes in the nation, with more than 500 rock 'n' roll souvenirs and plenty of food, drink, and music. It's open daily 11 a.m. to midnight. **Howl at the Moon Saloon**, upstairs at Church Street Market, 55 West Church Street, (407) 841-HOWL, features dueling grand pianos playing classic rock 'n' roll singalong tunes in a very popular bar open 6 p.m. Sunday through Thursday (5 p.m. weekends) to 2 a.m., with a varying cover charge.

An unusual nightlife stop is **Blazing Pianos**, 8445 International Drive, (407) 363-5104, a three-piano rock 'n' roll bar, complete with piano memorabilia and nonstop music, comedy, and audience interaction. It's open daily 7 p.m. to 1 a.m.; cover charge is $5 Sunday through Thursday, $7 on weekends.

Sports, sports, sports are the focus at **Friday's Front Row Sports Grill**, 8126 International Drive, (407) 363-1414, where you'll find an interactive game room, sporty gift shop, and 84 televisions; open daily 11 a.m. to 2 a.m., no cover. **Orlando Ale House**, 5573 Kirkland Road, (407) 248-0000, is a sports bar with light dining, 37 televisions, and 50 brands of beer that pop 11 a.m. to 2 p.m. daily here and at two other area locations.

If you never met a fast car you didn't love, join the wheels at **Race Rock Restaurant**, 8986 International Drive, (407) 248-9876, where owners Richard and Kyle Petty, Jeff Gordon, and Rusty Wallace have their stock cars crammed into every available space, allowing you the opportunity to wine and dine surrounded by trucks, hydroplanes, dragsters, motorcycles, and Indy cars.

Ybor's Cigar/Martini Bar, 41 West Church Street, (407) 316-8006, caters to those most-recent chic tastes and is open 4 p.m. to 2 a.m. Tuesday through Saturday.

APPENDIX

METRIC CONVERSION CHART

1 U.S. gallon = approximately 4 liters
1 liter = about 1 quart
1 Canadian gallon = approximately 4.5 liters

1 pound = approximately $\frac{1}{2}$ kilogram
1 kilogram = about 2 pounds

1 foot = approximately $\frac{1}{3}$ meter
1 meter = about 1 yard
1 yard = a little less than a meter
1 mile = approximately 1.6 kilometers
1 kilometer = about $\frac{2}{3}$ mile

90°F = about 30°C
20°C = approximately 70°F

Planning Map: South Florida and the Keys

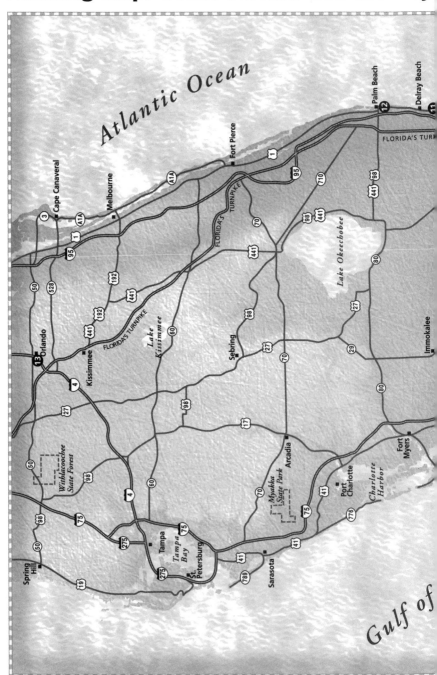

You have permission to photocopy this map.

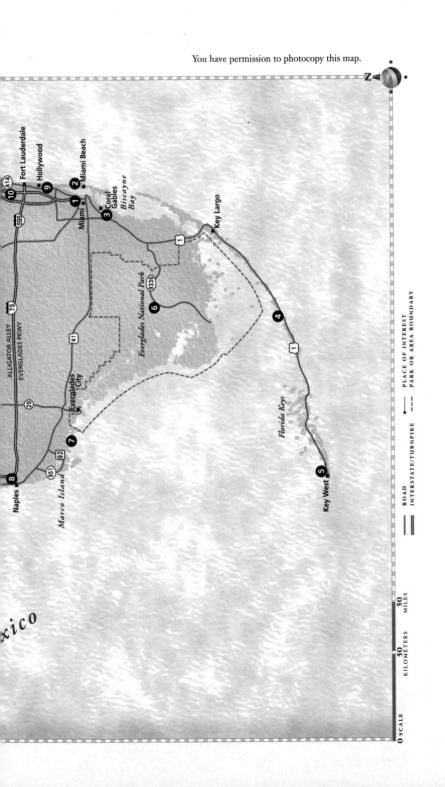

INDEX

Map Index

Books from John Muir Publications

Rick Steves' Books

Asia Through the Back Door, 400 pp., $17.95

Europe 101: History and Art for the Traveler, 352 pp., $17.95

Mona Winks: Self-Guided Tours of Europe's Top Museums, 432 pp., $18.95

Rick Steves' Baltics & Russia, 160 pp., $9.95

Rick Steves' Europe, 560 pp., $18.95

Rick Steves' France, Belgium & the Netherlands, 304 pp., $15.95

Rick Steves' Germany, Austria & Switzerland, 272 pp., $14.95

Rick Steves' Great Britain & Ireland, 320 pp., $15.95

Rick Steves' Italy, 224 pp., $13.95

Rick Steves' Scandinavia, 192 pp., $13.95

Rick Steves' Spain & Portugal, 240 pp., $13.95

Rick Steves' Europe Through the Back Door, 512 pp., $19.95

Rick Steves' French Phrase Book, 192 pp., $5.95

Rick Steves' German Phrase Book, 192 pp., $5.95

Rick Steves' Italian Phrase Book, 192 pp., $5.95

Rick Steves' Spanish & Portuguese Phrase Book, 336 pp., $7.95

Rick Steves' French/German/Italian Phrase Book, 320 pp., $7.95

Adventures in Nature Series

Belize: Adventures in Nature, 400 pp., $18.95

Guatemala: Adventures in Nature, 400 pp., $18.95

City•Smart™ Guidebooks

City•Smart Guidebook: Austin, 224 pp., $12.95

City•Smart Guidebook: Cleveland, 208 pp., $14.95

City•Smart Guidebook: Denver, 256 pp., $14.95

City•Smart Guidebook: Indianapolis, 224 pp., $12.95

City•Smart Guidebook: Kansas City, 248 pp., $12.95

City•Smart Guidebook: Memphis, 224 pp., $12.95

City•Smart Guidebook: Milwaukee, 224 pp., $12.95

City•Smart Guidebook: Minneapolis/St. Paul, 232 pp., $14.95

City•Smart Guidebook: Nashville, 256 pp., $14.95

City•Smart Guidebook: Portland, 232 pp., $14.95

City•Smart Guidebook: Tampa/St. Petersburg, 256 pp., $14.95

Travel+Smart™ Trip Planners

American Southwest Travel+Smart Trip Planner, 256 pp., $14.95

Colorado Travel+Smart Trip Planner, 248 pp., $14.95

Eastern Canada Travel+Smart Trip Planner, 272 pp., $15.95

Florida Gulf Coast Travel+Smart Trip Planner, 224 pp., $14.95

Hawaii Travel+Smart Trip Planner, 256 pp., $14.95

Kentucky/Tennessee Travel+Smart Trip Planner, 248 pp., $14.95

Michigan Travel+Smart Trip Planner, 232 pp., $14.95

Minnesota/Wisconsin Travel+Smart Trip Planner, 232 pp., $14.95

New England Travel+Smart Trip Planner, 256 pp., $14.95

New York Travel+Smart Trip Planner, 256 pp., $15.95

Northern California Travel+Smart Trip Planner, 272 pp., $15.95

Pacific Northwest Travel+Smart Trip Planner, 240 pp., $14.95

Southern California Travel+Smart Trip Planner, 232 pp., $14.95

South Florida and The Keys Travel+Smart Trip Planner, 232 pp., $14.95

Other Terrific Travel Titles

The 100 Best Small Art Towns in America, 256 pp., $15.95

The Big Book of Adventure Travel, 400 pp., $17.95

The Birder's Guide to Bed and Breakfasts: U.S. and Canada, 416 pp., $17.95

Costa Rica: A Natural Destination, 416 pp., $18.95

Indian America, 480 pp., $18.95

The People's Guide to Mexico, 608 pp., $19.95

Ranch Vacations, 632 pp., $22.95

Understanding Europeans, 272 pp., $14.95

Watch It Made in the U.S.A., 400 pp., $17.95

The World Awaits, 280 pp., $16.95

Automotive Titles

The Greaseless Guide to Car Care, 272 pp., $19.95

How to Keep Your Subaru Alive, 480 pp., $21.95

How to Keep Your Toyota Pick-Up Alive, 392 pp., $21.95

How to Keep Your VW Alive, 464 pp., $25.00

Ordering Information

Please check your local bookstore for our books, or call **1-800-888-7504** to order direct and to receive a complete catalog. A shipping charge will be added to your order total.

Send all inquiries to:
John Muir Publications
P.O. Box 613
Santa Fe, NM 87504

ABOUT THE AUTHOR

Marylyn Springer is a South Florida journalist and editor who has written about the region for many local, national, and international publications. She is the author or co-author of four other travel guides, including a guide to cruiseship travel, which won the Society of American Travel Writers' annual Lowell Thomas Award for Best Guidebook of the Year. She has also been the recipient of a number of state and local journalism awards for a variety of political and feature newspaper articles.

A graduate of the University of Miami, Springer has remained a resident of the region while traveling much of the world as part of her travel industry career. Also active in local community projects, she says that on those rare occasions when she isn't on a plane or in front of a computer, she plays Irish folk harp, crafts stained glass windows, and dreams of sloth, something she hopes someday to experience.